The ROAR
of the Crowd

following Scottish football down the years

David Ross

© David Ross 2005

First published in 2005
Argyll Publishing
Glendaruel
Argyll PA22 3AE
Scotland
www.argyllpublishing.com

The right of David Ross to be identified as the author of this work
has been asserted by him in accordance with the Copyright,
Designs and Patents Act of 1988

British Library Cataloguing-in-Publication Data.
A catalogue record for this book is available from
the British Library.

ISBN 1 902831 83 7

Photos: Newsquest (Herald & Times) Ltd

Origination: Cordfall Ltd, Glasgow

Printing: Bell & Bain Ltd, Glasgow

For Josephine

Contents

Hampden Park packed
with another huge crowd

All roads lead to Hampden.
Or so it seemed in the days when Scotland's national stadium
attracted crowds of over 100,000 on a regular basis

Acknowledgements

A book such as this inevitably requires help from a number of people in order to appear in print and I would like to express my appreciation and thanks to all who aided me.

The following individuals and the clubs they represent met my requests for information –
Ann Marie Ballantyne (Airdrie United),
John Reynolds (Albion Rovers),
John Glencross (Alloa Athletic),
Jim Mechan (Ayr United),
Dennis McCleary (Berwick Rangers),
Jim McAllister (Dumbarton),
Jim Dick (East Fife),
Jim Stewart (East Fife),
David Speed (Hearts),
Tom Brown (Kilmarnock),
Angela Burnett (Kilmarnock),
Andrew Stephen (Montrose),
Alan C Dick (Partick Thistle),
Stewart Duff (St Johnstone).

Online assistance came from Forrest Robertson, who was his usual fount of knowledge on matters both weighty and obscure, Ger Harley (www.scottishfitba.net), Davy Allan (www.LondonHearts.com) and 'BankieBill'.

The staff of the Mitchell Library in Glasgow and the National Library of Scotland in Edinburgh.

Douglas Stevenson of D&D Programmes in Kilmarnock gave me access to his collection.

The Scottish Football Association and the Scottish Football League were both extremely helpful and I would like to thank all their staff. I'm sure they won't mind if I give particular mention to Richard McBrearty of the Scottish Football Museum at Hampden Park for affording me access to players registration and gate book records as well as providing illustrations and David Thomson of the Scottish Football League for giving me access to their store of attendance records. And to both of the above named for dealing patiently with my many telephone calls.

Thanks to my publisher, Derek Rodger of Argyll Publishing, for taking it on in the first place and for his belief in the book.

Finally, I want to thank my wife Josephine for her support and encouragement.

David Ross

Introduction

NO ONE can say for certain who first had the idea of charging for admission to a football match. What we do know is that for centuries the game had been a participatory sport as much as a spectator one as entire towns gathered on feast days to watch a match which involved hundreds of players and lasted all day. There were no cups to be won and no money to be paid to the victors but the prize at stake was far greater than any amount of precious silver or grubby cash. Honour and local pride were the winners' laurels and these were beyond price.

But in the second half of the nineteenth century football began to change. Rules began to be drawn up and organisations established. Hitherto nebulous concepts such as the dimensions of the playing area and the number of players in a team started to be defined. As did such intangibles as rules regarding fouling and use of the hands. Innovations such as team colours and even the creation of football clubs that played specified opponents on specified pitches at specified times completed the transition from local pastime to national sport.

There remained one constant. One feature of the game played in towns and villages for hundreds of years transferred itself effortlessly to the 'new' sport. Local rivalry. Partisan passions remained undimmed by the new rules. If anything they grew stronger as games became more frequent and, thanks to the inventions of both car and train, opponents became more numerous and from much further afield. It was that rivalry at village, town, county and even national level that produced the great crowds generated at Scottish football matches over the past 130 years and which still sustains the game today.

There is something about being part of a football crowd which appeals to the inner psyche. A sense of belonging, of shared experience, of mutual support, of an almost primal human need to be with others just like ourselves while still retaining our individuality. Other opportunities for gathering in large crowds have existed – worship in churches, political meetings, trades union rallies for example. But these have been declining in both numbers and fervour for half a century and the football match is one of the few remaining occasions when people can gather together in large numbers on a regular basis and be part of a crowd.

How can there be such a financial crisis at top level professional football when there are more paying customers than ever before?

Today, more people watch League football in Scotland than at any time in the past forty years. Indeed, save for the periods after the end of both World Wars, more than at any time ever. Even if, in Scotland, there exists a 'two-party' system in football which has grown stronger and more dominant over the years, there are still forty alternatives on offer. Again, bar a few short years after World War I, the highest in history.

Today, the growth of competition means that the intrepid Scottish fitba' fan can follow their team anywhere in Europe. From Galway Bay to the Ural Mountains, from Lapland to the Straits of Gibraltar a supporter can traverse Britain, Ireland and all of continental Europe and not journey through a single country where more people, per head of population, watch football than in Scotland!

Yet more professional football clubs are in debt. In the summer of 2004 a quarter of the Scottish Premier League clubs were in administration. Yes, even amidst the gravest financial crisis in our game's history and the greatest shortage of playing talent ever known, the Scots and football are still, as they have been for over 130 years, wedded together.

Expressed as a percentage of population, attendance at League games in Scotland stands at the 80% mark over a season (ie over 4 million paying customers attend football matches during a Scottish football season). This is a far higher proportion than Germany which has the highest attendances. It is a third greater than England which has the biggest TV audience. Far more than Spain which has the best players. And easily larger than Italy which, next to Scotland, has the most passionate fans.

The only countries in Europe which outstrip the Scots are from the north-west and south-east fringes of the continent, Iceland and Cyprus. No country with a population of a million or more comes anywhere near.

This book tells the story of how we got to where we are today, the triumphs and the tragedies on the way, the peaks and the troughs along the journey, the joy and the tears behind the action on the pitch.

How, you might reasonably ask, can there be such a financial crisis at top level professional football when there are more paying customers than ever before?

The answer is two-fold. First, attendances form a significant part of clubs' income but not the only part. If clubs budget for TV deals that don't arrive or performance money that isn't earned, then they pay their players salaries that they can't sustain. Second, while more people than ever before are watching Scottish football, they are doing so at only two main venues – Ibrox and Celtic Park. Both Rangers and Celtic are attracting more supporters now than in their supposed heyday in the 1930s-50s. Elsewhere, though they are still nowhere near their worst, crowds are slipping.

While more people than ever before are watching Scottish football, they are doing so at only two main venues – Ibrox and Celtic Park.

There is so much confusion and myth surrounding football attendances in Scotland. 80,000 at Ibrox and Parkhead in the 1930s? More like 8000 for run-of-the-mill League games. For long periods until around 1960, clubs like Hearts, Hibs and Aberdeen could challenge the big two for support. At the other end of the scale the bottom division enjoyed a few golden years in the period immediately after World War II when some teams were capable of averaging five-figure gates over a season. Yet in the 1920s and 30s several clubs folded, some incapable of drawing as many as 100 spectators to their games.

This is the first comprehensive look at attendances in Scotland. Drawing on official Scottish League returns from 1961 and from clubs' own figures and newspaper estimates, this book looks at the highs and lows of every club and at trends in attendances. The phenomenon of Hampden Park is considered. For over forty years Hampden held the world attendance record and even today every significant crowd record in Europe is held by the home of Scottish football.

What this book doesn't do, what it cannot do, is to put into words that great communal elation expressed when a goal is scored. Nor can it explain that overwhelming unity which encompasses 50,000 supporters as they, unanimously, determine a penalty kick or an offside decision. And it makes no attempt to explain that seeming contradiction of distance which leads those same 50,000 to maintain that they are right and the man in black, standing a few feet from the incident in question, is wrong.

For that you need to be there in the flesh.

The most significant development in modern Scottish football, and the single act that has had the biggest impact on the state of the game in 2005 was initiated by those in charge of Scotland's biggest clubs. Inspired by the example of their counterparts in England they broke away from the Scottish League in 1998 and created their own Scottish Premier League – the SPL. The plan was to create a land of satellite-TV milk and honey in which the cream of continental talent would be lured to play for our clubs as they contended at the highest levels in Europe while maintaining an exciting and competitive domestic set-up.

It looks as if they'd been handed the wrong script.

Comparisons with England have not always been wise in Scottish football's 130-year history and the failure to appreciate the true value of the Scottish market – including the Old Firm impact – in television terms led to a drastic slump in revenue as clubs spent money that not only they didn't have but which they weren't ever going to get. The consequences of this judgement makes for the current Scottish football landscape – within the last year three of the leading clubs have been in administration and others have narrowly avoided disaster by taking drastic cost-cutting measures.

Did the game's leading lights need to do this? The previous four division set-up seemed to be working. Promotion/relegation play-offs between Aberdeen and Dunfermline and Airdrie and Hibernian brought out big crowds. Big names like Dundee United and Hibernian suffered relegation which, while it came as a blow to them, demonstrated a robust level of competition in the game and gave a huge boost to gates in the First Division. In season 1998-99, Hibs were the first side since Kilmarnock in 1954 to record a five-figure average outside the top flight.

The only area of the game which seemed set in stone was at the very top. As soon as Celtic started getting their act together the days of clubs like Motherwell or Aberdeen providing the principal challenge to Rangers were over. Celtic took second place in 1995-96 and neither of the Old Firm have finished any lower than second ever since. And the gap in attendances between them and the rest is every bit as big as it is in playing performance.

To begin to understand where football attendances might go in Scotland, it is instructive to look how we arrived at where we are today.

International Football Match, Scotland versus England
Hampden Park, Glasgow. Record Crowd, 125,000.

Hampden breaks its own record.
The 1912 match against England was one of
many to break the world attendance record

Crowded Houses: 1872-1918

T he first indication that there was a mass paying audience for Scottish football came on a dreich St Andrew's Day in 1872. This was the occasion of the first ever international football match. The Queen's Park Football Club, founded in 1867, responded to a challenge by Charles Alcock, Secretary of the English FA, and represented Scotland against England.

A century ago and crowds stream into the world's most modern football ground, Hampden Park, in 1905

Such was the interest shown in the fixture that the West of Scotland Cricket Club's ground at Hamilton Crescent in the Partick area of Glasgow was selected as the venue as no football club possessed a suitably enclosed ground in which to charge admission.

The match itself, though a 0-0 draw, was a tremendous success and the beginning of a series which lasted until 1989. There were around 4,000 spectators present which, for the 1870s, was considered a massive attendance. Certainly the cricketers had never enticed as many along to their ground. People hung from trees and climbed railings to gain a suitable vantage point.

Although club matches had been played before this, many of these were inter-club affairs between 'marrieds' and 'bachelors' or 'captain's picks' v 'vice-captain's picks' and so on. Even in games between clubs there is no evidence of spectators being charged for admission. The Scotland-England match is the first game for which there is any proof of money changing hands

Tickets for that game – describing it, oddly enough, as England v Scotland at 'foot-ball' – can still be found today though a twenty-first century collector will have to pay rather more than the one shilling (5p) they cost at the time.

The experience convinced Queen's Park that they needed a ground of their own through which they could charge for admission and they proceeded to build the first of three grounds to bear the name of Hampden Park.

Others soon followed. Within a few years many clubs possessed their own private grounds including still-familiar names like Rangers, Kilmarnock, Dumbarton and Morton while some who flourished then are scarcely remembered at all today. The Ramblers from the Gorbals have long since wandered off into oblivion while it's no great surprise that any team known as Albatross – as a Bridgeton club was designated – was a doomed venture from the outset.

Hearts and Hibs were among the unfortunates who had to share public parks with sides like Hanover and Swifts as the number of clubs mushroomed across Scotland.

This rapid expansion was the effect of another offshoot of that first international match – the establishment of the Scottish Football Association in 1873 and the founding of the Scottish Cup that same year. The popularity of the latter was so great that the number of entries rose massively, from sixteen in the initial competition to over 100 by its fifth year.

By 1876 the Scottish Cup Final was attracting a five-figure attendance and the addition of Wales to the international roster the same year helped crowds rise to 17,000, forcing the SFA to move its showpiece games away from Hamilton Crescent to the first Hampden Park.

Even then it was apparent that these international fixtures drew far greater support in Scotland than when the national eleven ventured south. It was only when the FA moved the England-Scotland fixture out of London and into the Lancashire heartland of the game in Blackburn in 1887 that the crowd hit five figures.

The bigger crowds brought problems with them. As early as January 1878 the SFA ordered a Scottish Cup match between Third Lanark and fellow Glasgow club South-Western to be replayed owing to the crowd encroaching on the pitch. Crowd interference was also blamed for Queen's Park's winning goal against Dumbarton in the 1881 Final which was also ordered to be replayed, although the outcome remained the same.

The Spiders remained Scotland's leading club until the advent of professionalism and in 1884 they moved to the second of their three Hampden Parks. This was, at the time, the most palatial building in Scottish football, containing changing rooms, baths and a gym – luxuries most clubs could only dream about. It was also the biggest ground in the country with 26,379 in attendance for the 1-1 draw between Scotland and England in April 1890. This was the largest crowd in Scottish football prior to the establishment of the Scottish Football League.

Interest in the game also burgeoned in the press. Before the 1872 international and even, to some extent, afterwards, the press ignored football, viewing it as a ruffian's game. It wasn't that they ignored sport – the average nineteenth century newspaper contained plenty of snippets of information on horse racing, cricket, billiards and even rounders! But football was usually restricted to paid advertisements for matches.

The growth in crowds altered the relationship irrevocably as newspapers fought out circulation wars to gain readers from an increasingly literate population. Match reports began to appear, then previews of games as football began to insinuate itself into the sporting columns. By the 1880s it had achieved the dominance in sports coverage it still enjoys today and the love-hate relationship between the media and the game was well under way.

The mutual feeding frenzy between the press and football was boosted in the 1880s with the establishment of publications such as the Scottish Athletic Journal, Scottish Sport and the Scottish Referee – dedicated sports papers which usually

In 1878 a Scottish Cup match between Third Lanark and fellow Glasgow club South-Western was ordered to be replayed owing to the crowd encroaching on the pitch

appeared twice weekly. Their presence only served to increase the coverage in the regular daily press, desperate to retain its hard-won readership.

It wasn't just the national press either. Local newspapers were in much more plentiful supply then as opposed to now and competition, even within small towns, was fierce. One way to get – and keep – readers was to identify with the local football club and provide the most up-to-date news on its activities. Every local paper had at least one – and often several – football correspondents, usually writing under a pseudonym bearing a classical allusion, such as 'Scrutator' or 'Horatio.'

These reporters liked to demonstrate their education by throwing the odd Latin phrase or quotation into their accounts of proceedings. Perhaps this helped convince them that the game wasn't as rough as had been supposed? At any rate their noms de plume provided them with an anonymity which came in useful when they wrote anything scathing about supporters' favourite players or clubs.

Establishing league football seemed like the next logical development in the game's progress if it wanted to keep and increase attendances

Establishing league football seemed like the next logical development in the game's progress if it wanted to keep and increase attendances. For competitive games would surely be much more attractive to spectators than the numerous friendlies which littered the fixture lists of the times?

Yet at the time it didn't appear quite so cut and dried. And powerful voices were raised in opposition to the League. Many in the SFA were against it. The country's most successful and most powerful club – Queen's Park – was implacably opposed. Many clubs too (chiefly those not invited to be involved) were aghast at the prospect. And the learned gentlemen of the press cried 'O Tempora, O Mores' at the very idea. Their main arguments were that it would be elitist, would lead to the death of minor clubs and – worst of all – would encourage professionalism.

They were right on all three counts. It was also, given the establishment of a league in England, inevitable. And indeed an argument can be advanced that without the establishment of a Scottish League the larger clubs would simply have joined the already-existing one in the south. Which would have created a bit of a headache for modern sports writers on a slow news day, removing, as it would have, that old standby of 'will the Old Firm join the Premiership?' (There are two potential answers to that question, the knowledge of which means never having to read another tedious article on the subject. These are 'no' and 'not unless Rupert Murdoch says so'.)

The boom of the 1880s had several downsides to it. Firstly, the success of the international team led to a migration south of many of the best Scottish players. From the late 1870s onwards clubs in North West England and the Midlands offered financial inducements to those willing to move even though professionalism wasn't officially recognised in England until 1885. Naturally, this had an effect on the quality of the game in Scotland. A way had to be found to stem the flow south.

Secondly, too many teams chased after supporters and there was a limit to how many sides could exist in any particular locality. Some teams faded away after a few short years. Others took longer, often decades, before giving up the ghost. The process, it can be argued, goes on to this day with the twenty-first century bringing top level football to Livingston and Inverness while Clyde left Glasgow after over 100 years and Clydebank failed to sustain League football for the second time in 70 years.

Thirdly, haphazard fixture lists played havoc with attendances. Gate money, far from being a useful addition to a club's coffers, had quickly become the main source of income and short notice alteration or cancellation of fixtures had a devastating effect on crowds. Again there is a parallel with our own times. Today, supporters get (rightly) annoyed when the date and time of a match is altered at short notice to suit the whim of a TV station. In the 1880s the fixtures for the season were published in advance only for a team to cancel at the last minute owing to some cup replay taking precedence. And not just the Scottish Cup either. It could be any one of the numerous county competitions which were popular at the time.

Then, as now, many fans were frustrated at the inability of their club to play its games on the stated date and time.

The difference is that while today it is League football which acquiesces in the ruination of the fixture card, back then it was seen as the game's saviour from such evils.

Just as it had done with the creation of an FA, a knockout cup and international football, it was England that led the way – albeit thanks to a Scot by name of William McGregor.

McGregor was a director of Aston Villa and his remedy for fixture losses and falling attendances was the creation of a league of clubs whose matches against each other would take precedence over all other competitions save for the FA Cup.

The Football League – the inspiration for all such competitions – was established in 1888 and by the end of its second season was an unqualified success. Thanks to its concentration in Lancashire and the West and East Midlands it provided plenty of 'derby' matches and allowed supporters to travel to away games in horse-drawn charabancs or 'brakes'. Attendances were excellent as a result. One club – Everton – boasted an average of 10,000 – a figure normally seen only at internationals or important cup ties. Even the most poorly supported teams were drawing in 3,000 for home games.

The Football League in England provided plenty of 'derby' matches

It was an idea whose time had come and, if the English experience was anything to go by, a concept that couldn't fail. And so on August 16th 1890 the Scottish Football League came into being with four matches involving eight of the unwieldy eleven clubs in membership. The League tried to replicate the English experience as closely as it could, containing four clubs from Glasgow – Celtic, Cowlairs, Rangers and Third Lanark, three from close by – Cambuslang and the Paisley pair of Abercorn and St Mirren, three from the chief pre-League rival to Glaswegian supremacy – Dumbarton, Renton and Vale of Leven from Dunbartonshire, and in its one concession to the rest of the country, Heart of Midlothian from Edinburgh.

This last was thought to be a great risk and many a sigh of relief was heard from the western clubs when Hearts' match away to Rangers on the opening day produced a gate of around 3,400. Gates for the other games were encouraging too with 3,000 attending Cambuslang's match with Vale of Leven and 2,000 for Dumbarton v Cowlairs. With the Paisley duo and Third Lanark inactive on the opening day it was the other game played which raised eyebrows among the members, offered a stinging rebuff to the sceptics and drew salivating gasps from those left out in the cold. Celtic v Renton drew an estimated 8,000.

Celtic were a new phenomenon in the Scottish game. While other clubs took years to patiently build up support they arrived, like Athena springing from the forehead of Zeus, fully-formed and armed as they took Scottish football by storm. There was nothing particularly unusual about their Irish and Roman Catholic ancestry. Many clubs represented the large Irish immigrant community in Scotland in the 1880s. Hibernian in Edinburgh are only the most obvious example. Any community in Scotland containing a sizeable population which was Irish in origin or by descent had a football team. Clubs with suffixes like Hibernians, Harp and Shamrock were dotted all over the country as were a few with the prefix Erin.

Celtic were different on three counts. Firstly they included charitable objectives amongst their aims. Secondly, rather than being a random bunch of young men kicking a ball about, theirs was an organised establishment with a decidedly focused aim on attracting support from within the largest Irish Roman Catholic community inside Scotland's largest city. Thirdly, they attempted from the outset to widen their appeal by not placing any religious requirements on their players and by adopting a name designed to resonate with the majority. It was not wholly successful as their support was drawn almost exclusively from the immigrant community.

Admitting an Edinburgh club into the League was thought to be a great risk

Celtic's success was such that they reached the Scottish Cup Final in their first season, had won the Cup by 1892 and the League a year later. Such success for what was seen by many as an 'alien' club reinforced the desire to find a champion for the majority Protestant population. That it would be another Glasgow club was obvious. Quite why this status ended up being conferred on a team which had no Scottish Cups and only a shared League title to show for twenty years of existence is another matter entirely.

The most popular theory is that, given their location close to the shipbuilding yards of Govan, Rangers drew support from another immigrant community, Ulster Protestants, who moved to Scotland in large numbers in the early 1900s. That may or may not be the case but Rangers were a well-supported side long before then and even in the early 1890s their meetings with Celtic drew far more supporters than clashes with Third Lanark, Clyde or Partick Thistle.

It is of course entirely feasible that had Queen's Park adopted professionalism they would have become the standard-bearers of Protestant Glasgow and that Rangers today would be a minor Third Division club, if indeed they existed at all.

It was Isaac Newton who said, 'To every action there is always opposed an equal reaction.' While the great scientist's powers may not have extended to forecasting the future of sport in Scotland, his famous statement certainly applies to it. As Celtic became ever more successful as a club representing immigrant Irish Catholics, so the clamour rose for a single alternative to represent native Scottish Protestants.

If it hadn't been Rangers it would have been Third Lanark or Queen's Park or maybe even long-dead Cowlairs. But such a club would have come into being. Of that there can be no doubt. The temperature of the times dictated it. But while it was inevitable that such a rivalry, forged on the anvil of mutual antipathy, should have come into being, it was not predestined to exert its baleful influence on our game down to the present day. That was the doing of the clubs themselves as they recognised their continued pre-eminence rested on joint exploitation of their shared antagonisms.

Dumbarton and Rangers shared the title at the end of a season which was an undoubted success. Celtic led the way in gates, averaging just over 5,500 with Rangers also edging over the 5,000 mark. Third Lanark were next, demonstrating the great appetite for football among the Glasgow public. But it was ravenous rather than gluttonous as Cowlairs found out. They were the worst supported side with an average of just over 1,500 and didn't re-appear the next season. Hearts' average of 3,400 was just less than that of the League as a whole so the imposition of an Edinburgh team hadn't been the disaster many feared. In fact Hearts' biggest gate of the season wasn't against a Glasgow team but came in their match with Dumbarton which drew takings of over £100.

The same teams met in the Scottish Cup Final and again, fears that lack of a Glaswegian presence would deter spectators from turning up weren't realised as 10,836 saw Hearts win the Scottish Cup for the first time.

The League's success was such – around 330,000 spectators

in total – that they decided to expand. Cowlairs were replaced by Renton (who had been expelled by the SFA for playing against a professional team) and Clyde and Leith Athletic were admitted, proving that while the League was prepared to expand numerically, they weren't as yet prepared to do so geographically.

While the League had happily copied many of their ideas from England, one that they singularly failed to reproduce concerned population. The twelve original members of the Football League all came from heavily populated towns. But unless one includes Midlands rivals Aston Villa and West Bromwich Albion as both being from Birmingham (a debatable point as any Baggies fan will tell you) no town provided more than one club.

In Scotland that was not the case. The legacy of this heavy concentration on Clydeside and Dunbartonshire can be seen today. Whereas only one of the original dozen English clubs (Accrington) no longer plays league football, only five of the Scottish originals (The Old Firm, Dumbarton, Hearts and St Mirren) are still around. And the Sons membership went into abeyance for almost a decade. Of the other six, four were gone as early as 1897 with Abercorn failing to re-appear after World War I and Third Lanark expiring in 1967.

The first sign of this high attrition rate came at the end of the second season when Cambuslang and Vale of Leven, the two worst supported teams, gave up the struggle. The League temporarily retrenched, sticking to just ten members, before – in another imitation of events south of the border – it took the bold step of introducing a Second Division in 1893. At the same time the inevitable was finally accepted and professionalism legalised in Scotland.

Bold may actually be too strong a word. The new division contained a number of sides from the 'traditional' areas – Cowlairs came back, and three other Glasgow teams, Thistle, Northern and Partick Thistle joined them. Hibs were the Edinburgh representatives. But there was some innovation as well. The larger towns in the west of Scotland were demanding membership and this was acknowledged by the admission of Morton from Greenock and Motherwell into membership. The

One idea from England that the Scottish League singularly failed to reproduce concerned population

Renfrewshire contingent was also strengthened by the addition of Port Glasgow Athletic.

The really striking move came in the First Division. Not so much in the demotion of Abercorn and Clyde to the lower league nor by the fast-tracking of St Bernard's from Edinburgh straight into the First Division but by the inclusion for the first time of a team from north of the Clyde-Forth line.

By admitting Dundee into the First Division the League gave a clear indication that it recognised the future lay in expanding into areas where support was plentiful. Dundee brought with them around 4,000 regular spectators, far in excess of most. Celtic were still the best supported team, beginning to nudge the 10,000 mark on average and Hearts were gaining fast on the terraces as they became successful on the pitch. With a League title in 1895, another Scottish Cup success a year later and a second championship in 1897 all ending up at Tynecastle, there was no indication that Scottish football was going down the century-long road of two-club dominance.

Hearts' 1896 Scottish Cup Final win brought home the sad fact that no ground outside of Glasgow was adequately equipped to cope with big games. Because the Final was against Edinburgh rivals Hibs, the SFA took the entirely logical decision to play the game in the capital. The only suitable venue was St Bernard's Logie Green. The game attracted 17,034 – a record for the ground – but with thousands locked out and many within unable to get a decent view this was the first and last time the Scottish Cup has been won on anything other than Glaswegian soil.

It wasn't that the SFA was particularly pro-Glasgow – though the influence wielded by that city was considerable – they tried to spread out the international matches against Wales and Ireland (who Scotland first met in 1884). As early as 1888 the Welsh match was taken to Easter Road where it attracted a respectable 8,000 to see Scotland win 5-1 and two years later the fixture was played in the unlikely setting of Abercorn's Underwood Park in Paisley where 7,500 saw a 5-0 Scottish triumph. But the 'touring' policy took a severe knock when only 600 saw the Welsh thrashed 6-1 at Tynecastle in 1892 despite the inclusion of four Hearts players in the Scotland eleven.

> **By admitting Dundee the League gave a clear indication that it recognised the future lay in expanding into areas where support was plentiful**

The simple truth was that games against Wales and Ireland were inevitably too one-sided to be attractive fare. The SFA got round the Irish question by taking the fixture to Celtic Park. Wales remained more of a problem. It wasn't always as bad as the Tynecastle game – there were 10,000 at Rugby Park to see the 5-2 win in 1894 and 11,700 at Dundee's Carolina Port ground for the 4-0 victory in 1896. Judicious use of players from the host clubs helped boost the gate on those occasions but when the match was taken to Fir Park in 1898 there were no representatives from Motherwell in the Scotland team and a mere 3,500 saw the home team win 5-2.

The lack of native players didn't hinder the fixture in Aberdeen in 1900 when Pittodrie staged its first international as 12,500 saw Scotland win by what was now the almost customary 5-2 scoreline. Yet with no Morton players taking part just 5,284 Greenock citizens could be persuaded to turn up at Cappielow to see a 5-1 Scottish victory in 1902.

In 1897 there was no indication that Scottish football was going down the century-long road of two-club dominance

One ground that didn't get a look-in was Hampden Park. After the record-breaking game of 1890 it was clear that the second ground of that name was too small to safely accommodate the prestigious England match. After going to Ibrox in 1892 the fixture took up residence at Celtic Park where it continued to set new Scottish records. 45,017 saw the teams draw 2-2 in 1894 and 56,500 saw the 2-1 Scots win two years later in the first match in which Scottish players from English clubs – 'Anglos' as they became designated – took part. There were fewer in 1898 but a new record was set when 63,000 saw a 4-1 home win in 1900. That was to be overtaken with tragic consequences two years later.

The 1890s saw a frenzy of stadium building as the League bug caught on. Many teams found their existing grounds too small for the new set-up. Queen's Park, denied permission to expand their existing ground, determined to erect a third Hampden Park to challenge the new rivals from the Scottish League. The first Rangers-Celtic Scottish Cup Final drew 17,000 to Second Hampden in 1894. Their next, five years later, attracted 25,000 and a semi-final at the old Ibrox stadium in 1900 saw 33,000 in attendance, almost twice as many as saw Celtic beat Queen's Park in the Final.

League attendances in games between Celtic and Rangers had rocketed too from around 8,000 in that first season to touching the 50,000 mark by the end of the decade. Exact figures for this period are hard to come by but gates of 40,323 and 44,868 were recorded for these games during the 1890s. The next most popular fixture was a visit from Hearts if the Edinburgh team were doing well. That could encourage as many as 25,000 along to Celtic Park and Ibrox.

So much for the doom-mongers who thought it was pushing it a bit to include an Edinburgh team in the League. Hearts' own derbies with Leith, St Bernard's and eventually Hibernian drew much smaller attendances, though Tynecastle was of course a much smaller ground. 17,500 against Hibs in 1895-96 was the best of the nineteenth century.

By the end of the 1890s the more populous towns in West-Central Scotland saw their teams gain entry to the League

By the end of its first decade the Scottish League was a still-expanding organisation. The Amateurs gave up their fight against the League that year. Faced with an ever-dwindling fixture list as the league sucked up their potential opponents, Queen's Park bowed to the inevitable and joined – albeit straight into the First Division – in 1900-01. It was too late to save their one-time dominance in the Scottish game but just in time to ensure they didn't go the way of Vale of Leven and Renton. It was also just in time for them to do Scottish football one last enormous service a few years later.

The Second Division had shed its Glaswegian excess as Northern, Thistle and Cowlairs all departed. Leaving too were former giants of the game Dumbarton and Renton (though the Sons would return).

The more populous towns in West-Central Scotland saw their teams gain entry. Airdrieonians joined in 1894 and Ayrshire was recognised when Kilmarnock were admitted a year later. But the League didn't get it right every time. Joining with Airdrie were Dundee Wanderers who lasted just twelve months and in with Killie came Linthouse, yet another Glasgow team, who lasted five years – they were based in Govan, an area of Glasgow already pretty much sewn up in terms of support by Rangers. The League extended into Stirlingshire when East Stirlingshire replaced them in 1900.

Other admissions were more long-lasting such as Ayr in

> **RANGERS AND CELTIC LTD**
>
> Some observed that the 1904 Scottish Cup Final between Rangers and Celtic was the third such contest in the past decade. And that occasion saw the first appearance of a new phrase to describe the pair.
>
> Supporters of both clubs were highly suspicious of the number of draws when these clubs met in cup ties which resulted in replays which were lucrative for the clubs but costly for the fans. On the day of the Final – April 16th – the 'Scottish Referee' published a cartoon depicting a man with a sandwich board upon which was written the legend 'PATRONISE THE OLD FIRM – RANGERS CELTIC LTD.'

1897 and Hamilton Accies who took over Renton's fixtures that year. And as the Victorian era gave way to the Edwardian, Arthurlie from Barrhead joined up in 1901.

The top division expanded rapidly in the early twentieth century. From ten in 1901 to twelve a year later then, with the admission of Lanarkshire pair Airdrieonians and Motherwell in 1903 to a new high of fourteen. The lower division recruited frantically as well. In 1902 the League ventured into Fife for the first time with the admission of Raith Rovers. Joining alongside them were Falkirk to give that town two League clubs. A year later Albion Rovers and Ayr Parkhouse were both admitted but the latter were replaced after just one year by a new club as the League made its boldest move yet and admitted Aberdeen into membership.

At the start of the 1904-05 season there were fourteen clubs in Division One and twelve in Division Two. After fourteen years of operation, six clubs could boast a League title to their name. Celtic and Rangers had four each (Rangers could add a joint title), Hearts two, Dumbarton one and one joint, Hibs and Third Lanark one apiece. Exactly the same number of teams had shared the first fourteen titles in England. The Scottish Football League appeared to be a healthy body, capable of attracting good crowds and full of competition.

Similarly six different clubs had won the Scottish Cup during the same period. Again, Rangers and Celtic had four wins each, Hearts had three and Hibernian, Queen's Park and St Bernard's one apiece.

HAMPDEN PARK

The third Hampden made its bow just in time. Although Ibrox and Celtic Park continued to vie for the big games, Hampden's position on the railway line direct to Glasgow Central ensured it would emerge successful in these 'ground wars.' It's eventual acceptance as the de facto national stadium was helped by the very fact that it WASN'T Ibrox or Parkhead. Celtic fans would never accept the former or Rangers supporters the latter while the rest of Scottish football wished a plague on both their houses.

Hampden became the spiritual home of Scottish football, at first by default then, as the ground grew in the affections of Scottish supporters, by desire.

The 1904 game with England had gone to Celtic Park but the SFA decided to take a chance on Hampden in 1906. It was a decision they were never to regret. Hours before the kick-off vast crowds could be seen making their way towards Mount Florida. Trains and trams were packed full. Horse-drawn carriages brought many more. Thousands arrived by the newest form of transport – the motor car and thousands more by the oldest – on foot.

In total the attendance numbered 102,741 – the first six-figure crowd in Scotland and a 50% increase on the old record. They enjoyed their day too as Scotland beat the Auld Enemy 2-1. This game set the seal on Hampden's position in the game and secured it the premier international. Whenever an England side set foot in Scotland over the next 83 years their destination was always Hampden Park.

Celtic Park, just as it is today, was easily the largest ground until the new Hampden came along but the growing rivalry with Rangers convinced that team they needed a bigger ground too and in 1900 they opened a new Ibrox Park, said to be capable of holding 75,000.

By a narrow vote it was decided to award the staging of the 1902 international against England to the new Ibrox and the 68,114 supporters there established a new Scottish record attendance.

But it isn't for the size of the crowd that this game is remembered. A section of the west terrace gave way under the pressure of the huge crowd and 26 spectators lost their lives with almost another 600 injured. The wooden construction of the terrace was blamed for the disaster. It was Scottish football's first great tragedy. Sadly, it wouldn't be the last. Quite incredibly the game restarted after an eighteen minutes delay and the sides fought out a 1-1 draw. Once the scale of the tragedy became clear the authorities decided to scrap the match from the

NEW SCOTTISH WORLD RECORD

Scotland had a new record to celebrate – a World record crowd.

The match against England at Hampden in 1908 wasn't the most enthralling of the century-long series, finishing in a 1-1 draw. But the crowd was spectacular. At 121,452 it not only broke the previous Scottish record, it exceeded the previous British and World best of 114,815 set by the 1901 FA Cup Final.

It was a true watershed in the game's development. For the next 42 years the World record would be held by Scotland and by Hampden Park. An enduring legacy of an otherwise unremarkable match.

record books and the teams met at the end of the season at Villa Park where they again drew.

The construction of the new Hampden Park was heavily influenced by the Ibrox disaster and its new terraces were built on solid earth. The ground opened in October 1903 with 40,000 present to see a rare Queen's Park victory over Celtic in the League.

The third Hampden hadn't been built to accommodate Queen's Park supporters though. A ground half the size could easily have done that and had plenty of room to spare. Queen's were determined to win back the Cup Finals and Internationals which had once been their birthright and the 1904 Final was the ground's first big test. With 64,472 inside it passed with flying colours. The spectators saw a thrilling match which Celtic won 3-2.

That game also marked the end of an era in which the Old Firm (as we must henceforth refer to them), while the leading lights, weren't the only stars of the show. In the years ahead other clubs would find it increasingly difficult to challenge for honours, particularly in the League which, with the sole exception of Motherwell's 1932 success, the Glaswegian pair dominated exclusively until 1948.

The phenomenal rise in attendances wasn't reflected evenly in the club game. That's not to say gates hadn't risen. They had actually doubled since the foundation of the Scottish League with both Old Firm clubs capable of averaging 10,000.

The construction of the new Hampden Park was heavily influenced by the Ibrox disaster and its new terraces were built on solid earth

Contained within that figure though were vast disparities. While they could draw gates of 50,000 and upwards for matches with each other, often their crowds could be as low as 2,000 for run-of-the-mill matches.

The other 'established' Glasgow Clubs – Queen's Park and Third Lanark – and those from Scotland's other large cities were the best of the rest. It was rare for a 'provincial' team to average as much as 5,000 and in the Second Division an average of 2,000 signified a successful season.

One of the reasons for the failure of the averages to rise more spectacularly was the continued increase in numbers. Games against Rangers and Celtic constituted over one fifth of total gates in 1900 in the ten-club First Division but only just over one tenth by 1914 when there were 20 clubs in the division. By the outbreak of World War I Scottish League membership numbered 34 in total.

An important factor for the future was Rangers ability to keep pace with Celtic's gates and even at times to outstrip them. This wasn't justified by results on the pitch as Celtic won six successive titles from 1904-1910. Ordinarily, such dominance by one club would lead to a drop in support for their rivals, especially if, as happened in these seasons, they were even eclipsed as chief challengers as sides like Dundee and Falkirk emerged as closest to Celtic.

That's certainly what happened and still happens in England in places like Manchester, Liverpool and North London when one of a pair of rivals is in the ascendancy. Of course there is no religious factor involved in these teams' battles for supremacy and it would seem it was this growing identification of Rangers with Protestantism which helped them to equal and even match Celtic in the attendances table even if they were woefully short of doing so on the field. Rangers went nine years without winning the League and were on course for a spell of 25 years without a Scottish Cup victory.

For a total of eight seasons from 1903-1911 they lifted neither League nor Cup, the most unsuccessful period in their history since the arrival of Celtic on the scene. Not even in the darkest days of Celtic's nine-in-a-row era or the sometimes dreadful Rangers teams of the pre-Souness days did they go for so long without having one or other of the top two trophies on display. And while it's difficult to prove for certain that the religious element is what kept their support not only stable but increasing, it's difficult to think of any other reason.

In 1909 the Old Firm met to contest the Scottish Cup Final for the fourth time in fifteen years. The match was an entertaining 2-2 draw and the teams assembled at Hampden for the replay seven days later. There were no provisions for extra time in the event of a draw but there had been much press speculation on the topic and many supporters clearly felt they were due a decision on the day.

When the second game finished 1-1 the fans took matters into their own hands. Frustrated by the failure to play extra time and angry at the prospect of paying for a third time, several thousand invaded the pitch and a full-scale riot broke out as supporters fought – not between themselves – but with the police. Even the fire brigade were attacked when they arrived on the scene to deal with the blazing turnstiles the mob had set alight. For over two hours the battle raged with some 5,000 supporters involved before police reinforcements forced them into the streets where windows were smashed and passers-by assailed as the mob retreated back to the city centre.

Religion played no part in the proceedings but the suspicions voiced in the Scottish Referee cartoon of 1904 were to the fore as supporters were convinced the clubs and the SFA were determined to milk them for as much as they could by taking the tie to a third game.

The SFA acted as promptly as Edwardian decency allowed. Which meant doing nothing on the Sabbath and convening a meeting on Monday morning. Both clubs were summoned to a further meeting that evening. It was the clubs themselves who petitioned for the Cup to be abandoned and medals withheld. And that was the decision agreed. But only after an amendment seeking a replay outside Glasgow on the grounds that Glaswegians were 'not capable of behaving themselves' was defeated by 15-11. At 8pm that night the SFA took the further step of denying all liability for claims pursued by injured spectators or for damage to property.

A sad footnote to the whole affair was the fate of the referee,

JB Stark. In April 1913 he was assaulted by a fan while officiating at Celtic Park. Later the same year, he (perhaps understandably) emigrated to Canada.

The aftermath of the riot saw the SFA reach an illogical conclusion. Hampden Park was no longer deemed suitable for the Scottish Cup Final. Yet it was still awarded the England game which attracted crowds twice as large. Even more illogically the Scottish Cup Final was awarded to the grounds of the very teams whose supporters had caused all the trouble!

Amidst the furore it was forgotten that Celtic had missed the chance to win the Scottish Cup for three years in succession. Almost a century later this is an achievement still beyond them.

No political cause could attract more than a fraction of the numbers intent on watching Scotland play football against England.

But the highlight of the sporting calendar remained the match against England and in 1912 the attendance rose to new heights as 127,307 saw another 1-1 draw. Speaking after the devastation of war, Albert Einstein described nationalism as 'an infantile disease – the measles of mankind'. Had the great physicist ever attended a Scotland-England game he may have made allowances for it. In a footballing sense nationalism was the engine of Scottish football. No political cause could attract more than a fraction of the numbers intent on watching Scotland play football against England.

Less remarked upon the same season but noteworthy nonetheless was the 32,000 crowd which saw Scotland beat Wales 1-0 at Tynecastle the same year – a far cry from the paltry 600 who had seen their first international at that venue.

Indeed, the years leading up to World War I saw big increases in attendances almost everywhere. Rangers led the way as they averaged over 20,000 for the first time. Half-day working on Saturdays had led to the first big crowds in the 1870s and 1880s and with more and more people having a Saturday off entirely there was an increase not just in gates but in travelling support too. 'Brake clubs' named after the horse-drawn charabancs which ferried supporters to away games became common in most clubs and their outings were adorned by elaborately designed banners such as were common at the time in the rapidly growing trades union movement.

They made for a colourful display of support and a

convenient rallying point for any fan who ended up lost after partaking of a little too much local hospitality on his travels.

And there were more travels to go on. The First Division had extended to twenty clubs by 1914 and the Second contained fourteen. But movement between the divisions was still subject to a vote by the top-flight clubs. This was a system that was not only unpopular but grossly unfair, and in the long run, unsustainable. It was a great pity that, having copied so much from south of the border, the Scottish League didn't follow the example of the Football League and introduce a system of automatic promotion and relegation.

The outbreak of war in August 1914 was, at first, thought to have had little impact on football. After all, hadn't the nation been assured that it would all be over by Christmas? But it soon became apparent that the war was not only going to be a lot longer but that it would also be a much more bloody affair than anyone had forecast.

Even although conscription wasn't introduced until 1916 there was great pressure brought to bear on the football authorities to close down or at least not to carry on as they had done hitherto.

Hearts would surely have won the League in 1915 had it not been for the loss of players to the WWI forces

It's one of the oddities of a nation at war that a shopkeeper who said 'business as usual' was regarded as 'doing his bit' while a footballer doing precisely the same was considered cowardly! Women were encouraged to hand out white feathers (denoting cowardice) to fit young men spotted not wearing uniform, even if these same young men happened to be part-time footballers whose day jobs as coal miners or shipyard workers exempted them from call-up after the imposition of conscription.

In any case clubs generally responded to the war effort favourably. Players were encouraged to volunteer for the services, most notably in the case of Hearts who would surely have won the League in 1915 had it not been for the loss of players to the forces. They are the best known example but every club no matter how high or how low lost players during the carnage of the war. The slaughter on the Western Front was so intense and so long-lasting that not one club in the land was left untouched.

The Scottish League, its two English counterparts (the Football League and the Southern League) and their Irish equivalent met with Government to thrash out an agreement for wartime activity. They were pleasantly surprised to find a level of support for the game's continuance in some shape or form as many in political circles could see the advantages of football as a diversion from bad news from the front.

But the response was confusing. The SFA suspended the 1914-15 Scottish Cup but let the Qualifying Cup carry on to its conclusion. Internationals ceased forthwith. While the Leagues in England shut down after 1915 the Scottish League continued. Or at least its First Division did as the League ruled out a request for regionalisation from the Second Division and that section closed for the duration (and for three years afterwards).

Crowds were falling badly though. Some teams were drawing under 3,000 – one match between Aberdeen and Ayr United was attended by just 250 according to a reporter – and transport difficulties forced the League to withdraw its three most northerly and easterly teams – Aberdeen, Dundee and Raith Rovers – in 1917. They were replaced by Clydebank whose league pedigree was scant – one season to be precise – but whose location at the centre of the munitions and shipbuilding industries meant it had a ready, willing and, most importantly of all, comparatively well-off population able to give a badly needed boost to gates.

Even though gates were well down the Old Firm still led the way. But a comparison of the last full season of war (1917-18) with that of peace (1913-14) shows just how drastic the reduction was. Rangers were down by over 6,500 per game and Celtic by over 4,500. Hearts, with a drop of over 5,500 were hit far harder proportionately than either of the Glasgow duo. Overall, the drop was over 2,000 per match – a severe blow to finances.

The worst season for attendances was during 1916-17 when the war was at its worst and home front morale was low too. But even the League average of around 5,300 that year was comparable with the best crowds at its inception back in 1890.

That showed how much interest in and attendances at

Scottish football had grown before meeting this temporary setback. As the guns finally fell silent across Europe and football faced an uncertain future, the game could pause for a brief reflection on what had gone before. Neither the Ibrox Disaster nor the Hampden riots had quelled the enthusiasm of the Scottish public, as a look at club record gates will show.

Unsurprisingly the Old Firm led the way. The game at Parkhead on New Year's Day 1914 drew 75,000 spectators, paying £1,650 at the gate and a further £530 at the stands, according to figures in the Glasgow Herald. At Ibrox 63,000 had watched the fixture earlier that season.

Other clubs could cite impressive statistics too. Queen's Park had that 40,000 crowd for the Hampden opener in 1903 and had drawn 30,231 for a visit from Rangers the next season. Hearts had played before 23,095, also against Rangers, while chasing the League in 1915. Celtic were the most popular visitors at Motherwell with 19,438 attending Fir Park in 1913-14.

For some it was the Scottish Cup which produced the biggest crowds – and the Old Firm didn't have to be present either. Kilmarnock's tie with Clyde in 1912 enticed 19,564 along to Rugby Park. Nor did the Old Firm have to be present for a big crowd to turn out at their own grounds. A Scottish Cup second replay between Aberdeen and Dundee was watched by 19,525 at Ibrox. The Second Division is much harder to quantify but the presence of Aberdeen for a single season boosted gates there with 5,924 watching the Dons introduction to league football against Falkirk.

What the clubs weren't as yet aware of was that gates were going to go higher. Much higher. Of the 42 clubs playing league football in Scotland today, 25 of them were League members in 1915. Of those 25, just one – Clyde – had already experienced their record attendance.

For the others the best was yet to come.

Th early twentieth century saw the rise of the motor car
and the demise of horse-drawn charbancs, allowing
spectators to travel from further afield

Growing in the Wind: 1918-1930

No one knew quite what was in store for football after World War I but there was evidence that numbers were rising, not just towards pre-war levels, but exceeding them. The Junior Cup Final was taken to Hampden for the first time in 1919 and 43,000 saw Rutherglen Glencairn draw with St Anthony's. That was more than twice as many as had attended any previous Junior Final. 38,000 saw Glencairn win the replay 1-0.

Further proof that the game was experiencing a boom came in 1919-20, the first real peacetime season since 1914. In the League, away games featuring the Old Firm hit new heights. Motherwell's pre-war record, set in 1913-14, was exceeded by over 4,000 as 23,750 saw them take on Celtic. Clydebank showed the wisdom, in the short term at least, of their elevation to the top flight when 18,021 attended their game with Rangers. The Ibrox club's presence set new records at other Glasgow grounds as 41,688 saw their match with Partick Thistle at Firhill and Third Lanark proved that it was possible after all to extend the second Hampden beyond the 25,000 limit when 30,213 were attracted to their game with Rangers at that venue, now renamed Cathkin Park after Thirds' original home.

It was the Scottish Cup though which broke all records. There were 30,000-plus gates at Dens Park and Tynecastle in the second round and 65,000 for Celtic v Partick Thistle in round three. At the same stage St Bernard's had to change the venue for their game, as their ground couldn't accommodate the anticipated 20,000 attendance. And who were their opponents? Hearts? Hibs? Rangers? No, their foes that day were Albion Rovers!

> St Bernard's had to change the venue for their Scottish Cup game, as their ground couldn't cope with the 20,000 attendance against Albion Rovers!

Rovers had, like Clydebank, struck lucky. Aberdeen, Dundee and Raith had all rejoined the League and one club was needed to make up the numbers. The Coatbridge side got the call and even though they were bottom of the single-division League this was to be their best season ever in the Scottish Cup.

The biggest eye-opener of them all came in the quarter-finals when an incredible 98,466 were present at Ibrox to see Rangers beat Celtic 1-0. It was a new record for a club game in Scotland and a sure sign that the arrival of the 100,000 attendance in club football was only a matter of time.

Over 120,000 in total watched the three games it took to decide the semi-final at Celtic Park between Rangers and Albion Rovers. Even more surprising than the crowd figures was the outcome of the tie as the team from Cliftonhill emulated Dumbarton in 1897 by reaching the Scottish Cup Final while anchored to the foot of the League.

The other semi-final was at Hampden where 50,000 saw Kilmarnock beat Morton and the identity of the two Finalists encouraged the SFA to take their showpiece game back to Hampden for the first time since the 1909 riots.

Their reasoning was that two such 'provincial' sides wouldn't attract more than 50,000 to the game. The last such 'provincial' Final, between Falkirk and Raith Rovers in 1913, had been watched by 45,000 and not even the Old Firm had attracted more than 70,000 to Hampden so to that extent their thinking was logical. It was also sadly outdated.

The SFA ignored the evidence of their own eyes. The evidence that an Old Firm quarter-final now attracted 30,000 more than the Final once did. The evidence that the 50,000 they expected for a 'provincial' Final had already turned up for the semi-final. The evidence that when a club has to look for a bigger ground because Albion Rovers are in town it could only mean a huge upturn in crowds.

And so, on April 17th 1920, Hampden Park was engulfed in another controversy. A massive 95,811 managed to get in to see the game but thousands more were locked outside. They missed a fine match which Killie won 3-2.

The SFA were better prepared the next year. Forewarned by

crowds such as 20,000 for Clydebank v Alloa, 54,000 at Ibrox to see Rangers take on the Wasps in the next round, 32,000 at the same venue when it was the neutral setting for a second replay between Hibs and Third Lanark and an amazing 22,000 at Cliftonhill for Albion Rovers v Armadale, the SFA knew precisely what to do. They doubled the admission price.

Not even Baldrick could have conjured up such a cunning plan. Phase One went into operation at the Scotland-England game a week before the 1921 Final. This was the first official meeting of the two countries north of the border since 1914. In keeping with the five previous occasions it had been played at Hampden, there should have been a massive six-figure crowd and perhaps a new world record.

Instead the price rises kept the crowd down to 85,000 – a figure considered disappointing at the time. The missing thousands lost out on one of the finest performances by a Scottish team in years as they put the Auld Enemy to the sword, winning 3-0.

Crowds stayed below the 100,000 mark for the next two visits from the English. Here was a stunning paradox. While teams like Albion Rovers, St Bernard's and Clydebank could scarcely accommodate their supporters, the biggest match in Britain, if not the world, was drawing 40,000-50,000 fewer people than it did pre-war!

Phase Two was even more successful. Not content with upping the prices, the SFA moved the Final – involving Rangers and Partick Thistle – to Celtic Park. This wasn't the most popular of venues with Rangers supporters at any time, but in 1921 with the political situation in Ireland worsening by the day and civil war looming in that troubled isle, many Gers fans decided they'd rather not give any of their money to the SFA as some of it would go to Celtic for the ground hire. For these supporters the distinction between a football club and the republican movement was clear. They didn't think there was one.

A transport strike on the day of the Final put a cap on matters, helping to reduce the attendance to 28,294, a figure which has not been 'beaten' for a Saturday Final since. In the same season 42,780 saw the same two teams at Firhill in the League.

Those who were there saw history made as Partick Thistle upset the odds to win 1-0. Some consolation for the thousands who missed the match was that, for the first time, Pathé News filmed the game and highlights could be seen in the local cinema. Unfortunately the Pathé cameramen missed the game's only goal!

The Qualifying Cup set a new high. There were 18,603 in attendance at Cowdenbeath this season to see East Fife beat Bo'ness in the Final. The Juniors remained healthy too. The 26,000 who saw Rob Roy beat Ashfield at Hampden closely challenged the Scottish Cup Final turnout.

'The crowd was somewhat disappointing. It barely touched 60,000.'

And League gates stayed high too. As usual the largest were for the Old Firm meetings with 1920-21 seeing 69,260 at Ibrox and 65,269 at Celtic Park. Apart from that huge crowd at Firhill, other clubs set new League highs. There were 15,013 at Rugby Park and 13,849 at Stark's Park as Kilmarnock and Raith Rovers entertained Rangers. Aberdeen demonstrated their potential with 23,566 for the visit of Celtic. But the most surprising attendance was once again at Cliftonhill where 20,615 saw Albion Rovers lose 2-1 to Rangers.

Another important development took place in the attendance charts as Celtic dropped out of the top two with Hearts taking their place. This was the first sign of a malaise which would affect Celtic for decades. Over a forty-years long period from 1926-1966 they would win the League just three times – a paltry total for a club that was part of a powerful duopoly. Apart from the odd occasion their rivalry with Rangers became sharply restricted to the games between the clubs. In terms of trophies the Ibrox side would eclipse their great rival for decades.

As a consequence Celtic's huge support manifested itself only for really important matches and their position in the attendance league reflects that as, while usually third, they dropped as low as seventh on occasion. They wouldn't regain their place in the top two until 1949. And after 1918 the next time they were the best supported side wasn't until their European Cup winning year of 1967.

Two seasons of post-war crowd success paved the way for the re-introduction of the Second Division. The Scottish League's failure to do so immediately at the end of the war had seen the stronger sides outside the League form their own set-ups and, freed from League rules, they were often able to lure top names to play for them. JR Smith left Scottish Cup holders Kilmarnock to sign for Cowdenbeath – an unthinkable move in pre-war days – before moving south and making history in 1923 when he became the first player to score in both Hampden and Wembley Cup Finals. Andy Wilson won six Scotland caps and captained his country while with Dunfermline Athletic.

This left the ex-Division Two and non-league teams in a strong bargaining position and their demand – automatic promotion and relegation – was conceded by a League worried enough about losing its top players to England, let alone to Fife.

Three teams would go down at the end of 1921-22 with one promoted, to allow the top division to revert to its 1914 complement of twenty. After that it would be a straight two up, two down, as in England.

This led to an even greater rise in attendances in the 22-club First Division as famous names like Queen's Park and Hearts became sucked into the relegation dogfight. Queen's Park's gates jumped by over 4,000 a game and while Hearts fell away slightly, at 17,000 they were easily the best supported side apart from Rangers.

In 1921-22 nine clubs averaged 10,000 or more – a tally which for the League's first twenty years had been the exclusive preserve of the Old Firm

Nine clubs averaged 10,000 or more – a tally which for the League's first twenty years had been the exclusive preserve of the Old Firm. In 1921-22 in addition to the big two, the Edinburgh pair, two other Glasgow clubs – Partick Thistle and Queen's Park – and the other 'big city' clubs, Aberdeen and Dundee all did so as well. But also included in their number was a 'provincial' team – St Mirren.

Attendances were so huge that when Rangers met Partick Thistle in the Scottish Cup, the reporter from the Sunday Mail could nonchalantly remark, 'The crowd was somewhat disappointing. It barely touched 60,000.'

The Second Division didn't do too badly either. Five of the fourteen clubs in that division in 1915 weren't there at the restart six years later. Albion Rovers and Clydebank were in Division One and Abercorn, Arthurlie and Leith Athletic were all posted missing. The latter pair would rejoin the League later but

Abercorn were finished. With only a few players still on their books and no ground they could call their own one of the founder members of the League called it a day.

If neighbours St Mirren sought to help out by ground sharing or loaning players then they kept pretty quiet about it. They were the chief beneficiaries of Abercorn's demise. Their attendance rise in 1921-22 was, proportionately, far greater than any other club's. They would offer Abercorn fans a home, it seems, but not their team.

The eleven new members of the League were to enjoy mixed fortunes over the years. Of the fourteen clubs in this division in 1915, eleven played in the top division at some stage of their history. But of the eleven new members, only four would ever do so and two of these – Alloa Athletic and Bo'ness – lasted no more than a season when they did.

Incredible as it seems, the most successful of the eleven new clubs were Arbroath and East Fife who went on to play in the top division for nine and fourteen seasons in total respectively. And of the others only Forfar Athletic and Stenhousemuir are still around today. Of the rest – Armadale, Bathgate, Broxburn United, Clackmannan and King's Park – only the last named managed to make it through to 1939.

The Second Division's best season for attendances in the inter-war period was its second season – 1922-23 – and this was solely due to the pulling power of what was by far the biggest fish in this particular pool – Queen's Park. Relegated alongside Clydebank and Dumbarton, the Spiders may have long since relinquished their position as Scotland's premier club but they were still a well-supported team and a big draw on their travels. This season they drew big crowds wherever they played and in a Scottish Cup tie at Hampden were watched by an amazing 55,000 against humble Bathgate.

Now that the lower league teams had been shorn of their best players, the gap between the divisions was all too apparent. Both Queen's Park and Clydebank regained their places – though Dumbarton would have to wait 50 years before doing so – and Alloa were relegated.

The Wasps consolation came in increased gates. Their first

home game in the top flight drew 10,783 for the visit of Celtic. They averaged over 4,500 for the season. Queen's Park drew twice as much but the lower division could still produce big gates even when the Hampden club weren't the star attraction as a crowd of 11,154 for St Johnstone v Clydebank showed. The Second Division averaged over 3,000 per game – a figure it wouldn't match again until after World War II when there were fewer clubs and it was easier to establish a higher average.

The post-war boom was over however, and although the decline in gates would be gentle and include upswings as well as downs it was clear a slide was in progress. First Division gates had dropped in 1922-23 and without Queen's Park, Second Division figures would have gone down also. But the most obvious indication that a peak had been passed came in the big showpiece occasions. The Scottish Cup Final between Celtic and Hibernian drew 15,000 less than the Kilmarnock-Albion Rovers game and the England international gate was down to just 71,000.

In these circumstances the Scottish League's next move was just baffling. It introduced a Third Division! Once again the League was mimicking events in England. A Third Division had been added there by the virtual assimilation of the Southern League in 1920 and the following year more clubs were added to the roster to create a Third Division North with the year-old third tier becoming the Third Division South.

The Scottish League followed suit by taking in much of the Western League which formed the backbone of the new division and even imitated England to the extent of granting associate status – as opposed to full membership – to the new clubs. Of the sixteen clubs forming the Third Division in 1923-24 only three – Arthurlie, Clackmannan and East Stirlingshire – had previous League experience. The bulk of the newcomers came from the west – Beith, Dykehead (Shotts), Dumbarton Harp, Galston, Helensburgh and Royal Albert (Larkhall) – and the far south-west – Mid-Annandale (Lockerbie), Nithsdale Wanderers (Sanquhar), Queen of the South (Dumfries) and Solway Star (Annan). Complicating the geography and adding to the travel burden were Borders club Peebles Rovers and the Angus pair of Brechin City and Montrose.

Few looked capable of attracting bigger crowds than the clubs at the bottom end of Division Two with Queen of the South being the obvious exception. Yet the first season progressed without much difficulty. Crowd figures – even estimates – are hard to come by for the Third Division as the national press tended to give it no more than a cursory mention and even locally many of the teams involved were obscured by more illustrious neighbours or came from communities so small they didn't even possess a local weekly paper.

Arthurlie won the title and they appear to have played before gates of between 1,500-2,000. It's reasonable to assume most clubs were drawing rather less than that and over the course of its troubled history there were several mentions of crowds of less than 200. Of course there were plenty of derby games and these helped mask the low figures.

The more successful a team the higher their gates is a good rule to follow and that was certainly the case in the Second Division in 1923-24 when St Johnstone won the title. They drew 11,155 for the visit of Albion Rovers and their away game at Dundee United attracted 12,862 to Tannadice. Those were gates most First Division clubs would have welcomed.

The Scottish Cup Final gate was again disappointing as only 59,218 turned up at Ibrox to see Airdrie beat Hibs. The poor turnout convinced the SFA to move the Final to Hampden where, save for three years in the 1990s when the old stadium was being rebuilt, it has remained ever since.

But the most significant event concerning crowds was the eclipse of the Old Firm by Hearts. For the first time ever the Edinburgh team was the best supported in the country. Hearts actually lost support but their drop of a few hundred was much less than that of Rangers who were down by over 6,000.

Rangers were still a successful club and won the title in season 1923-24 but the reasons for their drop aren't hard to discern. An unsuccessful Celtic was the main one. The Ibrox crowd for the Old Firm game this season was only 38,000 – half what it had been just a few years before. And as their chief rivals in the League were the comparatively poorly supported Airdrie, there was no compensation to be gained elsewhere as there would have been had either of the Edinburgh clubs, Aberdeen or Dundee been challenging.

It's harder to explain why Hearts were the best supported team. The Tynecastle club were a fairly ordinary outfit, rarely contending for honours in the inter-war era. They didn't make a single Scottish Cup Final and after their 1915 bid never finished as high as second in the table until 1938.

Yet all the available evidence suggests that for three seasons running from 1923-24 through to 1925-26 they were the best supported team. It may be that the figures from Ibrox and Parkhead for this period are heavily underestimated but nothing has appeared in print over the years to show that they drew bigger average gates than Hearts.

For seasons 1923-24 through to 1925-26 Hearts were the best supported team

Unless proof can be demonstrated to the contrary it's safe to say that these three years and one season in the 1930s are the only time in Scottish footballing history when any side other than the Old Firm topped the attendances table.

But when there was something at stake the Old Firm could still pull in the fans like no others as they proved in 1925 when the six-figure Rubicon was finally crossed in club football.

The pair were drawn together in the Scottish Cup semi-final and their Hampden meeting drew a crowd of 101,714. It was the first Scottish Cup tie to draw a six-figure gate, the first club match to do so and the first such crowd in Scotland since 1914. It was an attendance worthy of a great occasion. Sadly, the teams didn't provide one. It was embarrassingly one-sided but not, as might be expected, in favour of Rangers. Celtic, for once, rose to the occasion and crushed their rivals by a humbling 5-0.

But while the big two commanded huge audiences and promoted clubs received huge boosts in gates it was a different story elsewhere as the pathetic total of 841 to watch Arbroath against Clyde in Division Two testifies. In the Third Division it was even worse.

In moving from eighteen clubs in 1919 to 57 by 1924 Scottish football had over-reached itself. It had copied the English expansion without looking too closely at what was happening south of the border.

100,000 CROWDS

In season 1926-27 the Scotland-England match attracted its first six-figure gate since 1914 when 111,214 turned up in confident mood to see a Scotland team on a ten-match unbeaten run take on the Auld Enemy. An Alan Morton goal looked good enough to secure victory before an unheralded English youngster equalised on his debut and scored the winner with less than two minutes remaining.

It was England's first triumph on Scottish soil for 23 years and their first ever at the third Hampden Park. And they owed their success to a youngster who may have been unknown then but who made a name for himself the following season when he scored 60 League goals. William Ralph 'Dixie' Dean certainly made an impact on Scottish football that day.

The attendance was no fluke. The crowd at the England game didn't fall beneath 100,000 again until Hampden's capacity was reduced to below that number in the 1970s.

When the English set up their Third Division they brought League football to huge cities easily capable of drawing big gates. Whole swathes of southern England including places like Southampton, Brighton, Plymouth and Bristol gained League status, as did the previously unrepresented South London.

In Scotland the League thought that two clubs could prosper in a town as small as Dumbarton. Of the Third Division clubs only Peebles, Dumfries and the south-west didn't previously have a League club on their doorstep. A better comparison is with the English Third Division North which brought in clubs from areas with a strong existing League presence. It too struggled and several of its clubs fell by the wayside in the 1920s and 1930s.

The Scottish Third Division didn't last that long. Weighed under by the 'guarantee' which meant that turnstile cash from the first 300 paying adults was effectively paid to the away team, some clubs struggled to complete the 1925-26 season. At the end of that term the League pulled the plug on the set-up.

But the Third Division wasn't the unmitigated disaster it has been portrayed as over the years. By 1933 three teams that played in the Third Division – East Stirlingshire, Leith Athletic and Queen of the South – had risen to the First. That compares favourably with the four from the NEW Second Division members in 1921 that did the same and also with subsequent 'third' divisions.

With four of the original Third Division clubs still in the Scottish League today and several non-league senior and junior teams who owe their existence to their Third Division ancestors it could be said to be a case of 'right idea, wrong time'.

Popular myth has it that the miners strike of 1926 and the general strike of the same year played a part in this division's downfall but the final whistle sounded on the set-up BEFORE either of the industrial stoppages commenced and few Third Division clubs were from mining areas in any case.

Of course unemployment and industrial disputes impacted severely on what was still very much a working-class game but a club's playing status played a greater part in determining its survival. Thus Third Division Lochgelly faded away while First Division neighbours Cowdenbeath continued to struggle on.

But even in these dark days there were some clubs which prospered. In 1924-25 Dundee United – playing in the top league for the first time – drew some fantastic crowds. There were 20,059 at Tannadice for the first Dundee League derby and almost as many – 19,979 – when St Johnstone visited. The Perth team themselves were doing well at the gate in their first full season at Muirton Park and drew 15,879 for the visit of Rangers.

At the bottom of the League, Clydebank said goodbye to the top flight for the last time in 1925-26 but not before signing off with a record 23,193 for their game with Celtic.

TWO SIX-FIGURE CROWDS IN A WEEK

There were two famous victories in front of vast crowds at Hampden Park in 1929 inside the space of seven days.

The first was on April 6th in the first club match in Scotland to draw a six-figure gate in which one of the teams involved wasn't from the Old Firm. The other was and Rangers were heavy favourites to beat Kilmarnock in the Scottish Cup Final. It didn't work out that way. In an event-filled match, Killie triumphed 2-0 after keeper Sam Clemie saved a penalty with the game goalless and Rangers had Jock Buchanan sent off in the dying minutes – the first dismissal in a Scottish Cup Final. A magnificent crowd of 114,708 watched the spectacle.

Seven days later, almost as many turned up for the England game. 110,512 were inside the ground when Alex Jackson dislocated his elbow in the first half and left the pitch. With the game petering out to a 0-0 draw, ten-man Scotland won a corner in the 90th minute. With the last kick of the game Alex Cheyne's corner kick swerved past the keeper and into the net for a 1-0 triumph. So was born the Hampden 'swirl'.

Of even greater significance was simultaneous birth of the swirl's 'twin.' Sitting up in his hospital bed a mile away, Jackson heard the great noise that greeted the goal and declared to the hospital staff that Scotland had won.

Thus came into being the world-famous 'Hampden Roar'.

In 1928 the Scottish Cup Final reached the six-figure mark at last when the Old Firm met in the Final for the first time since the 1909 riots. After the teams had turned round level, Rangers went on the rampage to thrash their rivals 4-0 in front of 118,115 and win their first Scottish Cup for twenty five years.

Victory also gave them their first League and Cup 'Double'.

Such attendances are even more impressive considering the conditions of the time. There were no all-covered, let alone all-seated, grounds in the 1920s. Apart from the lucky few cocooned in the relative luxury of the stand and the tiny covered terraces of the day, the vast majority of supporters had to brave the elements.

Exposed not just to the wind and rain of Mother Nature, the supporter also had to withstand their human equivalents as thousands of fans, having partaken of a pre-match aperitif, reacted to the appalling lack of toilet facilities by relieving themselves as best they could.

Thousands of fans, having partaken of a pre-match aperitif, reacted to the appalling lack of toilet facilities by relieving themselves as best they could.

Often this involved re-filling empty bottles and disposing of them by throwing them as far away as possible – a unique approach to recycling which in other circumstances would have brought environmental plaudits, but which usually resulted in split skulls, hospital visits and urgent trips to the dry cleaners.

Alternatives included the pretence that urine contained similar qualities to cement as supporting walls received regular liquid reinforcement, or the old standby of simply emptying the bladder on the spot. Anyone contemplating this last in a public place would normally face the threat of arrest if spotted but when thousands are doing the same thing it becomes a risk-free activity.

All of which amply demonstrates why photographs of the time invariably show supporters dressed in cloth caps, old coats and trousers and muddy boots. No one attended a football match in their 'Sunday best.'

These conditions remained the rule right up to the dawn of the 1980s. And while they may seem fearsome to those too young to have watched football for more than a quarter of a century they did have some redeeming aspects. A good strong wind, for instance, did more than chill to the marrow. It also blew away the stench.

Even so, it still doesn't explain why so many long-time fans cast their minds back to this era and sigh, 'those were the days.'

The Hungry Thirties: 1930-39

While crowds at ordinary League games still slumped there were some welcome, and surprising, exceptions. Dundee United and St Johnstone were both at the wrong end of the table when 23,517 packed out Tannadice to see them draw 1-1 in November 1929. At the end of the season both were relegated. Their replacements were Leith Athletic and East Fife who fought out a 0-0 draw that year watched by 18,079. This gate was reckoned by some to be a record for the Second Division to that date but it's possible Queen's Park drew more the year they were in Division Two.

1930 saw a new crowd phenomenon – the six-figure midweek attendance

1930 also bore witness to a new crowds phenomenon – the six-figure midweek attendance. Rangers and Partick Thistle drew 0-0 in the Scottish Cup Final in a Saturday game watched by 107,475 and almost as many – 103,668 – came back four days later to see Rangers win 2-1. This was the first 100,000 crowd on a midweek anywhere in the world.

But if that was a good crowd it didn't begin to compare with 1931's match against England. Scotland gained a satisfying 2-0 victory in front of 131,273 supporters – a new world record, surpassing the previous Hampden best which had stood since 1912.

Such figures brought little rejoicing in some quarters however. In the five years since the demise of the Third Division five more League clubs had gone under. Broxburn United, Nithsdale Wanderers, Arthurlie, Bathgate and Clydebank all departed the League.

The loss of Clydebank was an indication of the times. In the boom period for shipbuilding during the war and shortly afterwards they had been a well supported side but the economic hardships of the late twenties and early thirties were just too much to bear and they slumped to close to the bottom both in performances and in crowds.

Forfar Athletic, Leith Athletic, Brechin City and Montrose were the ex-Third Division clubs clambering on the raft of that division's wreckage that were rescued to take the places of those Second Division clubs that had jumped ship.

But the replacement for Clydebank was one of the most truly mind-boggling decisions the Scottish League has ever taken. Into the League came Edinburgh City, the fifth League team in the capital and an all-amateur outfit with aspirations of being 'the Queen's Park of the east.'

They were more like the public park. In the eight seasons until World War II, they finished bottom six times, second bottom once and their best was finishing fourth from last. They conceded over 100 goals seven times, including a record 146 in their first term.

They were never watched by more than 6,000 fans, despite having plenty of Edinburgh derbies on the fixture card and played regularly before gates of below 100. On only two occasions did they ever look like justifying their inclusion. That was when they beat Hibs in the League in their first season and knocked the same team out of the Scottish Cup at Easter Road a few years later.

While they were creating all kinds of records at the wrong end of the game in their first year, a new midweek and aggregate best was set at the other. The 1932 Scottish Cup Final went to two games before Rangers defeated Kilmarnock and the 111,982 at the first game and 105,695 at the replay ensured the clubs their place in the contemporary record books.

1932 was also the year when Motherwell, after several years of knocking at the door, finally broke the Old Firm stranglehold on the game by winning the Scottish League title. They did so with an average gate of just over 8,000, the lowest since before World War I. No subsequent championship winners have played to lower home gates

Paradoxically, their success meant good crowds turned out to see them on their travels. A fine turnout at Tynecastle of 23,074 in the championship season was transformed into a superb 34,250 in 1932-33 as supporters thrilled to the luxury of watching a team designated Champions of Scotland that didn't hail (or even hail, hail) from Glasgow. That was more than watched either Rangers or Celtic at Tynecastle that season and a tribute not only to the men from Fir Park but to the discerning nature of the Scottish football fan.

In the days when grounds had big capacities and season tickets were the preserve of the middle-class, fans would not part with good money just to watch any old rubbish. Again, Hearts are the proof. When bottom club East Stirlingshire visited Tynecastle the gate was just 5,937 and – a year previously – when Leith Athletic provided the New Year fixture because Hibs were in Division Two, it wasn't just the Hi-bees who were missing. Around 15,000 supporters were too! Relief therefore in the Tynecastle boardroom when Hibs regained their place in 1933.

And joy the same year at the SFA whose coffers bulged with the proceeds from another monster Hampden gate. After waiting nineteen years to break the world record, Scotland did so again just two years later. Even though that time had elapsed, the 1933 game against England was actually their first Hampden international since the previous one as the policy of taking the Welsh and Northern Irish games elsewhere persisted. On this occasion Celtic's Jimmy McGrory was the hero of the day as his double strike gave Scotland a 2-1 win before the new record figure of 136,259.

In November that same year came a radical innovation. For the first time ever an opponent other than England played at Hampden. And for the first time ever Scotland met continental opposition on home soil. The opponents were the 'wunderteam' of Austria, respected throughout Europe and coached by the great Hugo Meisl, one of the foremost tacticians of the day. Yet the Scottish public remained unmoved by the prospect. Less than half the crowd for the England game – 62,000 – bothered to turn up to see the teams battle to a 2-2 draw.

Football was still a parochial affair in Scotland – as it was in the UK as a whole – and the World Cup, which had been launched in 1930, was regarded with derision if thought of at all. The attitude was simple. Beat the English and all's well with the world. It was not a way of thinking Scots would lightly discard.

But while victory and a new attendance record against England may have convinced some all was well it came against the backdrop of further losses at club level. Both Armadale and Bo'ness failed to meet their guarantees and were expelled from the League. That body learnt from the Edinburgh City debacle and chose not to replace the lost clubs, reducing the Second Division to a complement of eighteen. At first it seemed the wrong decision as average gates in the division fell to under 1,500 but these improved in the years before World War II, aided by a general economic upward trend and by some comparatively 'big' clubs suffering relegation. Falkirk, St Mirren, Airdrie and the biggest of them all, Dundee, all dropped into Division Two and their travelling support boosted crowds.

The economic boom prompted by fears of war undoubtedly contributed in large measure to the game's domestic revival

That wasn't to be known in 1933 though and with the First Division average slumping close to the 7,000 mark, this was the lowest point since 1918. Fortunately crowds had reached rock bottom. There were no more casualties in the League and an improving Celtic in the second half of the decade brought bigger crowds back to Parkhead and also re-invigorated their rivalry with Rangers. The return of Hibs reminded Edinburgh fans of what they had been, briefly, missing and their derby games with Hearts reached new heights too.

But the main reason for rising crowds in the latter part of the 1930s was down to a man with no known interest in the Scottish game. You can, if you are so inclined, read 'Mein Kampf' from cover to cover but while perusing its demented schemes for racial purity and world domination you will find not a single mention of any plan to increase Scottish football attendances.

Yet it was the rise of Adolf Hitler which finally dragged the game out of its slump. It may have taken some time for the myopic British political establishment to realise that Hitler actually meant what he had written but once the pfennig finally dropped a programme of re-armament meant more jobs and prosperity in munitions, shipbuilding, mining and steel.

It was too late to prevent the re-militarisation of the Rhineland, the Anschluss with Austria, the annexation of the Sudetenland, or the invasions of Czechoslovakia and Poland, but the economic boom prompted by fears of war undoubtedly contributed in large measure to the game's domestic revival.

Those increased crowds were badly needed too as the First Division was beginning to atrophy. There were twenty clubs and for many the season was effectively over by Christmas. They couldn't win the title and were in no danger of going down. There were no European places, no 'splits', no play-offs, so many League matches in the second half of the season were meaningless affairs. Without a decent Scottish Cup run there was little to enthuse supporters of at least half the division.

In 1933-34 for example Queen's Park drew just 3,624 for the visit of Aberdeen and even the short journey made by Rangers couldn't entice any more than 7,765. Kilmarnock's gate for the home game with Clyde was a mere 2,520 and for Falkirk just 2,591. But give the fans something to get excited about and they would respond. Killie's derby game with Ayr United drew 15,022 and a visit from the still-popular Motherwell lured 16,691 to Rugby Park.

The same pattern was repeated across the country. Hearts drew 32,853 for their first game with Hibs for three years but just 3,617 for Killie. Queen of the South, in the top flight for the first time, attracted 10,979 for Rangers' first trip to Dumfries and 10,948 for Celtic in the opening game of the season. Falkirk set a new League high at Brockville of 19,462 for Motherwell's visit.

The 1935 game with England, which Scotland won 2-0 thanks to two 'Dally' Duncan goals drew 129,693, not quite as many as before and that year's Scottish Cup Final between Rangers and Hamilton Accies was, at 87,286, the first (excluding replays) to fail to reach the 100,000 mark for eight years.

This was down to Accies' small support and lack of appeal rather than any underlying factor as 102,661 attended the semi-final between Rangers and Hearts with a further 90,428 taking in the replay.

The 1936 Scottish Cup Final also drew under 100,000 with 88,859 watching Rangers beat Third Lanark. Latecomers missed the only significant action as Bob McPhail scored the only goal of the game after just ninety seconds. This time the gate couldn't be contrasted with the semis as only 56,243 saw Rangers overcome Clyde. There were fewer people at the other semi-final – 47,796 – but that was an altogether better turnout for mid-ranking clubs Third Lanark and Falkirk at Tynecastle.

It meant that for the first time in ten years the Scottish football season hadn't experienced a 100,000 gate. This was to be a temporary blip as the supporters soon showed.

An astonishing 149,547 set a new world record attendance for the Scotland-England match at Hampden in 1937

The first indications that 1937 was going to be something special in the attendance stakes came on the year's first day. After a decade in the doldrums Celtic had staged a revival and won the title in 1935-36. They went into the 1937 Ne'erday game at Ibrox three points ahead of Rangers though the Gers had two games in hand. Giving the game added piquancy was the fact that both the Old Firm trailed Aberdeen though winning their games in hand would allow one – but not both – of them to leapfrog the Dons.

Those were the reasons why a grand total of 94,811 spectators made their way to Ibrox, establishing a new ground record and a new Scottish League one too. It was the home contingent who left with smiling faces as an Alex Venters goal gave Rangers a precious victory.

Rangers went on to win the League but their two rivals weren't content to stay in the Ibrox shadow as they both won through to contest the Scottish Cup Final.

Before that game though there was the England match to take in and this year the supporters outshone all previous occasions. Although the game was a 'dead rubber' with Wales having already won the International Championship an astonishing 149,547 set a new world record attendance. This match is dealt with in greater detail elsewhere in this book. Suffice to say it took crowd records to a level unsurpassed in Scotland to this day and because of modern stadia restrictions, is a record which will remain in perpetuity.

What was just as astonishing was that seven days later a crowd of almost similar size turned up at Hampden and, indeed, many of the 147,365 at the Scottish Cup Final had also been there the week previously.

Of course the Celtic revival had much to do with the size of the crowd but the Dons role shouldn't be underestimated. At long last this sleeping giant from the north had finally stirred from its slumbers.

In recent years Scottish football fans have had to listen to the complaints of Aberdeen supporters, spoiled by the riches of the Ferguson era, complain about not reaching their 'rightful' place in the game. Those supporters would do well to pause and consider their club's history. When they finished second in the table in 1937 it was only the second occasion in Aberdeen's thirty First Division seasons they had finished so high, the previous time being twenty-six years beforehand. And in twenty-nine attempts to win the Scottish Cup this was the first time they had reached the Final.

With a lack of success like that as their record, it's little wonder that the Aberdonian masses descended on Glasgow in their thousands. How many got to see the game is another matter for around 20,000 supporters – of both teams – were locked out of the ground at kick-off.

Those who did get in saw an explosive start as Celtic took an early lead after twelve minutes only for the Dons to equalise sixty seconds later. After that it was mainly a rearguard action from Aberdeen as Celtic pressed forward. The Bhoys' efforts were rewarded twenty minutes from time when, despite Aberdeen protests of handball, they secured the goal that won them the Scottish Cup.

The attendance remains a UK record for a club match and it held the world record for over a quarter of a century, being overtaken when Fluminense and Flamengo played out a 0-0 draw before 177,656 in a Rio State Championship game in December 1963 in the Maracana – the same match also took the world league attendance record away from Scotland.

That lay in the future. For now the records kept tumbling. The New Year fixtures at Parkhead in 1938 and Ibrox in 1939 set all-time ground records for the Old Firm. These are dealt with in the club section of this book.

Around 20,000 supporters were locked out of the ground at kick-off for the 1937 Scottish Cup final – with 147,365 inside!

We can't move on from this era without a look at a game that has been largely forgotten. On April 15th 1939 Scotland met England at Hampden. The Scots held the lead for a long period before being pegged back. Just when it looked like the game was heading for a draw, up popped English football's latest scoring sensation – Tommy Lawton – to snatch an 88th minute winner.

149,269 spectators watched this match, which is the second highest attendance for a football game anywhere in Europe. And that is the reason why it has been forgotten or ignored over the years rather than because it was a Scottish defeat or that it was the last official international to be played by Scotland for nearly seven years. It seems that the old adage that no one remembers who or what came second is, in this instance anyway, absolutely true.

149,269 watched Scotland vs England in April 1939 which is the second highest attendance for a football game anywhere in Europe

On the same day East Stirlingshire met Leith Athletic in a Second Division match which was watched by just 32 spectators, the lowest Second Division attendance ever.

While war clouds darkened the skies of Europe in the summer of 1939, the parochial little world of Scottish football could feel content with its lot. First Division attendances averaged just under 10,000 in 1938-39, their highest to that point. And if the Second Division figure of around 2,300 wasn't also a record at least it was the best in that section for thirteen seasons.

The Old Firm's share was around one in every six spectators. The game appeared to be in a healthy condition.

This last pre-war season now belongs as a memory only to those aged over 70 so it seems appropriate to bring this chapter to a close with a reminder to them and an illumination to the rest of us of what the authorities reckoned was a safe number for those largely open-air, windswept grounds to hold. These are the capacities and club records of the Scottish League grounds as they were at the outset of the doomed 1939-40 season.

Division One	Capacity	Club Record
Aberdeen	42,000	41,663
Albion Rovers	28,000	27,381
Alloa Athletic	20,000	13,000
Arbroath	15,000	12,092
Ayr United	28,000	23,561
Celtic	95,000	83,500
Clyde	55,000	46,000
Cowdenbeath	35,000	18,673
Falkirk	35,000	21,572
Hamilton Accies	30,000	28,690
Hearts	60,000	53,396
Hibernian	35,000	34,375
Kilmarnock	35,000	32,745
Motherwell	38,000	35,023
Partick Thistle	70,000	49,838
Queen of the South	12,000	13,000
Rangers	100,000	118,567
St Johnstone	30,000	21,843
St Mirren	50,000	47,428
Third Lanark	45,000	45,335

Division Two	Capacity	Club Record
Airdrieonians	28,000	25,000
Brechin City	5,000	4,500
Dumbarton	15,000	12,000
Dundee	40,000	38,099
Dundee United	25,000	23,517
Dunfermline Athletic	20,000	18,000
East Fife	20,000	18,642
East Stirlingshire	12,000	12,000
Edinburgh City	30,000	6,000
Forfar Athletic	10,000	6,000
King's Park	10,000	8,911
Leith Athletic	22,000	18,079
Montrose	10,000	6,389
Morton	25,000	23,500
Queen's Park	183,388	95,772
Raith Rovers	35,000	25,490
St Bernard's	40,000	15,000
Stenhousemuir	8,000	7,800

So it was the advent of all-seated grounds
that enticed more women to attend matches?
That's news to this crowd of Clyde supporters
on their way to the 1955 Cup Final

Higher and Higher: 1939-1960

War was imminent yet the 1939-40 season proceeded as scheduled. Hitler invaded Poland on September 1st but a full football programme was completed the next day though many teams were deprived of players due to national service call-ups. Next morning a sombre Neville Chamberlain announced Britain was at war.

Football authorities, mindful of the resentment felt by the League's continuation during the previous conflict, acted quickly to ensure there was no repeat. The SFA suspended all football on September 7th. The first major sporting casualty was the Old Firm match due three days later.

It wasn't just a desire to keep in step with government that sparked the shutdown. The carnage that could be wrought on heavily attended football matches by air assault was uppermost in everyone's minds – administrators, players and spectators alike.

When the anticipated attacks failed to materialise, the SFA relented. While still banning football played in the vicinity of– 'dangerous areas' such as military installations, munitions factories and shipbuilding, friendlies were given the go-ahead and on September 22nd the ban on competitive games was lifted, though crowds were limited to 50% of capacity.

Regional leagues were established in October but attendances were poor. Football had a great power to offer distraction at times of crisis but this was different. National survival itself was at stake and throughout the season the news from Europe got progressively worse. By the season's end, Poland, Denmark, Norway, Belgium, Holland and Luxembourg all lay prostrate at the jackbooted feet of Nazi Germany while British troops retreated to the Dunkirk beaches and France prepared for surrender.

Little surprise then that attendances plummeted. Dundee v Aberdeen was watched by only 4,297 while the New Year derby at Tannadice drew just 5,500. The following day a miserly 1,276 turned up for Dundee v St Bernard's.

Dundee averaged just 2,860, compared with 4,265 for 1938-39 in Division Two and 11,921 for 1937-38 in Division One. Rather than battle against the odds as in World War I, Dundee closed down in May 1940. It was four years before they resumed.

Attendances plummeted at the onset of World War II – a miserly 1,276 turned up at Dens Park

Aberdeen went into hibernation again. They averaged 14,211 in 1938-39 and 35,000 turned up in August 1939 for a match against Celtic but Aberdeen's best gate in 1939-40 was 8,841 for Albion Rovers in a cup tie.

Wartime cup games were better attended than League matches but crowds were still small by comparison with pre-war. The two-legged tie between Kilmarnock and Ayr United brought 8,631 and 9,941 to Rugby Park and Somerset respectively. On the surface, good attendances. Yet two years earlier the Scottish Cup had attracted 28,595 and 23,758 to the same venues to watch the same two teams.

The Dons were able to restart for 1941-42 but Killie closed down when Rugby Park was requisitioned by the army in May 1940, putting the Ayrshire team out of action for the duration of hostilities.

At Ibrox and Parkhead sub-5,000 gates were routine for League matches though big crowds still turned out for special games. In May 1940 63,004 saw Scotland v England and Hampden's official wartime capacity of 75,000 was breached in the Cup Final when 79,665 saw Rangers beat Dundee United.

Scotland escaped mildly compared to the south of England which bore the brunt of the blitz. Highbury for example was turned into an Air Raid Protection post and Arsenal were forced into the ignominy of playing home matches at White Hart Lane where a paltry 2,842 saw their New Year's Day 1940 fixture with Charlton.

Nor did the fear of air attacks on packed grounds become reality. The only ground in Scotland hit by a bomb was King's Park's Forthbank and that was both an accident and a blessing. An accident in that it was an unintentional target and a blessing because it allowed a new club – Stirling Albion – to set up in 1945 unencumbered by the debt of their predecessors.

As the grim days of 1940 retreated from view and Russian and American entry into the war brought certainty of eventual victory, so the crowds began to come back. When Dens Park opened its doors again in August 1944, allied troops had occupied Rome and were advancing on Paris. The Nazi legions were in headlong retreat along the Eastern Front and the war in the Pacific was turning in the Allies favour. The optimism on the battleground spread to the terraces. There were 16,132 at Dens to see Rangers visit and five years to the day of that miserable attendance for Dundee v Aberdeen, 19,098 spectators saw the same two teams in action. At over 12,000, Dundee's average was better than in peacetime.

137,363 watched the 1943 Scotland England match - in the middle of the War

The knockout tournaments saw good gates too. In May 1941 there were 65,054 for Rangers and Hearts at Hampden. The wartime-established Summer Cup wasn't as popular with just 36,734 attending the first Final when Hibs beat Rangers though that improved to 49,432 when the same teams met again a year on with Rangers winning on the toss of a coin. That was as good as it got for the new tourney. While big gates rolled up for the Southern League Cup Final, the summer equivalent suffered – the last Final, in June 1945, drawing the lowest crowd when 27,996 saw Partick Thistle pick up some rare silverware by beating Hibs 2-0. The Junior Cup Final came back to Hampden in 1943 and by 1945 was more popular than the Summer Cup as 32,224 saw Burnbank Athletic play Cambuslang Rangers.

But the fixture that drew the biggest wartime crowds was the same one that did so in peacetime. Even Adolf Hitler couldn't destroy the passion and excitement that came attached to Scotland v England. Crowds soared as capacity restrictions were lifted with 137,363 watching the 1943 match. Sadly for Scotland the crowd's enthusiasm wasn't matched by performances as the Scots went down to regular and often heavy defeats.

The first sign of a post-war boom came during the 'transition' season of 1945-46. Scotland played four internationals at Hampden, these demonstrating the enormous appetite for football. For the first time Hampden offered Wales a welcome to its steep sides and an astonishing crowd of 92,323 turned out to see Scotland win 2-0.

Belgium's visit in January 1946 was less attractive with just 48,830 seeing a 2-2 draw. But following the usual vast attendance (139,468) to see a Scottish win over England in April, proof of the increasing interest in the game arrived with the visit of Switzerland. An incredible 111,899 saw two goals from **Billy Liddell** and one from **Jimmy Delaney** give Scotland a 3-1 triumph.

Around 230,000 people watched a League game on Saturday August 10th 1946. Yet the largest gate was just 33,000 at Parkhead.

Many there that day had also been at Hampden four days previously when 119,880 saw Aberdeen hoist their first national trophy by defeating Rangers 3-2 in the Southern League Cup Final. Even in the middle of June 86,515 attended the Victory Cup Final to see Rangers beat Hibs. Fitba' was back and no doubt about it.

But was it just 'big' games that the public wanted to see? Or would every club see a boost in crowds? The answer came on Saturday August 10th 1946 – the first official League fixtures since September 2nd 1939. And while some of the results that day are of note like Celtic losing at home to Morton and Hibs crushing Queen of the South 9-1, it is the crowd figures that are intriguing. Around 230,000 people watched a League game that day. Yet the largest gate was just 33,000 at Parkhead.

The crowds flocked everywhere. 30,000 at Easter Road and a similar number at Fir Park where Rangers were the visitors, 18,000 at Brockville, 17,000 at Firhill, 16,897 at Hampden to see Third Lanark v Aberdeen and 15,000 to see St Mirren play Clyde. Lowest in the top division was 14,000 at Rugby Park.

The 'A' Division totalled 174,000, up 27,000 on the opening day in 1939-40 when there were two more games. The 1939 opening day average was under 15,000. In 1946-47 it was almost 22,000.

But the real sensation lies in the 'B' Division figures. In 1939 27,000 watched the opening day's games and 11,000 of those were at Dens Park. In 1946 51,000 attended with 13,000 at Tannadice, the highest. Yet there were two fewer games in 1946 than seven years earlier. The average leapt from 3,000 to 7,000.

The worst supported sides had been dumped into the 'C' division and if that footballing netherworld's opening day tally of around 5,000 is added it means more than twice as many fans watched lower league football on the first day of the season in 1946 than in 1939.

Yet 1946-47 was by no means the best year for attendances. Demobilisation wasn't complete, with British forces still serving in large numbers on mainland Europe and what remained of a fast-shrinking empire. Thousands of Scottish fitba' fans still wore khaki.

Then came one of the worst winters of the twentieth century, exacerbated by fuel shortages. Many matches were postponed and transport proved unreliable even when games did go ahead. When these postponed fixtures were eventually played they kicked off on midweek afternoons in this pre-floodlit era, further reducing the numbers willing and available to watch. Even a well-supported team like Hearts were watched by just 4,723 against Queen's Park and Third Lanark against Hamilton drew just 2,586 to Hampden Park. To give an example of what that looked like, imagine in your mind's eye the Celtic Park of today; fasten your gaze on its 60,000 seats. Now try and picture it with just 1,000 of those seats occupied!

Rangers remained the best-supported side. Hearts and Hibs showed big improvements but poor performances on the pitch were reflected in Celtic's gates which averaged under 20,000 – less than 400 ahead of Partick Thistle.

The other Glasgow clubs did well with Clyde averaging over 12,000 and Third Lanark, who shared Hampden this season, actually drew more (12,981) on average than Queen's Park (10,868). Kilmarnock were relegated yet their average of 13,755 was the best in their history to this point and has only been beaten once in nearly 60 years since!

Dundee, with 13,440, were easily the best-supported 'B' Division team and had higher crowds than nine 'A' Division sides. Only Motherwell and Hamilton of the top-flight teams averaged less than five figures. Reflecting the huge increases in the 'B' Division, Stenhousemuir were the only team to average less than 3,000.

The largest Scottish Cup crowd wasn't at the Hampden Final but at Ibrox. Rangers started with 74,606 for a visit from Clyde then packed in 95,000 for Hibs. The game was drawn and 48,816 saw Hibs win the replay

81,284 watched the League Cup Final (a continuation of the wartime Southern League Cup) in which Rangers beat Aberdeen. The new competition produced the biggest domestic crowd of the season when 123,654 saw goals from **Torry Gillick**, **Willie Waddell** and **Willie Thornton** give Rangers a 3-1 semi-final win over Hibs.

This match came just two weeks after Hibs had won their Scottish Cup tie. The chance for revenge motivated Rangers supporters to turn out in droves.

Just one international was played with an with amazing 97,326 watching a 0-0 draw at Hampden against Northern Ireland.

But the biggest crowd of the first post-war season was for another Hampden international game – in which only three Scots featured, only one of whom actually played in Scotland. **Archie Macaulay**, **Billy Liddell** and solitary home Scot **Billy Steel** were the caledonian contingent in a Great Britain side which thumped a Rest of Europe selection 6-1 in a game to mark the home nations return to FIFA (and also to boost the coffers of the then cash-poor international association), watched by 129,117.

The record post-war crowd in Scotland wasn't for an international match, nor for a Cup Final, nor even for an Old Firm game. The biggest gate since 1939 was on March 27th 1948 when a massive 142,070 turned up to see Rangers and Hibs in a Scottish Cup semi-final tie. Again, Rangers emerged victorious – a solitary **Willie Thornton** strike separating the sides.

Celtic had fallen behind Hearts and Hibs and were on a par with Dundee, Aberdeen and Partick Thistle for crowds. But the merest whiff of success in the air drew the Parkhead punters back in their thousands. The 1948 Scottish Cup started with a modest 19,931 watching Celtic beat Cowdenbeath but that

The biggest gate since 1939 was on March 27th 1948 when a massive 142,070 turned up to see Rangers and Hibs in a Scottish Cup semi-final

jumped to 55,231 for the visit of Motherwell in the next round. Even 'C' Division Montrose drew 39,077 for a quarter-final tie and there were 80,000 inside Ibrox for the semi-final to see Celtic's dreams shattered by an extra-time goal from Morton.

Rangers couldn't convince fans to part with hard cash for unattractive ties. Just 17,000 saw their match with Leith Athletic but the better the opposition the greater the crowd. 68,000 saw the Gers defeat Partick Thistle and there were 90,000 inside Ibrox to see the victory over East Fife.

Little wonder then that the 1948 Final established a new aggregate record. 130,129 saw a 1-1 draw between Rangers and Morton. Four days later a crowd of 132,103 saw Rangers prevail in extra time. It was only the third (and last) occasion when the Final replay drew a bigger gate than the first match. After the comparatively small gates of 1947, the Scottish Cup seemed back on track as a major crowd-puller.

1948-49 was the high-water mark for football attendances – in Scotland the estimated total was around 6.2million

League gates stayed buoyant with only Airdrie of the 'A' Division sides recording an average of less than 10,000. Relegation still hit crowds though. Only Dundee United drew more than Kilmarnock's 6,718 average in the 'B' Division yet the Rugby Parkers tally was less than half the number who watched them in the top league. The boom extended all over Scotland with Highland League champions Clachnacuddin averaging over 3,000.

1948-49 was the high-water mark for football attendances in Britain. Documented evidence from the Football League showed total attendances in England of over 41 million. In Scotland the estimated total was around 6,200,000. There were 39,975 at Dens Park for the vital League game between Dundee and Rangers. This pair fought for the flag all season with Dundee, a point ahead going into the last game, blowing it by losing at Falkirk while Rangers beat Albion Rovers. Hearts pulled in over 40,000 for the Old Firm and Hibs, 39,389 for Dundee and only fell below 20,000 twice with 18,966 for Queen of the South and 10,002 for the last match of the season, against Albion Rovers.

Stirling Albion's lowest was 3,313 v Arbroath while 7,589 saw their promotion clash with Raith Rovers. Raith had a sizeable travelling support and a season's best of 9,169 attended Hampden for their match with Queen's Park. The Amateurs were in the lower division for the first time since 1923 and while crowds were down their gate book still shows them averaging 5,929 that season.

In the Scottish Cup Leith Athletic enticed 11,625 to see their tie with Raith. Also in Edinburgh that day 29,388 saw Hearts against Airdrie. And 14,269 were at Love Street to see St Mirren v Stirling Albion. 25,000 saw lower league Dundee United knock out Celtic at Tannadice.

Raith were back in Leith in the next round where 26,538 saw them draw with Hibs. Somerset Park was heaving with 20,589 for the visit of Morton and Central Park, Cowdenbeath groaned under the weight of 23,350 bodies as East Fife prevailed in the county derby.

Edinburgh though was Scottish football's boom town. 30,241 saw Hearts beat Dumbarton and over 60,000 watched football in the city on the same day when Hearts met Dundee (37,356) and Hibs took on East Fife (24,946).

There was an exception to this massive growth in the capital and, unsurprisingly, this was Edinburgh City. In the season when Scottish crowds reached an all-time high the amateur outfit posted a record low. Just twenty-two paying spectators witnessed City's 'C' Division 11-1 thrashing by Brechin City. The Edinburgh amateurs quit at the end of the season and joined the Juniors.

There were two six-figure Scottish Cup gates – 103,458 for the Rangers v East Fife semi-final and 108,662 to see the Ibrox team beat Clyde in the Final. While the League Cup still lagged behind, it also drew a 100,000-plus crowd when 105,000 saw Rangers meet Celtic in the group stage. There was also a huge gate of 76,466 at Ibrox for the visit of Hibernian and if attendances in the latter stages weren't quite as good, the new competition was paying its way.

But the most popular competition apart from the Scottish Cup was the Junior Cup which eclipsed League Cup Final gates for some years. In 1949, 66,377 saw Auchinleck Talbot beat Petershill.

Internationally, an all-time friendly record was set when 123,970 saw Scotland beat France 2-0.

> Central Park, Cowdenbeath groaned under the weight of 23,350 bodies as East Fife prevailed in the county derby

The most compelling evidence that the estimated total wasn't far from the truth comes by comparison with the present day. English and Scottish gates tend to go hand in hand. The same factors which apply to both rising and falling crowds (increased prosperity, job security, onfield entertainment on the one hand and unemployment, recession and matchday violence on the other) tend to apply to both countries at the same time. The crash in the early 1980s is one example. This immediate post-war boom is another.

English gates over the past few seasons have been running at slightly less than 70% of the record figure of 1948-49. Taking 6,200,000 as the Scottish figure, crowds north of the border are within two percentage points of the English figure.

In 1949, 66,377 saw Auchinleck Talbot beat Petershill in the Junior Cup final

The 'B' Division peak was in 1949-50 with attendances averaging over 5,500. There was a cluster of west-central clubs – Airdrie, Ayr United, Kilmarnock, Hamilton, Morton and Queen's Park – all recently relegated (in Ayr's case by League diktat) and desperate to get back to the top. Add in others capable of attracting crowds if going well (Dundee United, Dunfermline, St Johnstone) and more than half the division were aiming for promotion.

Scotland's lower orders had never been so healthy. There were 19,245 at Rugby Park for Killie's game with Morton and an amazing 23,520 when Ayr United came calling in the Ayrshire derby match. But even those figures were beaten by a match at Hampden in January 1950. Kilmarnock were involved again – this time against Queen's Park. The match between Scotland's two oldest clubs, both fallen on hard times, evoked memories of better days when 27,602 saw Killie win 3-1. It was – and remains – the largest recorded crowd for a League match in Scotland outwith the top division.

And, proof once more, that what attracts crowds best is to have something at stake. The same teams met at the same ground earlier that season in the League Cup. On that occasion with both sides effectively already eliminated the attendance was just 4,776. The team that won that League Cup section – Dunfermline Athletic – marched all the way to the Final where their opponents were East Fife. Scottish football was well used to derbies – but of the Glasgow variety. An all-Fife Final was a novelty, but not enough of one to entice a large crowd along. Just 38,897 saw East Fife win the League Cup for the second time.

There were almost 80,000 more inside Hampden when East Fife next visited, 118,615 to be precise, for the 1950 Scottish Cup Final. The Fifers couldn't make it a Cup double though as Rangers beat them 3-0.

Seven days earlier Scotland drew their record attendance for a World Cup qualifier when 133,991 saw England win 1-0. The Scots still qualified to go to Brazil for the finals but declined as they had not finished the group as British champions! Imagine any country refusing to take their place at the World Cup nowadays because they were unhappy with their qualifying record!

Alas, not only were the Scots absent in Brazil, the World Cup also witnessed the end of a remarkable sequence. The world attendance record had been held by Hampden Park since 1908 but on July 13th 1950 it was lost for good when 152,260 saw Brazil beat Spain in the Maracana in Rio. The 200,000 capacity stadium, built for the 1950 tournament, held an even larger number three days later when the all-time world record of 199,854 saw Uruguay defeat Brazil to win the World Cup.

'A' Division gates fell slightly thanks to a decline at Parkhead as the promised Celtic resurgence failed to materialise and in 1950-51 another small drop was recorded, this time on account of Rangers crowds slumping as Hibs ran away with the title, finishing ten points clear. For the second successive season every top division team recorded a five-figure average. Cup competitions continued to attract what would have been unbelievable figures in the pre-war era, with 21,619 for Airdrie v Clyde – one tenth of that total would constitute a good crowd if the same teams met now.

International football was less popular this season. Scotland's failure to go the World Cup may not at first looked to have an impact – 122,351 saw a win over Switzerland eleven days after the defeat by England – but as the season progressed there was a notable drop in support. 67,693 saw Scotland's first defeat by a continental country at home when Austria won 1-0 at Hampden in December 1950. In the space of four days in

May 1951 the Scots recorded victories over Denmark and France but the crowds – 74,747 and 74,412 respectively – were comparatively poor. These gates may look massive to the modern eye but the attendance at the France game was almost 50,000 down on two years previously.

The Juniors still thrived though. Bo'ness United were a case in point. 54,114 saw their semi-final against Renfrew in 1947, almost as many as attended the Final (54,903) against Shawfield.

That match was drawn and the replay – won by Shawfield – drew a smaller, but still respectable, total of 26,218. Bo'ness tried again in 1948. They clashed with Shawfield at Hampden again, in the last four, and won through before 29,434 before going on to clinch the trophy, beating Irvine Meadow 2-1 in front of 54,072. Yet this was essentially the same Bo'ness club that had been forced to leave the Scottish League in 1932 because they weren't attracting enough supporters to pay visiting teams the minimum guarantee!

The apotheosis of the Junior game was reached in 1951. For the first – and last – time both semi-finals were taken to Hampden. 29,135 saw Petershill beat Armadale Thistle and 31,785 were there to see Meadow draw with Broxburn Athletic. 27,502 saw the Ayrshire team win the replay but there must have been wry recollections among long-time supporters as they wondered where all these people had been when, like Bo'ness, Armadale and Broxburn lost their battle for survival in the League.

There were more people at the Junior Cup Final than at any of Scotland's three home internationals in season 1950/51

Meetings between Glasgow's best and Ayrshire's finest guaranteed big gates as when Talbot beat the Peasies in 1949. Add in the fact the Meadow were also recent runners-up (1948) and all the ingredients were there for a classic occasion.

The 76,314 supporters at the Final established a new record – one likely to stand for all time. Sadly, they didn't see a classic game, with Petershill winning 1-0 but that magnificent attendance is a tribute to the strength of the Junior game in Scotland. There were more people at the Junior Cup Final than at any of Scotland's three home internationals this season and for the fourth season in succession they had attracted more than the League Cup Final.

If 1950 was the year of the 'B' Division and 1951 that of the Juniors then 1952 was the year when the 'A' Division teams – the Old Firm apart – took centre stage. Hibs retained the title and their average League attendance nudged past the 30,000 mark – the only time a team outside the Glasgow giants did so.

The Hi-bees' pulling power can be gauged from a cup tie against Raith Rovers. A second replay, at Tynecastle of all places, drew a crowd of 33,614 to see an uncharacteristically out-of-sorts Hibernian beaten 4-1.

Hibs averaged over 30,000 – the only time a team outside the Old Firm did so

Hearts fans turned out in numbers to greet their rivals' conquerors in the next round. 47,150 saw Raith fail to complete a capital double, losing 1-0. And just to prove the big Edinburgh clubs didn't have it all their own way, 'C' Division Leith Athletic drew 9,250 the same day to see Dundee United end their cup dreams 4-1.

It wasn't just the city teams that experienced great attendances. It was all over the country. In Inverness over 8,000 saw Morton beat Clachnacuddin while more than 9,000 turned up down in Wigtown where the local side were thrashed by Dundee. The same afternoon saw 29,651 at Love Street where Motherwell beat St Mirren 3-2.

The Fir Parkers were a big attraction. In the next round at Dunfermline 22,295 saw the home team hold 'Well to a draw. And two grounds that day – Gayfield and Palmerston Park – saw the biggest crowds in their history for the visits from Rangers and Hearts. When Hearts travelled to Airdrie in the next round, Broomfield also played host to its record gate.

On the same day over 40,000 were at Dens for the visit of Aberdeen, more than 80,000 saw Rangers play Motherwell while even the comparatively modest affair between Third Lanark and Falkirk enticed 24,487 to Cathkin.

For the first time since 1947 there was no Old Firm presence in the last four. Unlike that year supporters still turned out in huge numbers. At Easter Road where Dundee defeated Third Lanark there was a modest 23,615 but the Hampden turnout was phenomenal.

98,208 saw Motherwell and Hearts draw 1-1 and that was the same result after extra time in the replay when 80,141 were there. A hastily-arranged second replay two days later saw Motherwell emerge victorious in front of 60,290. In eleven days an amazing 238,639 spectators attended these games.

Both finalists were popular and successful clubs. Dundee were League Cup holders, having succeeded Motherwell in winning that trophy. 'Well had narrowly lost the previous year's Cup Final and this was their fifth Final appearance since 1931 in the one tournament they had yet to win. Dundee had experienced the last-day heartbreak of losing the League in 1949.

Yet no one could have anticipated just how many were determined to watch this match. By the time the teams kicked off there were 136,495 inside Hampden. It was – and remains – a post-war record for a Scottish Cup Final. It will remain in perpetuity the fourth biggest attendance in Scotland since the war and the eighth biggest of all time. And not a Rangers or Celtic scarf in sight.

Motherwell vs Dundee was a record crowd (136,495) for a post-war Scottish Cup Final

After a scoreless first half, Motherwell ran rampant, chalking up four goals without reply to take the Scottish Cup for the first time.

The record breaking days weren't over and the Scottish Cup continued to see new highs established. In 1952-53 Dens Park and Brockville set new records, covered in detail in the club section. Others recorded figures which startle the modern eye. 19,210 for Hamilton v Kilmarnock, 34,301 at Firhill for Partick v Clyde, 24,763 crammed into Annfield as Stirling Albion faced up to Celtic, 17,986 to see Clyde against Ayr United, 26,234 for Third Lanark and Hamilton and 29,041 for Hearts v Queen of the South. Most impressive of all was the quarter-final between Aberdeen and Hibs. 47,585 at Easter Road and 41,880 at Pittodrie for the replay where the Dons won through.

But the first signs that the boom days wouldn't last forever began to appear.

An attendance of just 18,468 at Ibrox for the Scottish Cup semi-final clash between Third Lanark and Aberdeen in 1953 provided the first evidence that the appetite for football wasn't insatiable and the following season's League Cup Final drew a disappointing 38,560 to see East Fife beat Partick Thistle.

Thanks to a misprint this figure entered the record books as having almost 90,000 in attendance and has gone unchallenged for over fifty years – until now.

But where the Old Firm were concerned support was as strong – if not stronger – than before. The thrilling conclusion to the 1952-53 title chase when Rangers edged out Hibs on goal average saw gates at Ibrox rise by over 6,000 a game to climb back over the 40,000 mark. And when Celtic won their first post-war title in 1954 and also clinched the double for the first time in forty years they closed the gap between themselves and their great rivals to under 2,500.

Both Scottish Cup semi-finals were taken to Hampden for the first time and two six-figure gates were recorded. 102,444 for the draw between Celtic and Motherwell – 92,639 saw Celts win the replay – and 110,982 for one of the most amazing results in post-war football as Aberdeen demolished Rangers 6-0. Both Aberdeen and Third Lanark set all-time records for home attendances in cup ties this season. In the 'B' Division, Kilmarnock won promotion playing to an average of 11,643 – greater than that of five 'A' Division sides.

The national team continued to draw huge crowds for the England match with 134,892 watching the England game yet a month later just 25,869 saw Scotland beat Norway 1-0 in their final match before the World Cup Finals in Switzerland. It was the lowest attendance for a Hampden international to that point but a poor performance in the Finals in Switzerland meant crowds would soon slump further.

While crowds had peaked in 1948-49 those of subsequent seasons had still been higher than in the best pre-war years. 1954-55 proved to be a watershed. For only the second time (and to date the last) the Old Firm failed to get their hands on a single trophy. Yet while some matches continued to draw vast crowds, others were worryingly low, even by pre-war standards.

In the League Cup Motherwell advanced to the final after beating holders East Fife before a poor gate of just 18,816. A big crowd was expected for the Final against Hearts. Here were trophyless Hearts, striving to end nearly half a century of failure, the third best supported club in the land, up against Motherwell, winners of both League and Scottish Cups just a few seasons before, a rejuvenated Motherwell after a brief sojourn in the 'B' Division, a Motherwell who had entertained that massive crowd less than three years previously.

The attendance was just 55,642. An **Alfie Conn** hat-trick and a goal from **Jimmy Wardhaugh** helped Hearts end their 48-year trophy drought as they beat Motherwell 4-2 and the celebrations in Edinburgh were both genuine and long-lasting. But the feeling lingers, especially in view of the 1952 Scottish Cup Final attendance and also that of 1956 that this still wasn't regarded as a 'big' prize. Nice to win, yes, but not the same as the League or the Scottish Cup.

Internationally, the appearance of foreign nations at Hampden was no longer a novelty but a frequent occurrence and the loss of mystique surrounding such fixtures led to a sharp drop in attendance. Crowds were also affected by the dawning realisation that Scotland's place in world football was nowhere near as high as had been blithely assumed in the semi-isolation of the inter-war years. Big attendances were still recorded for worthy opposition as when Hungary – Wembley conquerors of England, unlucky beaten finalists in the 1954 World Cup and still widely regarded as the best eleven on the planet – visited in December 1954. A massive 113,180 attended an entertaining match which the Scots lost 4-2. But such gates were now exceptional. At the end of the season Scotland beat Portugal 3-0 in front of a paltry 20,834.

This was also the season in which television first made an

SCOTLAND FOREVER

Internationally, Scotland remained poor yet somehow managed to win when it counted most. Against a Spanish side packed with stars from Real Madrid and Barcelona, they pulled off a World Cup qualifying win by 4-2 in front of 88,873. But against sides lacking the Spaniards' glamour, supporters were less keen to part with their money. Just 56,714 were there for the vital World Cup match against Switzerland which the Scots won to book their place in the 1958 finals in Sweden. Even the lustre of the Hungarians had begun to pall. 55,337 – fewer than half the 1954 figure – saw another 1-1 draw in May 1958. Only the England game remained the same – 127,874 turned out this year. From Scotland's point of view the outcome wasn't much different either though the 4-0 defeat was heavier than usual.

The Scotland international supporter though is forever optimistic, too optimistic, many would argue. Despite the defeats, despite the poor performances, the moment it looked like the team was on an upward slope the supporters would turn out in vast numbers.

That was the story in 1958-59 when, chastened by yet another poor World Cup, Scotland decided to blood new, youthful talent like Denis Law. His presence against Northern Ireland helped swell the gate to 72,713. Unfortunately he couldn't score and the game finished 2-2.

The only other Scotland international in season 1958-59 was a friendly against West Germany. They had won the 1954 World Cup and finished fourth in 1958. In Schnellinger, Rahn and Seeler they had some of the best players in Europe. By contrast Scotland handed debuts to three players from Motherwell and one from newly-relegated Falkirk

Within a minute of kick-off the debutant from Brockville had put the Scots ahead. He was John White, destined for greatness with Scotland and Tottenham Hotspur and along with Bill Brown the first Scot to gain a winners medal in a European trophy. Tragically struck dead by lightning on a golf course, aged just 27, White was one of a rare breed which burst into full bloom in the 1960s, giving Scottish football some of the greatest names in its history.

Another first-timer, Motherwell's Andy Weir, put Scotland two up after six minutes and though the Germans came back strongly, the Dave Mackay-led and inspired Scots recorded a famous 3-2 victory in front of a superb crowd of 103,415. This was the last six-figure gate for a friendly international.

impact on the game. The first step was in November 1954 when the BBC screened the second half of the Scotland v Northern Ireland game live. The 2-2 draw was watched by just 44,229, easily the lowest for any post-war home international up to that point.

Undeterred, the SFA reached agreement for the 1955 Scottish Cup Final to be televised live. To modern eyes the attendance of 106,234 for the 1-1 draw between Celtic and Clyde seems massive. In fact it was the lowest post-war crowd for a Cup Final involving an Old Firm side and would remain so until capacity restrictions were imposed in the mid-1970s.

The SFA had anticipated at least 120,000 for the match and while the Glasgow press had little to say about the attendance, The Scotsman was not as reticent, commenting

'The attendance of 106,234 was smaller than anticipated. In view of that the replay may not be televised. Talks are being held today to decide the matter. Officials could not be happy about the returns from the other grounds on Saturday for the crowds at league matches were about the lowest of the season. Obviously many thousands stayed at home to watch the final on TV screens.'

The replay went ahead without the cameras. Clyde won the trophy in front of just 68,801. It was the lowest Scottish Cup Final crowd since 1924 and the smallest at Hampden since 1909. Indeed, less than three weeks later that figure was nearly beaten by the Juniors when 64,841 saw Kilsyth Rangers play Duntocher Hibs!

Nor could TV be blamed for the attendance at Cliftonhill the same evening as the replay when a meagre 172 attended Albion Rovers' match against Brechin City.

Other factors were responsible for these low attendances. Lack of floodlighting meant kick-off times had to be arranged to ensure matches finished in daylight. And in the open-air grounds of the 1950s the weather was all-important. In the first few months of 1955 it was absolutely atrocious. Even in late March much of Scotland was covered in a blanket of snow and when that subsided it gave way to horrendous wind and rain.

With more and more households possessing TV sets it didn't need a live football match to keep spectators by their firesides. Programmes like 'Dixon of Dock Green' and 'This Is Your Life' (both of which first aired in 1955) were popular enough to keep thousands indoors of an evening.

But the most important factor of all in determining whether or not a supporter keeps coming back for more is the quality of the game. If the football on display is exciting and skilful then fans will appreciate it. Supporters will even put up with dull, defensive drabness if the match means something. A 0-0 bore draw to the uncommitted can be 90 minutes of electrifying drama to supporters if the title, promotion or relegation hinges on the outcome.

In what was laughably termed the Spring of 1955 all the negative factors came together. There was snow, rain and wind in abundance. There was too little to play for in too many matches. Supporters began to seek out alternatives and once the habit of attending regularly was broken it was often broken for good.

Hibernian provide the most graphic example of what lay ahead. In the space of 48 hours in March 1955 they played two games at Easter Road, both of which were – on the face of it – meaningless fixtures. One was a friendly, the other an end-of-season League game. But their supporters' vastly differing attitudes to the games is telling.

On Monday March 21st Hibs lined up against Arsenal under

the Easter Road floodlights. Even though the Gunners were missing some of their regulars their presence was enough to entice a gate of 24,000 along to see an entertaining 2-2 draw Despite the arrival of driving snow during the game, few left before the conclusion.

On Wednesday 23rd the Hi-bees took on Stirling Albion. Hibs had fallen back since the heady days of the early fifties and gates were down though they still averaged over 20,000. Albion were rock bottom of the table. There was nothing at stake. The lights stayed off as the game kicked off at the grossly inconvenient time of 5pm on a miserably cold and wet evening. Hibs won easily enough, 4-1, but the game was played in a deathly quiet ground. Only 875 spectators – 667 adults and 208 juveniles – could be bothered to turn up. The total receipts came to just £63 with Albion due the minimum guarantee of £300 regardless. Writing in the Sunday Post four days later, Jack Harkness confirmed that it was 'the lowest-ever gate for an 'A' Division match, according to the League.'

If the end of the post-war boom can be given a time, date and place then it was surely 5pm on Wednesday March 23rd 1955 at Easter Road

23,000 of the Hibs fans who had enjoyed the spectacle against Arsenal turned their backs on their team just two days later. If the end of the post-war boom can be given a time, date and place then it was surely 5pm on Wednesday March 23rd 1955 at Easter Road.

Hibs heeded the warning. Invited to take part in the inaugural European Cup in 1955-56 they willingly accepted the role of Scotland's standard-bearer. Just 5,000 saw their debut – a 4-0 win over West Germany's Rot Weiss Essen but a healthy gate of 30,000 made the Easter Road return which finished 1-1.

The next round saw Hibs pitted against Swedish outfit Djurgardens. Their season was in winter hibernation so Djurgardens were happy to play their 'home' leg in Scotland. Consequently, Firhill hosted European Cup football before Hampden, Ibrox or Parkhead and 21,962 saw Hibs win 3-1. Five days later the second leg took place at Easter Road with Hibs winning 1-0 in front of 31,346.

That was in November and it was April before the Hi-Bees played again. Semi-final opponents Stade De Reims won the first leg 2-0 with 35,486 watching. The second leg demonstrated the huge potential of European football when a massive 44,941 saw Hibs struggle in vain to overturn the deficit, losing 1-0 on the night and 3-0 on aggregate. It was the largest crowd Hibs had drawn for a floodlit match.

Floodlighting revolutionised football in the 1950s. Clubs possessing lights had a great advantage in enticing fans along to games. Apart from the sheer novelty, it allowed games to kick-off later in the evening at a more convenient time for supporters who had been working through the day.

Certainly, early evening kick-offs, scheduled to catch daylight hours, took their toll on crowds and afternoon cup replays in winter were even worse. Now, postponed matches and replays could kick-off at a more civilised hour.

Some clubs still held out against them and it was the 1960s before floodlighting became universal but the crowd for Hibs v Reims showed what was possible under lights.

And clubs needed to do everything possible to attract support. Five 'C' Division sides were admitted to the 'B' Division in 1955-56 when the third tier was scrapped but while that signalled survival for the clubs concerned it depressed gate figures at that level. The top division struggled too with only Rangers, Hearts and the promoted pair of Airdrie and Dunfermline recording increases.

The story was much the same for the rest of the decade. A gradual but definite decline in gates occasionally offset by success on the field followed by a sharper drop when success proved unsustainable. Aberdeen are a case in point. League champions in 1955 and League Cup winners the following season their league gates fell by over 5,000 the year after that. That same season – 1956-57 – saw Celtic reach their post-war low of 17,706 – less than half the number that watched their successful rivals over in Govan.

Hearts had taken over from Hibs as chief challengers to Rangers and they ran away with the title in 1957-58, watched by an average of over 24,000. While that figure looks huge to 21st century supporters, others wouldn't seem out of place today. Aberdeen attracted an average of 11,618 and in the lower division Dunfermline were the best supported with just 4,944. It was the first time since 1939 that no club in that sphere had averaged 5,000.

The League Cup, previously so ill-regarded by Celtic, suddenly flowered into a tournament of distinction in green-and-white eyes. It wasn't that the competition was getting any better, merely that for the first time ever the League Cup Final was an Old Firm affair and Celtic slaughtered their old rivals 7-1. But even that great occasion, one eulogised still today by Parkhead punters whose PARENTS weren't even born then, didn't really pack in the fans.

The attendance was a respectable 90,185 but considering this was the first Old Firm showdown in a Hampden final since 1928 the crowd wasn't spectacular even if it was around three times as many has had watched Celtic beat Partick Thistle in a final replay the previous season. Around 30,000 more could have been expected if it had been the Scottish Cup Final. Although it's only fair to add that there must have been 30,000 Rangers fans at the game who wished they weren't there and another 30,000 absent Celts who wished they were!

Poor old Thistle lost a third League Cup Final in six seasons when Hearts strolled to a 5-1 win in 1958-59 before 59,960. Yet again the Junior Cup Final topped the League Cup. And again it was a Glasgow-Ayrshire confrontation that brought out the fans. 65,211 were in attendance as Irvine Meadow finally atoned for previous failures by beating Shettleston 2-1.

But the signs of malaise affecting the senior game were starting to spread into the Juniors too. This was the last time that over 50,000 attended the final. The last time it drew more than the League Cup Final. Indeed, with one or two notable exceptions, the following decade would see a massive slump in crowds at this level.

Hearts retained the League Cup in 1959-60, again beating one of the 'lesser' Glasgow teams – Third Lanark – in the Final. Hearts won 2-1 to complete the first leg of a League Cup/League double while Thirds slipped away to lick their wounds, unaware that the grand old famous name of Third Lanark which had first appeared in a national final as far back as 1876, had just added their name to the scroll of finalists for the last time.

The experience of 1955 made the SFA wary about live TV coverage and it was over two decades later before the Final was screened live again. This played a major role in preventing the decline in gates from developing into a full-scale slump. When Hearts beat Celtic to win the trophy for the first time in half a century in 1956 the gate was a massive 133,583 – a figure that hasn't been beaten since.

The following three seasons were unusual in that there was no Old Firm presence in any of the Finals. In fact since the establishment of the Scottish League there have been only five Scottish Cup Finals in which the cities of Glasgow, Edinburgh, Dundee and Aberdeen lacked representation. And in each of these Finals either Falkirk or Kilmarnock have taken part. In 1957 both did and the aggregate of over 160,000 for the Final and replay was a respectable total for the times. Falkirk took the trophy that year and they were succeeded by Clyde in 1958 who defeated Hibs before over 95,000 – another fine figure. But both those finals were eclipsed by that of 1959 when 108,591 saw St Mirren beat Aberdeen 3-1. It was to be the last time a six-figure crowd attended a Scottish club match without an Old Firm presence.

Yet while the Final was well attended the tournament as a whole wasn't impervious to the drop in gates. Cowdenbeath drew a splendid 10,206 to see their tie against Dunfermline this season but a poor 3,823 watched the replay. St Mirren began their defence of the trophy in 1960 in front of just 7,449 who watched Gerry Baker establish a 20th century record by scoring ten times as Saints overwhelmed Glasgow University 15-0. On the same day calamitously low figures were recorded at Peebles where just 615 saw the local side take on First Division Ayr United and at Cliftonhill. That bastion of big gates in the 1920s drew just 572 to see Albion Rovers against non-league Tarff Rovers.

Even the Old Firm were no longer immune. They clashed in the semi-finals for the first time since 1925. On that occasion they had performed before the first six-figure crowd for a club match in Scotland. Now, even the mighty Rangers and Celtic failed to fill Hampden. 79,768 saw the ancient enemies draw 1-1 and 72,710 were at the replay to see Rangers win 4-1. Or, as many to see the Old Firm as would have turned out for the Junior final a decade previously.

Rangers beat Kilmarnock 2-0 in the Final, watched by 108,017 – less than 2,000 more than had watched the 1955 Final. And in 1960 there were no TV cameras to blame.

The Ibrox club had followed Hibs onto the European stage but if they expected the same success they were in for a rude awakening. 65,000 saw their first match, against Nice in 1956-57 but only 8,439 saw the French team take the tie to a play-off. This was staged in Paris but the gate wasn't much of an improvement. A mere 11,908 saw Nice put an end to Rangers' ambitions.

It was the following season that really exposed the Gers limitations both on the field and as crowd-pullers. There were full houses at Ibrox as 85,000 roared Rangers on against St Etienne and AC Milan. 29,517 in the return leg in France wasn't too bad. But the trip to Italy was a disaster. Rangers had blown the tie in the first leg when, after leading 1-0, they lost four goals inside the last fifteen minutes.

There was no way back but it must have been a shock for the Glasgow club to turn up in Milan and find a miserable 3,000 there to watch the local side add two to their tally without reply. The weather was abominably bad with heavy rain threatening to have the match postponed. Even so, it was clear that while the usually insular Scottish supporters may have embraced European competition, their continental counterparts had a long way to go. Additionally, it was a huge blow to the Ibrox club's ego to discover that the team 'follow followed' by thousands all over Scotland were considered so insignificant by the Italians.

By the end of the decade the effects of the decline were beginning to show more sharply domestically. League crowds at Ibrox dropped by 4,000 per game. At the other end of the division, Arbroath were watched by scarcely more than the Rangers loss. At 4,780 their average was the first post-war sub-5,000 figure in the top flight – the first in fact since Arbroath themselves in 1939.

In the Second Division (the more normal names had been restored in 1956-57) the 'sleeping giants' of St Johnstone and

Dundee United finally stirred into promotion positions. There were 16,900 at Tannadice the day they reclaimed their place in the big time.

But this pair were an exception. The writing on the wall for Scottish football could be seen in the returns from Hampden. As recently as 1957 Queen's Park had enjoyed average gates of 11,644 and pulled in over 30,000 for big matches. On five occasions this term they were watched by under 1,000 spectators, the lowest coming against Forfar Athletic when the vast, cavernous bowl that was Hampden Park was eerily speckled by little knots of supporters spread thinly around the stadium as Queen's counted the meagre takings from a total of just 536 in attendance.

Those few there that day had glimpsed the future – and it was bleak.

RANGERS CROWDS IN EUROPE

Rangers returned to Europe in 1959-60 and enjoyed a heady run to the semi-finals of the European Cup.

69,423 saw them get their bid for glory under way when they thrashed Anderlecht 5-0. Red Star Bratislava were beaten in front of 80,000 and 82,587 saw them lose to Sparta Rotterdam, forcing the tie to a Highbury play-off. A curious mix of London-based Gers fans, those travelling down from Scotland and the odd local helped the gate to a respectable 34,176 – more than watched five Arsenal league games that season – as Rangers won through to the last four.

Rangers were taught a football lesson by Eintracht Frankfurt, losing 6-1 in Germany before 72,000 supporters. Undaunted, 69,000 turned up at Ibrox hoping for a miracle. They didn't get one as the Germans won comprehensively, 6-3.

If that was what Eintracht did to them then it's probably just as well they didn't make the final which was held at Hampden for the first time. The old ground may have lost its world record but the European Cup gave it new targets to aim at and the 127,621 who saw four goals from Ferenc Puskas and three from Alfredo Di Stefano as Real Madrid destroyed Eintracht 7-3, established a new – and still unbeaten – record for a European Cup Final.

Who cares if they're cold, wet and exposed to the elements?
Not these fans

Statistics

Finding accurate information about attendance figures isn't always easy. In many cases club records have either been lost, never recorded or withheld from public view.

Nor are newspapers a guaranteed reliable source. In the early days they tended to report gate receipts rather than numbers and when they did issue a figure it was often an estimated one. This remained the case until comparatively recent times. Many such estimates are fairly reliable, particularly if coming from regular reporters familiar with the ground they're covering or local newspaper correspondents who could probably also give a full breakdown of pie sales by individual kiosk!

But not all press reports are as accurate and a match which featured as 5,000 in one paper could be twice that number in another. There was, for many years, a tendency to quote crowds in chunks of 1,000 a time until reaching 10,000 when it would become 2,000 a time before moving to increments of 5,000 once the gate reached 20,000.

It wasn't just reasonably big crowds either. Generations of readers of one particular Sunday newspaper have grown up believing Stenhousemuir are the most consistent club in the land in terms of support. Week in, week out, it didn't matter who they played, this paper always gave them an attendance of 500.

Then there is the problem of who to actually count as part of the crowd. Paying fans and season ticket holders go without saying. But what about the generations of children whose plaintive cry of 'Gonnae gie's a lift ower, Mister?' may have gained them admission but never registered a single click on the turnstile? As for complimentaries, I've tried to address this issue in the main body of the text.

I don't think it's slurring the character of turnstile operators of the past 130 years to suggest there were times when friends and relatives found a place in the crowd if not in the official figures and stewards too have occasionally opened the gate either as an act of friendship or for a small consideration. Before any steward gets overly offended by the above, let me just add that these words come from one who worked as a steward and on the turnstiles in his youth.

There were also occasions when fans would scale walls or barge through en masse to get in to a game yet their presence has gone unrecorded.

On the other hand the story that a certain Third Division club adds everyone in the ground to its attendance, including the players, has never been verified. Nor, it has to be said, has it been disproved either.

People will always have their own interpretation. The figures have been taken as issued by the Scottish League from 1961 onwards, except where club information is available and differs from that of the League. In these circumstances the club figures have been taken. For the period before 1961 I've relied on club information and where that has not been available, contemporary reports from both national and local press. Where there have been major discrepancies between papers over the same game I have opted for the figure cited by most publications.

It hasn't been possible to compile an exhaustive list as many Second Division matches before 1915 were ignored and even some First Division matches too. I have only included seasons for which I have a record of an attendance for every League match played by every club. To do otherwise would be to distort the figures and render them meaningless. By this method I have been able to compile what I believe to be reasonably accurate annual averages for the past 100 years as well as for the first three seasons of the Scottish League's existence.

Both the Third Division from 1923-26 and the 'C' Division of 1946-55 were virtually ignored by the press and although some information is available there isn't enough of it to permit their inclusion in the attendance tables. Readers should be able to glean some idea of these clubs' crowds from reading the Clubs section of the book.

Finally, while I believe these figures to be as accurate as possible, please bear in mind that this is the first time ever that such a mass of statistical detail on attendances in Scotland has been published and I freely acknowledge there are bound to be errors. I would also be delighted to be proven wrong if it meant adding to the store of our knowledge of the game's past through the release of hitherto unpublished club records. Anyone with any such information should contact the author via his website www.scottishleague.net

1905-06		1906-07		1907-08		1908-09	
Rangers	10500	Celtic	13118	Celtic	13618	Rangers	16706
Celtic	10000	Rangers	12706	Rangers	13588	Celtic	11676
Dundee	8045	Dundee	8452	Dundee	9845	Dundee	9518
Hearts	7666	Hearts	5835	Hearts	8706	Hearts	7794
Aberdeen	6900	Clyde	5765	Queen's Park	7353	Aberdeen	7676
Queen's Park	6533	Queen's Park	5676	Aberdeen	7000	Clyde	6882
Airdrieonians	5833	Hibernian	5529	Falkirk	6735	Queen's Park	6718
Hibernian	5467	Airdrieonians	5312	Clyde	6047	Hibernian	6206
Third Lanark	5318	Third Lanark	5294	Kilmarnock	5894	Falkirk	5912
St Mirren	4533	Aberdeen	5159	Third Lanark	5882	Third Lanark	5883
Falkirk	4433	Motherwell	4529	Hibernian	5853	Motherwell	5676
Motherwell	4167	St Mirren	4500	Motherwell	5471	Kilmarnock	5335
Partick Thistle	3947	Falkirk	4353	St Mirren	4853	St Mirren	5118
Kilmarnock	3933	Kilmarnock	3912	Morton	4000	Airdrieonians	4371
Morton	3918	Morton	3559	Airdrieonians	3912	Hamilton Acad	4176
Port Glasgow	3227	Partick Thistle	3529	Hamilton Acad	3265	Morton	3235
Vale of Leven	2045	Hamilton Acad	3235	Partick Thistle	3141	Partick Thistle	2312
Clyde	2036	Port Glasgow	2618	Port Glasgow	2835	Port Glasgow	2294
Leith Ath	1955	Vale of Leven	2409	Dumbarton	2045	Dumbarton	2273
Cowdenbeath	1818	Dumbarton	1927	Ayr	2000	Vale of Leven	2018
Albion Rovers	1773	St Bernard's	1909	Vale of Leven	1955	Raith Rovers	1882
Ayr	1682	Ayr	1773	Raith Rovers	1555	Abercorn	1795
Arthurlie	1636	Leith Ath	1682	Cowdenbeath	1455	Ayr	1455
Abercorn	1500	Cowdenbeath	1436	St Bernard's	1355	Cowdenbeath	1409
Raith Rovers	1455	Raith Rovers	1364	Ayr Parkhouse	1318	Albion Rovers	1373
St Bernard's	1409	Ayr Parkhouse	1309	Abercorn	1273	Arthurlie	1091
Hamilton Acad	1327	East Stirling	1109	East Stirling	1045	Leith Ath	1091
East Stirling	1264	Albion Rovers	1100	Leith Ath	909	St Bernard's	1091
		Abercorn	909	Albion Rovers	727	East Stirling	1055
		Arthurlie	864	Arthurlie	727	Ayr Parkhouse	782

1909-10		1910-11		1911-12		1912-13	
Rangers	14471	Rangers	16147	Rangers	20529	Rangers	21471
Celtic	12059	Partick Thistle	11029	Celtic	14206	Celtic	14471
Dundee	9000	Celtic	9324	Partick Thistle	11882	Hearts	10676
Partick Thistle	8382	Aberdeen	9088	Hearts	10529	Partick Thistle	9588
Hearts	7853	Hearts	9088	Queen's Park	8235	Aberdeen	8518
Aberdeen	7359	Dundee	7588	Clyde	7647	Third Lanark	8353
Clyde	6559	Clyde	7294	Third Lanark	7029	Queen's Park	7529
Falkirk	5794	Third Lanark	6824	St Mirren	6853	St Mirren	7294
St Mirren	5559	Queen's Park	6294	Aberdeen	6676	Motherwell	7235
Hibernian	5353	Falkirk	6235	Dundee	6618	Dundee	7059
Third Lanark	5265	Hibernian	6059	Morton	6353	Morton	6882
Morton	5205	Raith Rovers	5941	Hibernian	6324	Clyde	6559
Queen's Park	5176	Kilmarnock	5659	Motherwell	6176	Falkirk	6441
Motherwell	5000	Motherwell	5500	Falkirk	6059	Hibernian	6265
Kilmarnock	4882	St Mirren	5500	Raith Rovers	5659	Airdrieonians	5824
Hamilton Acad	3647	Morton	5382	Airdrieonians	4588	Hamilton Acad	5382
Airdrieonians	3500	Hamilton Acad	4176	Kilmarnock	4453	Raith Rovers	5353
Port Glasgow	2706	Airdrieonians	3676	Hamilton Acad	4412	Kilmarnock	5121
Leith Ath	2455	Dumbarton	2136	Dumbarton	2818	Dunfermline	2446
Dumbarton	2136	East Stirling	1773	Ayr Utd	2773	Dumbarton	2392
Vale of Leven	2000	Vale of Leven	1773	Cowdenbeath	2545	Ayr Utd	2308
Raith Rovers	1909	Ayr Utd	1591	St Johnstone	2200	Cowdenbeath	2269
Cowdenbeath	1818	Albion Rovers	1545	Leith Ath	2045	Vale of Leven	1846
Abercorn	1773	Cowdenbeath	1545	Dundee Hibs	2000	Abercorn	1792
St Bernard's	1682	Abercorn	1318	Abercorn	1864	St Johnstone	1481
Ayr	1591	Dundee Hibs	1318	Albion Rovers	1773	Leith Ath	1269
Albion Rovers	1273	Leith Ath	1227	East Stirling	1682	Arthurlie	1115
Arthurlie	1000	Arthurlie	1136	Vale of Leven	1455	St Bernard's	1100
East Stirling	927	St Bernard's	1091	St Bernard's	1409	Dundee Hibs	1042
Ayr Parkhouse	900	Port Glasgow	782	Arthurlie	1182	Johnstone	1038
						East Stirling	992
						Albion Rovers	695

1913-14		1914-15		1915-16		1916-17	
Rangers	21395	Rangers	14947	Rangers	12221	Rangers	12526
Celtic	19684	Celtic	13563	Celtic	11789	Celtic	12316
Hearts	13131	Hearts	11157	Partick Thistle	9237	Partick Thistle	7079
Partick Thistle	11211	Partick Thistle	10368	Hearts	7631	Third Lanark	6895
Dundee	10316	Third Lanark	6632	Dundee	5684	Hearts	6289
Queen's Park	9632	Queen's Park	6421	Queen's Park	5684	Morton	6000
Third Lanark	8842	Aberdeen	5974	Hamilton Acad	5421	Queen's Park	5632
St Mirren	8158	St Mirren	5842	Third Lanark	5421	Clyde	5500
Hibernian	8079	Morton	5474	Morton	5333	St Mirren	5158
Clyde	7921	Hibernian	5394	Aberdeen	4684	Motherwell	4895
Aberdeen	7763	Motherwell	5342	Clyde	4632	Dundee	4747
Morton	7579	Dundee	5316	St Mirren	4526	Hibernian	4368
Airdrieonians	6186	Ayr Utd	5053	Motherwell	4500	Aberdeen	3803
Hamilton Acad	6158	Falkirk	4868	Hibernian	4421	Hamilton Acad	3684
Motherwell	6158	Hamilton Acad	4832	Kilmarnock	4368	Kilmarnock	3474
Falkirk	5974	Clyde	4789	Ayr Utd	3789	Airdrieonians	3211
Raith Rovers	5474	Airdrieonians	4420	Falkirk	3711	Ayr Utd	3053
Ayr Utd	5421	Kilmarnock	4168	Dumbarton	3447	Falkirk	2921
Dumbarton	5316	Dumbarton	3684	Airdrieonians	3395	Dumbarton	2632
Kilmarnock	5263	Raith Rovers	3553	Raith Rovers	3105	Raith Rovers	2395
Cowdenbeath	2364	Cowdenbeath	3385				
Dunfermline	2118	Clydebank	2769				
St Johnstone	1673	Dunfermline	2115				
Albion Rovers	1655	Leith Ath	1885				
Dundee Hibs	1636	St Johnstone	1846				
Vale of Leven	1436	St Bernard's	1731				
St Bernard's	1136	Albion Rovers	1454				
Abercorn	1064	Lochgelly Utd	1446				
East Stirling	1045	Vale of Leven	1269				
Arthurlie	955	Abercorn	1000				
Leith Ath	909	East Stirling	915				
Johnstone	764	Dundee Hibs	892				
		Arthurlie	869				
		Johnstone	669				

1917-18		1918-19		1919-20		1920-21	
Celtic	15059	Rangers	21118	Rangers	21381	Rangers	23489
Rangers	14765	Celtic	17059	Celtic	17000	Hearts	17928
Partick Thistle	11294	Queen's Park	11529	Hearts	16223	Celtic	16775
Hearts	7500	Partick Thistle	11000	Dundee	14667	Dundee	14572
Queen's Park	7235	Hearts	9735	Partick Thistle	12891	Partick Thistle	13504
Clydebank	7159	Third Lanark	7647	Aberdeen	12262	Aberdeen	13374
Third Lanark	6647	Clyde	7059	Hibernian	11190	Hibernian	10714
Motherwell	6235	Motherwell	7000	Queen's Park	10571	Motherwell	10048
Morton	6000	Morton	6765	Motherwell	9083	Clyde	8857
St Mirren	5941	Clydebank	6529	Morton	8095	Morton	8476
Hibernian	5882	Hibernian	6471	Third Lanark	7963	Third Lanark	7810
Hamilton Acad	5529	St Mirren	5765	St Mirren	7190	Queen's Park	7810
Kilmarnock	5000	Hamilton Acad	5412	Raith Rovers	6857	Albion Rovers	7386
Clyde	4588	Kilmarnock	5353	Clyde	6429	Raith Rovers	7305
Airdrieonians	4235	Falkirk	4912	Albion Rovers	6329	Hamilton Acad	7238
Dumbarton	3588	Ayr Utd	4824	Kilmarnock	6286	Kilmarnock	7143
Falkirk	3529	Airdrieonians	3765	Clydebank	5477	Falkirk	7071
Ayr Utd	2647	Dumbarton	3353	Falkirk	5081	Airdrieonians	6238
				Airdrieonians	5047	St Mirren	6238
				Ayr Utd	4619	Clydebank	6048
				Hamilton Acad	4571	Ayr Utd	5048
				Dumbarton	3571	Dumbarton	3762

1921-22		1922-23		1923-24		1924-25	
Rangers	23857	Rangers	22632	Hearts	16368	Hearts	17500
Hearts	17071	Hearts	17105	Rangers	16000	Rangers	17263
Partick Thistle	14564	Dundee	15623	Dundee	12421	Hibernian	13842
Dundee	14429	Aberdeen	13831	Aberdeen	12211	Aberdeen	12684
Celtic	14381	Hibernian	13632	Celtic	11568	Dundee	12132
Aberdeen	13452	Celtic	11579	Queen's Park	11368	Partick Thistle	12105
Queen's Park	12000	Partick Thistle	11263	Hibernian	10263	Celtic	11000
Hibernian	11619	Falkirk	9368	Partick Thistle	9737	St Johnstone	9895
St Mirren	10109	Queen's Park	9158	Raith Rovers	7947	Queen's Park	9632
Raith Rovers	8166	Third Lanark	8947	Third Lanark	7421	Cowdenbeath	9211
Third Lanark	8095	St Mirren	8342	Kilmarnock	7316	Third Lanark	8579
Falkirk	7905	Clyde	8053	St Mirren	7000	Airdrieonians	8552
Hamilton Acad	7714	Kilmarnock	7868	Airdrieonians	6895	Falkirk	8211
Morton	7452	Morton	6895	Falkirk	6737	Hamilton Acad	7289
Clyde	7190	Motherwell	6711	St Johnstone	5904	St Mirren	7263
Kilmarnock	6952	Airdrieonians	6526	Hamilton Acad	5789	Raith Rovers	6974
Motherwell	6619	Raith Rovers	6526	Motherwell	5789	Kilmarnock	6632
Airdrieonians	6143	Albion Rovers	6158	Clyde	5474	Ayr Utd	5816
Albion Rovers	6119	Hamilton Acad	5579	Morton	5132	Dundee Utd	5289
Clydebank	5143	Ayr Utd	5184	Cowdenbeath	4842	Motherwell	4897
Ayr Utd	4857	Alloa Ath	4594	Ayr Utd	4737	Morton	4794
Dumbarton	4190	Cowdenbeath	4316	Dunfermline	4395	Clydebank	3474
Cowdenbeath	4026	St Johnstone	4298	Dundee Utd	4142	Clyde	2921
Alloa Ath	3868	Dunfermline	4158	Clydebank	4132	Dunfermline	2889
St Johnstone	3684	King's Park	3416	King's Park	3857	Alloa Ath	2842
Dunfermline	3526	Clydebank	3105	East Fife	2895	East Fife	2747
Dundee Hibs	3211	East Fife	2984	Arbroath	2781	King's Park	2554
East Fife	3184	Lochgelly Utd	2947	Stenhousemuir	2305	Arbroath	2488
East Stirling	3000	Dumbarton	2842	Bathgate	2263	Bo'ness	2316
King's Park	2737	Bathgate	2789	Alloa Ath	2237	East Stirling	2305
Arbroath	2593	St Bernard's	2737	Albion Rovers	2026	Albion Rovers	2158
Lochgelly Utd	2395	East Stirling	2474	St Bernard's	2026	Dumbarton	2132
Armadale	2342	Bo'ness	2395	Forfar Ath	2000	St Bernard's	1974
Broxburn Utd	2211	Arbroath	2211	Bo'ness	1868	Bathgate	1947
Bathgate	2158	Armadale	2184	Armadale	1842	Arthurlie	1895
Bo'ness	2079	Stenhousemuir	2042	Vale of Leven	1711	Stenhousemuir	1895
St Bernard's	2079	Vale of Leven	2026	Dumbarton	1632	Armadale	1868
Stenhousemuir	2053	Johnstone	1947	Broxburn Utd	1605	Forfar Ath	1684
Vale of Leven	2000	Broxburn Utd	1901	Johnstone	1342	Broxburn Utd	1632
Johnstone	1737	Forfar Ath	1737	Lochgelly Utd	1316	Johnstone	1184
Forfar Ath	1632						
Clackmannan	1495						

1925-26		1926-27		1927-28		1928-29	
Hearts	18474	Rangers	17579	Rangers	21263	Rangers	19737
Rangers	17605	Hearts	17026	Hearts	16763	Hearts	18921
Hibernian	13289	Aberdeen	12974	Celtic	13684	Aberdeen	13474
Celtic	13211	Hibernian	12342	Partick Thistle	11474	Queen's Park	12316
Aberdeen	13184	Celtic	12211	Aberdeen	11105	Celtic	10237
Partick Thistle	11526	Partick Thistle	10789	Hibernian	10895	Hibernian	8737
Queen's Park	11316	Dundee	10447	Queen's Park	9474	Dundee	8474
Dundee	10632	Queen's Park	9053	Motherwell	7368	Third Lanark	8000
Dundee Utd	10002	Motherwell	8895	St Mirren	6895	Kilmarnock	7516
St Mirren	9316	St Mirren	8263	Dundee	6816	Ayr Utd	7326
Airdrieonians	8026	Dundee Utd	7974	Kilmarnock	6734	Falkirk	7158
St Johnstone	7467	Falkirk	7211	Falkirk	6579	Partick Thistle	6879
Motherwell	7421	Clyde	6789	Clyde	6158	Morton	6526
Falkirk	7263	Kilmarnock	6632	St Johnstone	5579	Motherwell	6526
Kilmarnock	7158	St Johnstone	6526	Raith Rovers	5474	St Mirren	6158
Cowdenbeath	6105	Airdrieonians	5789	Dundee Utd	5368	St Johnstone	5421
Clydebank	5389	Hamilton Acad	4895	Third Lanark	5211	Clyde	5368
Raith Rovers	5342	Dunfermline	4868	Hamilton Acad	4421	Dundee Utd	4816
Hamilton Acad	5316	Morton	4474	Ayr Utd	4263	Hamilton Acad	4474
Dunfermline	4632	Cowdenbeath	4368	Airdrieonians	4053	Raith Rovers	4195
Morton	4553	Third Lanark	3947	Cowdenbeath	3947	Airdrieonians	3737
Ayr Utd	4421	Raith Rovers	2868	Bo'ness	3895	Albion Rovers	3053
Clyde	4368	East Fife	2726	Dunfermline	3474	QoS	2711
Third Lanark	3684	QoS	2632	Arbroath	2500	Arbroath	2673
QoS	3368	Bo'ness	2605	QoS	2447	Cowdenbeath	2600
East Fife	3053	East Stirling	2579	Morton	2358	East Fife	2289
Arbroath	2947	Arbroath	2474	East Fife	2079	East Stirling	2263
King's Park	2684	Ayr Utd	2332	King's Park	2026	Leith Ath	2132
East Stirling	2547	King's Park	2158	East Stirling	2000	King's Park	2079
Stenhousemuir	2126	Clydebank	1921	Forfar Ath	1868	St Bernard's	1978
Alloa Ath	2079	Alloa Ath	1816	Alloa Ath	1816	Dumbarton	1737
Nithsdale W	2079	Arthurlie	1711	Leith Ath	1684	Clydebank	1694
Dumbarton	2000	St Bernard's	1658	Arthurlie	1658	Dunfermline	1621
St Bernard's	1842	Albion Rovers	1632	Albion Rovers	1632	Alloa Ath	1605
Arthurlie	1789	Forfar Ath	1553	St Bernard's	1526	Bo'ness	1556
Albion Rovers	1685	Armadale	1532	Clydebank	1500	Forfar Ath	1421
Bo'ness	1658	Dumbarton	1300	Stenhousemuir	1426	Stenhousemuir	1368
Armadale	1474	Stenhousemuir	1289	Dumbarton	1395	Arthurlie	933
Bathgate	1447	Bathgate	1263	Armadale	1000	Bathgate	922
Broxburn Utd	1158	Nithsdale W	1237	Bathgate	847	Armadale	905

Note: Arthurlie
completed 15 home
League games
Bathgate completed 12
home League games

1929-30		1930-31		1931-32		1932-33	
Rangers	21579	Rangers	20184	Rangers	20368	Rangers	16632
Hearts	16737	Hearts	17789	Hearts	15449	Hearts	16134
Aberdeen	14800	Celtic	17395	Aberdeen	12947	Aberdeen	12211
Celtic	11263	Aberdeen	12868	Celtic	12053	Celtic	11553
Queen's Park	9816	Partick Thistle	12442	Partick Thistle	11211	Partick Thistle	10632
Partick Thistle	9263	Dundee	9789	Third Lanark	10053	Motherwell	7063
Morton	8474	Hibernian	9053	Queen's Park	8842	Third Lanark	6684
Dundee	8158	Motherwell	7447	Motherwell	8237	Falkirk	6526
Hibernian	8132	Morton	7263	Dundee	7789	St Mirren	6526
Dundee Utd	7501	Queen's Park	6974	St Mirren	7316	Queen's Park	6289
Kilmarnock	6895	Kilmarnock	6895	Kilmarnock	7053	Hibernian	6236
St Mirren	6789	St Mirren	6526	Dundee Utd	6300	Kilmarnock	6211
Clyde	6526	Ayr Utd	6105	Falkirk	6263	St Johnstone	6079
Motherwell	6342	Clyde	5868	Ayr Utd	5947	Ayr Utd	5684
Ayr Utd	6105	Leith Ath	5474	Morton	5474	Clyde	5447
Falkirk	5342	Falkirk	5236	Clyde	5316	Morton	4816
Hamilton Acad	4895	East Fife	4763	Hamilton Acad	4947	Dundee	4611
Leith Ath	4635	Dundee Utd	4563	Leith Ath	4289	Hamilton Acad	4089
Airdrieonians	4000	Hamilton Acad	4500	Hibernian	4211	QoS	3306
St Johnstone	4000	Third Lanark	4026	St Johnstone	4184	East Stirling	3274
Third Lanark	3842	Airdrieonians	3711	Airdrieonians	4079	Airdrieonians	3221
East Fife	3395	St Johnstone	3237	QoS	2595	Cowdenbeath	2063
Albion Rovers	3000	Cowdenbeath	2842	Cowdenbeath	2584	Raith Rovers	1871
Raith Rovers	2789	QoS	2763	Raith Rovers	2442	St Bernard's	1847
Cowdenbeath	2737	Dunfermline	2500	East Stirling	2316	Leith Ath	1753
King's Park	2079	Dumbarton	2369	East Fife	2195	Alloa Ath	1722
QoS	2053	Raith Rovers	2216	Dunfermline	2121	King's Park	1694
Alloa Ath	1958	Alloa Ath	2026	Alloa Ath	2053	Dunfermline	1678
East Stirling	1884	King's Park	1853	King's Park	1921	East Fife	1547
Montrose	1747	Arbroath	1611	Arbroath	1689	Dundee Utd	1535
Arbroath	1584	East Stirling	1595	St Bernard's	1626	Albion Rovers	1506
Brechin City	1568	Montrose	1495	Dumbarton	1537	Stenhousemuir	1506
St Bernard's	1542	Albion Rovers	1295	Albion Rovers	1400	Arbroath	1500
Dumbarton	1526	Brechin City	1142	Brechin City	1379	Dumbarton	1316
Dunfermline	1437	Forfar Ath	1142	Stenhousemuir	1332	Montrose	1244
Bo'ness	1226	St Bernard's	1132	Montrose	1232	Brechin City	889
Forfar Ath	1195	Bo'ness	1047	Bo'ness	1189	Forfar Ath	781
Stenhousemuir	1032	Stenhousemuir	905	Forfar Ath	1042	Armadale*	689
Armadale	942	Clydebank	868	Armadale	805	Bo'ness**	633
Clydebank	884	Armadale	705	Edinburgh City	429	Edinburgh City	464

* only played 9 homes
** only played 6 homes

91

1933-34		1934-35		1935-36		1936-37	
Rangers	16895	Rangers	19526	Hearts	18363	Rangers	20253
Hearts	14400	Hearts	18655	Rangers	18105	Hearts	20087
Aberdeen	11795	Celtic	14421	Celtic	16579	Celtic	17526
Hibernian	11263	Aberdeen	10868	Aberdeen	13899	Aberdeen	17342
Celtic	9579	Partick Thistle	10500	Hibernian	10069	Hibernian	11341
Dundee	9203	Hibernian	10370	Partick Thistle	9779	Dundee	10195
Motherwell	8552	Dundee	9079	Dundee	9737	Falkirk	8737
Partick Thistle	7947	Clyde	8158	Queen's Park	9622	Partick Thistle	8632
Kilmarnock	7128	Queen's Park	7949	Clyde	7895	Queen's Park	8141
Queen's Park	7013	Motherwell	7500	Ayr Utd	7053	Third Lanark	8000
Ayr Utd	6895	Ayr Utd	6947	Third Lanark	7000	St Mirren	7789
Falkirk	6814	QoS	6874	QoS	6679	Clyde	7632
QoS	6180	Kilmarnock	6105	Kilmarnock	6658	Kilmarnock	6105
Clyde	5342	St Mirren	6053	Dunfermline	6158	Motherwell	6053
St Mirren	5158	Albion Rovers	6000	Motherwell	5895	QoS	5521
Third Lanark	4816	Dunfermline	5868	St Mirren	5441	Dunfermline	5211
St Johnstone	4632	Falkirk	5789	St Johnstone	5021	Hamilton Acad	4895
Hamilton Acad	3816	St Johnstone	5695	Dundee Utd	4376	Ayr Utd	4765
Morton	3382	Hamilton Acad	5158	Arbroath	4311	St Johnstone	4711
Airdrieonians	2937	Dundee Utd	4382	Falkirk	4294	Arbroath	4121
Arbroath	2312	Airdrieonians	4026	Hamilton Acad	4289	Albion Rovers	3932
Dundee Utd	2300	Morton	3206	Airdrieonians	4158	Morton	3824
Albion Rovers	1971	Third Lanark	3000	Albion Rovers	4079	Raith Rovers	3187
Cowdenbeath	1763	Arbroath	2624	Morton	3853	Dundee Utd	3088
Dunfermline	1718	East Fife	1900	Alloa Ath	2382	St Bernard's	2912
East Fife	1624	Alloa Ath	1794	East Stirling	2035	Airdrieonians	2676
Alloa Ath	1618	St Bernard's	1759	East Fife	1935	East Fife	2559
Raith Rovers	1588	King's Park	1582	Cowdenbeath	1853	Cowdenbeath	2512
Leith Ath	1524	Raith Rovers	1335	Raith Rovers	1653	Alloa Ath	2118
King's Park	1365	Dumbarton	1265	St Bernard's	1476	Dumbarton	1941
Dumbarton	1276	Leith Ath	1241	Stenhousemuir	1471	Leith Ath	1850
Montrose	1259	Cowdenbeath	1194	Leith Ath	1247	King's Park	1347
St Bernard's	1100	Montrose	1147	Dumbarton	1241	Montrose	997
East Stirling	1071	East Stirling	1059	King's Park	1129	Stenhousemuir	947
Brechin City	976	Brechin City	894	Montrose	1100	East Stirling	935
Stenhousemuir	700	Stenhousemuir	841	Brechin City	882	Brechin City	835
Forfar Ath	653	Forfar Ath	694	Forfar Ath	835	Forfar Ath	776
Edinburgh City	302	Edinburgh City	387	Edinburgh City	494	Edinburgh City	444

1937-38		1938-39		1946-47		1947-48	
Rangers	21579	Rangers	23158	Rangers	28467	Rangers	28400
Hearts	20173	Hearts	18309	Hibernian	24225	Hibernian	27950
Celtic	14737	Celtic	15892	Celtic	19860	Hearts	22694
Aberdeen	14368	Aberdeen	14211	Hearts	19570	Celtic	21000
Dundee	11921	Hibernian	12895	Partick Thistle	19467	Dundee	20800
Hibernian	11163	Partick Thistle	12526	Aberdeen	18900	Aberdeen	20395
Queen's Park	9168	Queen's Park	11012	Kilmarnock	13755	Partick Thistle	20267
Falkirk	9111	Falkirk	8895	Dundee	13440	Clyde	14227
Kilmarnock	8615	Raith Rovers	8711	Third Lanark	12874	St Mirren	13567
Third Lanark	8474	St Mirren	8211	Clyde	12067	Third Lanark	13067
Ayr Utd	8368	Clyde	8158	St Mirren	11267	Motherwell	12567
St Mirren	8158	Ayr Utd	8079	Queen's Park	10464	Queen's Park	12027
Partick Thistle	8000	Kilmarnock	8079	QoS	10233	Falkirk	11333
Motherwell	6789	Third Lanark	7342	Falkirk	10167	QoS	11033
Clyde	6763	QoS	7016	Morton	10000	Morton	10900
Morton	6737	Motherwell	6447	Dundee Utd	9769	Airdrieonians	9500
QoS	6589	Hamilton Acad	5842	Motherwell	9667	Dundee Utd	8333
Raith Rovers	5982	Albion Rovers	5000	Airdrieonians	8385	Kilmarnock	6718
Hamilton Acad	4842	St Johnstone	4763	Hamilton Acad	6567	East Fife	6600
St Johnstone	4737	Dundee Utd	4341	Ayr Utd	6385	Ayr Utd	6433
Arbroath	4242	Dundee	4265	Raith Rovers	5962	St Johnstone	6047
Albion Rovers	3412	Arbroath	4079	East Fife	5423	Cowdenbeath	5633
East Fife	3412	Cowdenbeath	4059	Albion Rovers	5392	Raith Rovers	5500
Airdrieonians	3294	East Fife	3624	St Johnstone	4962	Albion Rovers	5167
Cowdenbeath	3118	Morton	3159	Cowdenbeath	4600	Stirling Albion	4953
Dumbarton	3000	Alloa Ath	3147	Arbroath	4462	Hamilton Acad	4800
St Bernard's	2200	Dumbarton	3059	Dunfermline	3962	Alloa Ath	4700
Dunfermline	2012	Airdrieonians	2971	Alloa Ath	3823	Dunfermline	3900
Alloa Ath	1835	Dunfermline	2776	Dumbarton	3038	Arbroath	3673
Dundee Utd	1385	King's Park	2176	Stenhousemuir	1823	Dumbarton	3267
King's Park	1182	St Bernard's	1829			Leith Ath	2700
Leith Ath	1047	Leith Ath	1188			Stenhousemuir	1533
Montrose	1012	East Stirling	1101				
East Stirling	924	Montrose	988				
Brechin City	729	Brechin City	888				
Forfar Ath	694	Forfar Ath	788				
Stenhousemuir	612	Stenhousemuir	712				
Edinburgh City	394	Edinburgh City	491				

1948-49		1949-50		1950-51		1951-52	
Rangers	44600	Rangers	44933	Rangers	35933	Rangers	34867
Celtic	37205	Celtic	29867	Celtic	28786	Hibernian	30700
Hearts	28195	Hibernian	29157	Hibernian	28333	Celtic	29568
Hibernian	27267	Hearts	27811	Hearts	23917	Hearts	25238
Dundee	24532	Partick Thistle	24413	Dundee	22160	Dundee	20467
Aberdeen	24200	Dundee	21967	Aberdeen	19767	Partick Thistle	17933
Partick Thistle	20233	Clyde	17900	Partick Thistle	19467	Aberdeen	17067
Clyde	16667	St Mirren	17333	Third Lanark	15433	St Mirren	15533
St Mirren	16533	Aberdeen	17200	St Mirren	14600	East Fife	12133
Third Lanark	14233	Raith Rovers	14387	Raith Rovers	14167	Third Lanark	11900
Morton	13467	Stirling Albion	13360	Clyde	13000	Motherwell	11867
East Fife	13133	East Fife	12846	Morton	12933	Raith Rovers	11280
Motherwell	13000	Third Lanark	12687	East Fife	11573	Airdrieonians	10667
Falkirk	12233	Motherwell	12200	Motherwell	11267	Stirling Albion	9934
QoS	11980	Falkirk	11600	Falkirk	10433	Morton	9833
Raith Rovers	8967	QoS	10660	Airdrieonians	10400	Kilmarnock	9776
Kilmarnock	8477	Kilmarnock	10338	Ayr Utd	8900	QoS	9600
Dundee Utd	8100	Morton	9800	Dundee Utd	8800	Falkirk	8500
Albion Rovers	7883	Dundee Utd	8867	Kilmarnock	8016	Dundee Utd	8280
Airdrieonians	7433	Queen's Park	7546	Stirling Albion	7867	Clyde	8033
Ayr Utd	6795	Airdrieonians	6567	QoS	7642	Ayr Utd	8000
St Johnstone	6233	St Johnstone	6333	St Johnstone	5780	Dunfermline	5333
Dunfermline	6000	Ayr Utd	6033	Queen's Park	5591	Queen's Park	4854
Queen's Park	5929	Dunfermline	4933	Hamilton Acad	4973	St Johnstone	4787
Stirling Albion	5478	Hamilton Acad	4833	Dunfermline	4533	Dumbarton	3633
Hamilton Acad	4633	Cowdenbeath	4600	Dumbarton	3767	Cowdenbeath	3580
Alloa Ath	4333	Albion Rovers	4200	Cowdenbeath	3467	Hamilton Acad	3553
Cowdenbeath	4080	Arbroath	3867	Alloa Ath	3000	Alloa Ath	2933
Arbroath	3700	Alloa Ath	3847	Albion Rovers	2967	Arbroath	2767
Dumbarton	2833	Dumbarton	2660	Arbroath	2953	Albion Rovers	2513
East Stirling	2573	Forfar Ath	2577	Forfar Ath	2127	Forfar Ath	2247
		Stenhousemuir	1927	Stenhousemuir	1653	Stenhousemuir	1953

1952-53		1953-54		1954-55		1955-56	
Rangers	40667	Rangers	30467	Rangers	34120	Rangers	36294
Hibernian	29800	Celtic	28067	Celtic	30654	Hearts	23588
Celtic	23933	Hearts	26248	Hearts	23133	Celtic	21467
Hearts	22377	Hibernian	22020	Hibernian	22825	Hibernian	20224
Dundee	19667	Dundee	19100	Aberdeen	20667	Aberdeen	19235
Aberdeen	19267	Aberdeen	17400	Partick Thistle	17592	Partick Thistle	14209
St Mirren	16800	Partick Thistle	16204	Dundee	16100	St Mirren	13000
Partick Thistle	16305	St Mirren	13800	Kilmarnock	15504	Dundee	12912
Clyde	15333	Clyde	13528	St Mirren	15204	Kilmarnock	12600
Third Lanark	13170	Falkirk	12333	Clyde	14267	Motherwell	11559
Motherwell	12235	Raith Rovers	11967	Falkirk	13282	Clyde	10559
East Fife	12213	Kilmarnock	11643	Motherwell	12733	Falkirk	9912
Falkirk	11300	Stirling Albion	10767	Raith Rovers	10300	Airdrieonians	9324
Raith Rovers	11200	QoS	10633	East Fife	9167	Raith Rovers	9118
Airdrieonians	10900	East Fife	9607	QoS	8567	Dunfermline	8989
QoS	9387	Hamilton Acad	9033	Stirling Albion	6387	QoS	8471
Kilmarnock	9122	Airdrieonians	8467	Airdrieonians	6333	East Fife	7694
Stirling Albion	7433	Motherwell	7433	Dundee Utd	6067	Queen's Park	6893
Ayr Utd	7353	Dundee Utd	7200	Third Lanark	5147	St Johnstone	6006
Hamilton Acad	6167	Ayr Utd	6540	Hamilton Acad	4967	Ayr Utd	5639
Dundee Utd	5640	St Johnstone	6533	St Johnstone	4773	Stirling Albion	5549
St Johnstone	4313	Third Lanark	5367	Queen's Park	4340	Dundee Utd	5083
Queen's Park	4303	Queen's Park	5065	Dunfermline	4207	Third Lanark	4750
Dunfermline	4200	Dunfermline	5013	Ayr Utd	4080	Dumbarton	3917
Morton	4187	Morton	4867	Morton	3467	Hamilton Acad	2838
Arbroath	3302	Albion Rovers	4600	Albion Rovers	3398	Arbroath	2471
Alloa Ath	3067	Cowdenbeath	3433	Cowdenbeath	2737	Morton	2428
Cowdenbeath	2800	Arbroath	3039	Arbroath	2722	Cowdenbeath	2378
Dumbarton	2620	Alloa Ath	2867	Alloa Ath	2367	Berwick Rang	2266
Stenhousemuir	2300	Dumbarton	2633	Brechin City	1740	Albion Rovers	2028
Albion Rovers	2267	Stenhousemuir	2433	Forfar Ath	1725	Brechin City	1861
Forfar Ath	1600	Forfar Ath	1967	Stenhousemuir	1627	Stranraer	1726
						Alloa Ath	1639
						Forfar Ath	1328
						Montrose	1297
						Stenhousemuir	1222
						East Stirling	1206

1956-57		1957-58		1958-59		1959-60	
Rangers	35888	Rangers	30765	Rangers	35353	Rangers	31501
Hearts	23882	Hearts	24118	Hearts	21471	Hearts	23059
Hibernian	18176	Hibernian	20206	Celtic	18411	Celtic	20588
Celtic	17706	Celtic	18348	Hibernian	14618	Hibernian	16559
Partick Thistle	13782	Clyde	12353	Motherwell	13034	Kilmarnock	13158
Aberdeen	13706	Dundee	12118	Aberdeen	12588	St Mirren	12500
Motherwell	13243	Partick Thistle	12029	Partick Thistle	11781	Partick Thistle	12353
Kilmarnock	12594	Third Lanark	12029	St Mirren	11765	Dundee	12118
Raith Rovers	12059	Kilmarnock	11637	Dundee	11471	Motherwell	12118
Dundee	12000	Aberdeen	11618	Clyde	10735	Aberdeen	11529
Queen's Park	11644	Motherwell	11241	Falkirk	10353	Ayr Utd	10353
St Mirren	11453	St Mirren	10794	Kilmarnock	10330	Third Lanark	9882
Falkirk	11235	Falkirk	10176	Third Lanark	8765	Clyde	8677
Ayr Utd	9794	Raith Rovers	9529	Airdrieonians	8559	Dunfermline	8590
Airdrieonians	8588	Airdrieonians	8265	Dunfermline	8324	Raith Rovers	7647
Dunfermline	7588	QoS	6941	Raith Rovers	7753	St Johnstone	7451
QoS	7441	Queen's Park	6471	Ayr Utd	6291	Airdrieonians	6912
East Fife	6853	East Fife	5529	Stirling Albion	6143	Stirling Albion	6187
Clyde	6222	Dunfermline	4944	QoS	5588	Dundee Utd	5861
Third Lanark	5500	Dumbarton	4389	St Johnstone	3961	QoS	4917
Dumbarton	4194	Dundee Utd	3678	Morton	3944	Arbroath	4780
St Johnstone	4144	Ayr Utd	3556	Arbroath	3304	Falkirk	4694
Dundee Utd	3656	Arbroath	3133	Dumbarton	3144	Hamilton Acad	3306
Stirling Albion	2833	Stirling Albion	3095	Dundee Utd	2961	Morton	2806
Arbroath	2792	St Johnstone	2932	East Fife	2950	Queen's Park	2174
Morton	2767	Cowdenbeath	2528	Hamilton Acad	2828	Dumbarton	2142
Cowdenbeath	2583	Morton	2444	Queen's Park	2096	Montrose	2078
Hamilton Acad	1883	Hamilton Acad	2417	Cowdenbeath	1444	East Fife	2000
Albion Rovers	1878	Alloa Ath	1556	Brechin City	1386	Stenhousemuir	1972
Alloa Ath	1806	Brechin City	1372	Forfar Ath	1364	Alloa Ath	1611
Stranraer	1757	Montrose	1347	Stranraer	1275	Berwick Rang	1521
Brechin City	1614	Forfar Ath	1344	Montrose	1223	East Stirling	1278
Montrose	1467	Stranraer	1300	Berwick Rang	1193	Albion Rovers	1267
Berwick Rang	1367	East Stirling	1206	Albion Rovers	1139	Brechin City	1226
Stenhousemuir	1367	Stenhousemuir	1194	Alloa Ath	1111	Cowdenbeath	1169
Forfar Ath	1217	Albion Rovers	1131	Stenhousemuir	856	Stranraer	1137
East Stirling	994	Berwick Rang	1012	East Stirling	736	Forfar Ath	1042

1960-61		1961-62		1962-63		1963-64	
Rangers	35596	Rangers	35917	Rangers	30685	Rangers	30659
Hearts	20294	Celtic	25332	Celtic	24643	Celtic	19800
Celtic	19324	Dundee	15934	Hearts	12778	Hearts	14037
Hibernian	15471	Hearts	13592	Aberdeen	11717	Dundee	13947
St Mirren	13059	Kilmarnock	10478	Dundee	11421	Hibernian	11972
Aberdeen	12618	St Mirren	10359	Partick Thistle	10590	Aberdeen	9084
Kilmarnock	12451	Partick Thistle	9825	Hibernian	9096	Dundee Utd	9047
Dundee	12247	Hibernian	9763	St Mirren	9087	Kilmarnock	8891
Partick Thistle	12205	Dundee Utd	9380	Dundee Utd	9080	Partick Thistle	8548
Motherwell	11859	St Johnstone	8750	Kilmarnock	8777	Morton	8339
Dundee Utd	11382	Motherwell	7952	Dunfermline	7562	Dunfermline	8001
Third Lanark	11088	Dunfermline	7910	Motherwell	6518	St Johnstone	7318
St Johnstone	10503	Aberdeen	7762	QoS	5952	St Mirren	7075
Dunfermline	10191	Third Lanark	7108	St Johnstone	5871	Motherwell	5956
Clyde	9735	Falkirk	6477	Morton	5801	Falkirk	5916
Airdrieonians	7659	Stirling Albion	5289	Third Lanark	5148	Third Lanark	4715
Ayr Utd	7559	Morton	5031	Clyde	4839	QoS	4153
Raith Rovers	6559	Airdrieonians	4464	Falkirk	4828	Airdrieonians	3797
Falkirk	5722	Raith Rovers	4318	Airdrieonians	3492	East Stirling	3270
QoS	3972	QoS	4050	Raith Rovers	3182	East Fife	2159
Stirling Albion	2961	Clyde	2786	Hamilton Acad	2031	Clyde	1766
Arbroath	2029	Ayr Utd	2689	East Stirling	1928	Arbroath	1663
Morton	2011	East Fife	2047	East Fife	1727	Queen's Park	1491
Hamilton Acad	1972	Arbroath	1749	Ayr Utd	1674	Montrose	1333
Stenhousemuir	1667	Queen's Park	1622	Arbroath	1652	Raith Rovers	1268
Montrose	1650	Hamilton Acad	1608	Queen's Park	1612	Dumbarton	1204
Cowdenbeath	1583	Berwick Rang	1505	Montrose	1332	Ayr Utd	1188
East Fife	1583	Dumbarton	1408	Alloa Ath	1303	Hamilton Acad	1072
Dumbarton	1456	Montrose	1396	Stirling Albion	1283	Stirling Albion	1041
Stranraer	1436	Alloa Ath	1350	Dumbarton	1213	Berwick Rang	938
East Stirling	1300	Stranraer	1214	Stranraer	1128	Alloa Ath	882
Queen's Park	1247	Albion Rovers	798	Forfar Ath	977	Stranraer	877
Berwick Rang	1162	Forfar Ath	739	Albion Rovers	841	Albion Rovers	748
Forfar Ath	1144	East Stirling	700	Cowdenbeath	835	Brechin City	607
Brechin City	1044	Cowdenbeath	675	Berwick Rang	811	Forfar Ath	549
Alloa Ath	1039	Brechin City	539	Stenhousemuir	590	Cowdenbeath	519
Albion Rovers	619	Stenhousemuir	469	Brechin City	544	Stenhousemuir	435

1964-65		1965-66		1966-67		1967-68	
Rangers	29089	Rangers	24441	Celtic	31082	Rangers	34980
Celtic	18284	Celtic	24102	Rangers	28573	Celtic	31373
Hearts	16682	Hearts	12120	Hibernian	12321	Hibernian	11475
Hibernian	13826	Hibernian	11664	Aberdeen	11787	Hearts	11136
Dundee	12028	Dundee	9009	Hearts	10188	Aberdeen	10056
Kilmarnock	10476	Dundee Utd	8783	Dundee	9036	Dundee	7608
Morton	9873	Kilmarnock	8706	Kilmarnock	8439	Dunfermline	7329
Dundee Utd	9051	Aberdeen	8291	Dundee Utd	7342	Partick Thistle	7091
Dunfermline	8166	Dunfermline	7168	Partick Thistle	6316	Dundee Utd	6268
Aberdeen	8161	Partick Thistle	6872	Dunfermline	6191	Morton	6125
Partick Thistle	6006	Morton	6518	Motherwell	5341	Kilmarnock	5694
St Johnstone	5630	Motherwell	5154	St Johnstone	5006	Raith Rovers	5644
St Mirren	5075	St Johnstone	4966	Airdrieonians	4714	Falkirk	4666
Motherwell	4930	St Mirren	4834	Falkirk	4666	Motherwell	4870
Clyde	4591	Falkirk	4419	Clyde	4638	St Johnstone	4670
Falkirk	4195	Stirling Albion	4222	Ayr Utd	4613	Clyde	3873
Airdrieonians	3671	Clyde	3920	St Mirren	4424	Airdrieonians	3791
Third Lanark	2701	Ayr Utd	3707	Morton	3824	St Mirren	3158
QoS	2596	Hamilton Acad	3132	Stirling Albion	3586	Stirling Albion	2895
ES Clydebank	2064	QoS	2364	Raith Rovers	2744	Ayr Utd	2351
Stirling Albion	1744	Airdrieonians	1710	QoS	1662	QoS	1958
Queen's Park	1354	Arbroath	1195	Clydebank	1545	East Fife	1416
Hamilton Acad	1337	Raith Rovers	1108	East Fife	1480	Arbroath	1387
East Fife	1333	Dumbarton	1081	Arbroath	1233	Queen's Park	1348
Dumbarton	1049	East Fife	1032	Queen's Park	1077	Clydebank	1108
Ayr Utd	1034	Queen's Park	987	Hamilton Acad	1019	Dumbarton	858
Raith Rovers	954	Berwick Rang	846	Berwick Rang	782	Hamilton Acad	704
Berwick Rang	951	Third Lanark	823	Montrose	738	Alloa Ath	659
Arbroath	934	Montrose	815	Dumbarton	724	Montrose	647
Montrose	766	Albion Rovers	806	Alloa Ath	713	Albion Rovers	610
Stranraer	755	Stranraer	686	Stranraer	707	Berwick Rang	585
Alloa Ath	697	Alloa Ath	569	Third Lanark	703	Forfar Ath	569
Forfar Ath	630	East Stirling	421	Albion Rovers	642	Stranraer	430
Albion Rovers	533	Cowdenbeath	395	Cowdenbeath	550	East Stirling	401
Brechin City	444	Forfar Ath	387	Forfar Ath	498	Cowdenbeath	385
Cowdenbeath	416	Brechin City	384	East Stirling	409	Brechin City	362
Stenhousemuir	266	Stenhousemuir	268	Brechin City	400	Stenhousemuir	233
				Stenhousemuir	270		

1968-69		1969-70		1970-71		1971-72	
Celtic	34740	Rangers	33634	Celtic	29647	Celtic	31241
Rangers	33747	Celtic	33188	Rangers	29471	Rangers	26199
Hearts	11544	Hibernian	13128	Aberdeen	15917	Aberdeen	17993
Aberdeen	11343	Hearts	12473	Hearts	11668	Hibernian	14057
Hibernian	10835	Aberdeen	10436	Hibernian	10541	Hearts	11196
St Mirren	9430	Dundee Utd	8327	Dundee Utd	6987	Partick Thistle	10172
Dundee Utd	8307	Ayr Utd	8077	St Johnstone	6912	Dundee	8020
Kilmarnock	8294	Dundee	6946	Dunfermline	6898	Ayr Utd	7552
Dunfermline	7110	St Mirren	6814	Dundee	6746	Dunfermline	6804
Dundee	7003	Motherwell	6811	Ayr Utd	6620	Dundee Utd	6766
Partick Thistle	6236	Kilmarnock	6724	Falkirk	6353	Falkirk	6703
Morton	5839	Dunfermline	6448	St Mirren	6192	St Johnstone	6198
St Johnstone	5338	St Johnstone	6290	Kilmarnock	5933	Motherwell	6002
Raith Rovers	5177	Partick Thistle	5704	Motherwell	5877	Kilmarnock	5717
Falkirk	5096	Morton	4782	Morton	4416	East Fife	5664
Clyde	4538	Clyde	3955	Partick Thistle	4256	Airdrieonians	5379
Airdrieonians	4307	Falkirk	3834	Airdrieonians	4219	Morton	4947
Arbroath	3347	Raith Rovers	3725	Clyde	3357	St Mirren	3816
Ayr Utd	2707	Airdrieonians	3535	Cowdenbeath	3350	Clyde	3634
Motherwell	2667	Cowdenbeath	2194	East Fife	3119	Dumbarton	3217
QoS	1677	QoS	2129	Raith Rovers	1975	Raith Rovers	2285
East Fife	1397	Alloa Ath	1401	Arbroath	1811	QoS	2179
Stirling Albion	1199	Arbroath	1309	Dumbarton	1600	Arbroath	1982
Queen's Park	1176	East Fife	1213	QoS	1413	Stirling Albion	1743
East Stirling	983	Dumbarton	1170	Clydebank	1375	Cowdenbeath	1539
Clydebank	823	Stirling Albion	1079	Alloa Ath	1074	Clydebank	1335
Hamilton Acad	811	Berwick Rang	896	Queen's Park	1042	Montrose	1328
Dumbarton	799	Queen's Park	796	Stranraer	976	Forfar Ath	1123
Forfar Ath	749	Clydebank	732	Montrose	898	Stranraer	1068
Alloa Ath	710	East Stirling	723	Stirling Albion	846	Alloa Ath	983
Stranraer	698	Montrose	676	Hamilton Acad	715	Queen's Park	931
Albion Rovers	558	Forfar Ath	636	Forfar Ath	707	Hamilton Acad	896
Montrose	510	Stranraer	517	Berwick Rang	528	East Stirling	591
Cowdenbeath	450	Hamilton Acad	514	Albion Rovers	516	Berwick Rang	532
Berwick Rang	427	Stenhousemuir	346	East Stirling	487	Brechin City	520
Brechin City	321	Brechin City	329	Stenhousemuir	422	Albion Rovers	515
Stenhousemuir	286	Albion Rovers	319	Brechin City	330	Stenhousemuir	445

1972-73		1973-74		1974-75		1975-76	
Rangers	27469	Celtic	24762	Rangers	32855	Rangers	30648
Celtic	26606	Rangers	22356	Celtic	22775	Celtic	28066
Hibernian	16100	Hibernian	14339	Hibernian	13721	Hibernian	13797
Aberdeen	13733	Hearts	11733	Hearts	12225	Hearts	12677
Hearts	10213	Aberdeen	8657	Aberdeen	9673	Aberdeen	11774
Dundee	7884	Dundee	6948	Dundee	7336	Motherwell	9575
Partick Thistle	7398	Partick Thistle	6618	Kilmarnock	7022	Dundee	8767
Dundee Utd	6925	Motherwell	6309	Dundee Utd	6629	Dundee Utd	7617
Ayr Utd	6393	Ayr Utd	6112	Partick Thistle	6136	Ayr Utd	6895
Dumbarton	5772	Dunfermline	5785	Motherwell	5833	Partick Thistle	4841
Motherwell	5227	Dundee Utd	5468	Ayr Utd	5800	St Johnstone	4787
Falkirk	5127	Dumbarton	4422	Dunfermline	4822	Kilmarnock	4239
East Fife	4903	Falkirk	4342	Airdrieonians	4401	St Mirren	3698
Airdrieonians	4855	St Johnstone	3855	Dumbarton	4343	Falkirk	2524
St Johnstone	4658	Kilmarnock	3639	St Johnstone	4243	Airdrieonians	2513
Kilmarnock	4489	East Fife	3612	Morton	3300	Dunfermline	2488
Morton	4239	Arbroath	3104	Clyde	3246	QoS	2222
Dunfermline	4219	Clyde	3005	Arbroath	2874	Dumbarton	2137
Arbroath	3590	Morton	2839	Falkirk	2618	Raith Rovers	2064
St Mirren	2979	Airdrieonians	2758	St Mirren	2396	Hamilton Acad	1977
Raith Rovers	2095	Hamilton Acad	2324	Hamilton Acad	2334	East Fife	1830
Stirling Albion	2019	St Mirren	2267	QoS	1874	Arbroath	1696
Hamilton Acad	1774	QoS	2006	East Fife	1852	Montrose	1669
Clyde	1760	Raith Rovers	1765	Raith Rovers	1562	Morton	1453
QoS	1320	Stirling Albion	1291	Montrose	1332	Clyde	1418
Clydebank	1298	Clydebank	1281	Stirling Albion	1247	Clydebank	1391
Cowdenbeath	1238	Stranraer	1004	Clydebank	1185	Stirling Albion	1131
Montrose	1196	Montrose	941	East Stirling	1166	Alloa Ath	904
Forfar Ath	1008	Alloa Ath	884	Stranraer	799	Stranraer	880
Stranraer	986	East Stirling	798	Cowdenbeath	726	Cowdenbeath	721
Alloa Ath	852	Cowdenbeath	790	Meadowbank	677	Queen's Park	609
Queen's Park	734	Queen's Park	683	Alloa Ath	640	Forfar Ath	588
Stenhousemuir	675	Berwick Rang	667	Queen's Park	578	East Stirling	556
East Stirling	628	Forfar Ath	598	Forfar Ath	570	Meadowbank	463
Berwick Rang	464	Albion Rovers	596	Berwick Rang	522	Stenhousemuir	432
Brechin City	438	Stenhousemuir	450	Albion Rovers	519	Albion Rovers	402
Albion Rovers	426	Brechin City	440	Stenhousemuir	451	Brechin City	340
				Brechin City	439	Berwick Rang	324

1976-77		1977-78		1978-79		1979-80	
Celtic	28063	Celtic	29568	Rangers	25628	Celtic	28499
Rangers	21692	Rangers	28083	Celtic	25303	Rangers	20405
Aberdeen	13798	Aberdeen	16115	Aberdeen	14171	Aberdeen	12944
Hearts	11696	St Mirren	11793	Hearts	10831	St Mirren	10343
Hibernian	10003	Hearts	9863	St Mirren	10694	Dundee Utd	9977
Motherwell	7170	Hibernian	9647	Hibernian	9794	Hibernian	9564
Dundee Utd	7127	Dundee Utd	8411	Dundee Utd	9101	Dundee	9434
Ayr Utd	6751	Partick Thistle	8381	Partick Thistle	7966	Morton	8051
St Mirren	6415	Motherwell	8235	Morton	7927	Partick Thistle	7273
Partick Thistle	6287	Dundee	6729	Motherwell	7740	Kilmarnock	6990
Kilmarnock	5849	Ayr Utd	6196	Dundee	5971	Hearts	5735
Dundee	4518	Clydebank	4484	Ayr Utd	3193	Motherwell	2920
Clydebank	3045	Morton	4002	Kilmarnock	3033	Ayr Utd	2654
Raith Rovers	2219	Kilmarnock	2834	Dunfermline	2450	Airdrieonians	2633
Morton	1959	Stirling Albion	2161	Falkirk	2131	Dunfermline	2597
QoS	1882	St Johnstone	2103	Hamilton Acad	2109	Raith Rovers	2340
Hamilton Acad	1808	Hamilton Acad	1942	Raith Rovers	1847	St Johnstone	2245
Airdrieonians	1757	Raith Rovers	1908	St Johnstone	1789	Hamilton Acad	2139
St Johnstone	1694	Dunfermline	1903	Clydebank	1533	Falkirk	1909
Falkirk	1663	Dumbarton	1848	Airdrieonians	1387	Dumbarton	1471
East Fife	1660	Arbroath	1791	Clyde	1238	Berwick Rang	1384
Dunfermline	1573	Falkirk	1777	Stirling Albion	1196	Stirling Albion	1279
Stirling Albion	1511	East Fife	1766	Arbroath	1192	Clydebank	1209
Montrose	1481	QoS	1659	QoS	1171	Arbroath	1174
Arbroath	1375	Alloa Ath	1528	Dumbarton	1127	Forfar Ath	1081
Dumbarton	1363	Montrose	1351	Forfar Ath	1024	Clyde	1030
Stranraer	1245	Airdrieonians	1232	Berwick Rang	990	QoS	1018
Alloa Ath	1211	Forfar Ath	1108	East Fife	981	Stranraer	775
Queen's Park	675	Stranraer	1067	Montrose	913	East Fife	723
Clyde	673	Berwick Rang	1041	Stranraer	855	Montrose	700
Forfar Ath	628	Clyde	992	Alloa Ath	819	East Stirling	680
Cowdenbeath	583	Cowdenbeath	834	Cowdenbeath	543	Alloa Ath	669
Meadowbank	574	Queen's Park	652	Brechin City	484	Brechin City	617
East Stirling	516	East Stirling	625	Queen's Park	476	Cowdenbeath	524
Stenhousemuir	427	Albion Rovers	529	East Stirling	470	Queen's Park	513
Albion Rovers	418	Meadowbank	503	Meadowbank	464	Meadowbank	428
Berwick Rang	380	Brechin City	447	Albion Rovers	429	Albion Rovers	417
Brechin City	327	Stenhousemuir	446	Stenhousemuir	418	Stenhousemuir	394

1980-81		1981-82		1982-83		1983-84	
Celtic	22836	Celtic	22718	Celtic	23740	Rangers	21996
Rangers	18328	Rangers	16400	Rangers	17681	Celtic	18390
Aberdeen	12315	Aberdeen	11360	Aberdeen	15534	Aberdeen	17138
St Mirren	7859	Dundee Utd	9416	Dundee Utd	11133	Hearts	11914
Hearts	7759	Dundee	7570	Dundee	7929	Dundee Utd	10894
Dundee Utd	7716	Hibernian	7445	Hibernian	7109	Hibernian	8334
Morton	6004	St Mirren	6955	Motherwell	6509	Dundee	7442
Partick Thistle	5481	Hearts	5157	Hearts	5908	Motherwell	5566
Airdrieonians	4965	Partick Thistle	5117	St Mirren	5846	St Mirren	4900
Dundee	4951	Morton	3872	Morton	4237	St Johnstone	4859
Kilmarnock	4507	Airdrieonians	3821	Kilmarnock	3463	Partick Thistle	2419
Hibernian	4460	Motherwell	3317	St Johnstone	2943	Morton	1857
Raith Rovers	2644	Kilmarnock	2609	Partick Thistle	2303	Falkirk	1832
St Johnstone	2465	Ayr Utd	2122	Airdrieonians	1653	Ayr Utd	1423
Ayr Utd	2455	St Johnstone	1957	Falkirk	1562	Kilmarnock	1358
Motherwell	2397	Falkirk	1950	Raith Rovers	1484	Airdrieonians	1096
Dunfermline	2356	Dunfermline	1930	Dunfermline	1415	Forfar Ath	1072
Falkirk	2137	Raith Rovers	1673	Ayr Utd	1244	Hamilton Acad	1059
Hamilton Acad	1967	Hamilton Acad	1349	Alloa Ath	1190	Dunfermline	1090
QoS	1247	Forfar Ath	1146	Hamilton Acad	1054	Raith Rovers	1000
East Stirling	1178	QoS	1130	Queen's Park	1001	Clydebank	837
Berwick Rang	988	Queen's Park	974	Forfar Ath	935	QoS	829
Stirling Albion	953	Clydebank	886	Clydebank	932	Dumbarton	827
Clydebank	917	Berwick Rang	796	Clyde	809	Brechin City	780
Forfar Ath	873	Alloa Ath	704	Dumbarton	728	East Fife	780
Queen's Park	781	Brechin City	679	Arbroath	696	Alloa Ath	772
Alloa Ath	731	Arbroath	659	QoS	689	Clyde	687
Dumbarton	731	East Stirling	633	Brechin City	671	Arbroath	584
Arbroath	662	Stranraer	579	Stirling Albion	609	Meadowbank	538
Brechin City	648	Clyde	537	East Fife	585	Berwick Rang	531
Cowdenbeath	560	Dumbarton	510	Berwick Rang	581	Stirling Albion	514
Stranraer	550	East Fife	502	Meadowbank	546	Queen's Park	494
Clyde	513	Stirling Albion	479	Stranraer	446	Stranraer	476
East Fife	508	Albion Rovers	382	Montrose	343	Albion Rovers	370
Montrose	457	Cowdenbeath	361	Stenhousemuir	325	Cowdenbeath	348
Meadowbank	376	Montrose	354	Cowdenbeath	323	Stenhousemuir	336
Albion Rovers	331	Stenhousemuir	324	Albion Rovers	267	Montrose	286
Stenhousemuir	286	Meadowbank	275	East Stirling	214	East Stirling	246

1984-85		1985-86		1986-87		1987-88	
Rangers	20963	Celtic	25335	Rangers	36152	Rangers	38568
Celtic	20827	Rangers	25146	Celtic	25311	Celtic	33199
Aberdeen	15877	Hearts	16198	Hearts	14531	Hearts	16633
Hearts	11305	Aberdeen	14326	Aberdeen	12595	Aberdeen	13460
Dundee Utd	10666	Dundee Utd	10842	Dundee Utd	10432	Hibernian	11590
Dundee	8439	Hibernian	9135	Hibernian	9154	Dundee Utd	10462
Hibernian	7425	Dundee	8950	Dundee	7513	Dunfermline	9245
St Mirren	5902	St Mirren	6405	Falkirk	6274	Dundee	8595
Morton	3467	Motherwell	5572	St Mirren	5865	St Mirren	7386
Dumbarton	3451	Clydebank	3669	Motherwell	5398	Motherwell	6660
Motherwell	2509	Dunfermline	2872	Hamilton Acad	4239	Falkirk	6659
Dunfermline	2329	Falkirk	2359	Dunfermline	4145	Morton	4933
Partick Thistle	1931	Kilmarnock	1949	Clydebank	3182	Ayr Utd	2796
Falkirk	1849	Partick Thistle	1868	Morton	1932	Raith Rovers	2109
Ayr Utd	1564	Hamilton Acad	1675	Kilmarnock	1899	Hamilton Acad	2044
Airdrieonians	1517	Ayr Utd	1519	Partick Thistle	1756	Partick Thistle	1972
St Johnstone	1385	QoS	1511	QoS	1743	St Johnstone	1946
Kilmarnock	1351	Airdrieonians	1333	Ayr Utd	1553	Kilmarnock	1846
Hamilton Acad	1235	Morton	1256	Raith Rovers	1436	Airdrieonians	1414
Forfar Ath	1194	Dumbarton	1170	Airdrieonians	1430	QoS	1282
East Fife	1113	Raith Rovers	975	East Fife	1250	Clydebank	1064
Clydebank	1080	St Johnstone	957	Dumbarton	1077	Clyde	1051
Alloa Ath	960	Clyde	950	St Johnstone	1074	East Fife	980
Raith Rovers	893	East Fife	917	Clyde	915	Dumbarton	836
Clyde	840	Forfar Ath	858	Forfar Ath	877	Stirling Albion	760
Brechin City	727	Alloa Ath	757	Stirling Albion	725	Forfar Ath	739
Montrose	625	Montrose	694	Montrose	648	Meadowbank	734
QoS	599	Brechin City	665	Brechin City	613	Queen's Park	610
Meadowbank	585	Stenhousemuir	643	Alloa Ath	577	Arbroath	587
Queen's Park	543	Arbroath	612	Queen's Park	538	Alloa Ath	570
Stirling Albion	537	Stirling Albion	605	Stranraer	525	Stranraer	493
Cowdenbeath	508	Berwick Rang	588	Albion Rovers	497	Brechin City	474
Arbroath	486	Queen's Park	557	Arbroath	475	Berwick Rang	448
Berwick Rang	454	Meadowbank	536	Meadowbank	411	Montrose	420
Stranraer	449	Cowdenbeath	525	Cowdenbeath	384	Albion Rovers	358
Stenhousemuir	431	Stranraer	508	Berwick Rang	380	Stenhousemuir	358
Albion Rovers	422	Albion Rovers	414	Stenhousemuir	365	East Stirling	354
East Stirling	388	East Stirling	331	East Stirling	345	Cowdenbeath	268

1988-89		1989-90		1990-91		1991-92	
Rangers	39189	Rangers	38436	Rangers	35969	Rangers	37701
Celtic	31713	Celtic	28616	Celtic	29012	Celtic	25086
Hearts	15367	Hearts	15694	Aberdeen	15273	Hearts	13317
Aberdeen	14107	Aberdeen	15445	Hearts	13232	Aberdeen	11798
Hibernian	13896	Dunfermline	10989	Dundee Utd	10089	Hibernian	9841
Dundee Utd	12830	Hibernian	10705	Hibernian	9257	Dundee Utd	8088
Dundee	9352	Dundee Utd	10719	Dunfermline	8257	Motherwell	6686
St Mirren	8398	Dundee	8884	Motherwell	7787	Dunfermline	6366
Motherwell	7254	Motherwell	8632	St Johnstone	7755	St Johnstone	6246
Dunfermline	6605	St Mirren	7646	St Mirren	7612	Falkirk	6234
Hamilton Acad	4979	St Johnstone	5866	Kilmarnock	4939	St Mirren	5043
Falkirk	3782	Partick Thistle	3778	Falkirk	4505	Airdrieonians	5012
Ayr Utd	3541	Kilmarnock	3247	Partick Thistle	3700	Kilmarnock	4388
St Johnstone	2946	Falkirk	3061	Dundee	3636	Partick Thistle	3990
Partick Thistle	2686	Ayr Utd	2677	Airdrieonians	3183	Dundee	3690
Kilmarnock	2488	Airdrieonians	2280	Ayr Utd	2766	Ayr Utd	2530
Airdrieonians	2355	Hamilton Acad	1739	Morton	1886	Hamilton Acad	1886
Raith Rovers	2160	Raith Rovers	1683	Raith Rovers	1841	Morton	1725
Morton	2091	Morton	1572	Hamilton Acad	1779	Raith Rovers	1663
Clydebank	1550	Albion Rovers	1191	Clydebank	1410	Clydebank	1103
Forfar Ath	1162	Clydebank	1117	Clyde	1127	Stirling Albion	1103
Clyde	1148	Alloa Ath	1057	Forfar Ath	1018	Montrose	953
QoS	987	Clyde	1050	Stirling Albion	793	Forfar Ath	846
Meadowbank	848	Forfar Ath	1009	Brechin City	766	Dumbarton	829
Stranraer	733	Stranraer	789	Meadowbank	763	Alloa Ath	786
Stirling Albion	676	QoS	737	East Fife	662	East Fife	770
Queen's Park	641	Stirling Albion	708	QoS	619	QoS	609
East Fife	627	East Fife	696	Queen's Park	602	Meadowbank	574
Alloa Ath	609	Meadowbank	691	Stranraer	588	Stranraer	517
Albion Rovers	561	Brechin City	613	Dumbarton	502	Clyde	511
Dumbarton	506	Dumbarton	607	Stenhousemuir	482	Arbroath	500
Arbroath	476	Queen's Park	591	Alloa Ath	458	Queen's Park	481
Brechin City	472	Stenhousemuir	556	Montrose	457	Brechin City	449
Berwick Rang	406	Arbroath	526	Berwick Rang	429	Cowdenbeath	448
Montrose	388	Berwick Rang	495	Arbroath	395	Stenhousemuir	424
Stenhousemuir	371	Montrose	400	Albion Rovers	321	East Stirling	305
Cowdenbeath	315	East Stirling	315	Cowdenbeath	295	Berwick Rang	294
East Stirling	271	Cowdenbeath	290	East Stirling	256	Albion Rovers	287

1992-93		1993-94		1994-95		1995-96	
Rangers	40737	Rangers	43345	Rangers	44062	Rangers	44661
Celtic	22684	Celtic	22637	Celtic	24601	Celtic	34342
Aberdeen	11176	Aberdeen	12723	Aberdeen	13424	Aberdeen	12764
Hearts	9829	Hearts	11010	Hearts	10123	Hearts	12078
Hibernian	8791	Hibernian	9718	Kilmarnock	9530	Hibernian	9842
Dundee Utd	8404	Kilmarnock	9161	Hibernian	8782	Kilmarnock	8719
Dundee	6785	Dundee Utd	8596	Dundee Utd	8500	Dundee Utd	7283
Motherwell	6277	Motherwell	7897	Falkirk	7807	Motherwell	7222
Partick Thistle	5940	Partick Thistle	6730	Motherwell	7778	Partick Thistle	6458
Falkirk	5769	St Johnstone	5877	Partick Thistle	6941	Dunfermline	5899
St Johnstone	5603	Dundee	5646	Dunfermline	5633	Falkirk	5885
Kilmarnock	4694	Raith Rovers	4880	Raith Rovers	4070	Raith Rovers	5784
Airdrieonians	4520	Dunfermline	4496	St Johnstone	3791	Morton	4104
Dunfermline	3486	Falkirk	3936	Dundee	3667	St Johnstone	3776
St Mirren	3178	St Mirren	2593	St Mirren	2674	Dundee	3608
Raith Rovers	2929	Airdrieonians	2369	Morton	2092	St Mirren	2835
Ayr Utd	2376	Ayr Utd	1815	Ayr Utd	2044	Livingston	1978
Morton	1925	Clyde	1709	Airdrieonians	1821	Ross County	1749
Hamilton Acad	1802	Hamilton Acad	1687	Ross County	1566	Airdrieonians	1711
Dumbarton	1143	Morton	1541	Hamilton Acad	1557	Inverness	1579
Clydebank	1068	Clydebank	1523	Inverness	1276	Ayr Utd	1380
Stirling Albion	865	Stirling Albion	1206	QoS	1209	Clydebank	1378
Cowdenbeath	841	Dumbarton	1117	Clyde	1134	Dumbarton	1352
Arbroath	742	QoS	981	Clydebank	1060	Hamilton Acad	1305
Clyde	700	Stranraer	892	Stranraer	1010	QoS	1189
Stranraer	649	East Fife	780	Dumbarton	925	Clyde	1004
East Fife	629	Brechin City	677	Stirling Albion	880	Stirling Albion	934
Montrose	618	Arbroath	643	Montrose	811	East Fife	919
Meadowbank	600	Montrose	566	East Fife	758	Stranraer	624
Forfar Ath	598	Queen's Park	546	Forfar Ath	683	Montrose	559
QoS	586	Forfar Ath	533	Stenhousemuir	590	Stenhousemuir	536
Brechin City	566	Alloa Ath	507	Berwick Rang	589	Forfar Ath	534
Alloa Ath	503	Berwick Rang	465	Arbroath	556	Queen's Park	523
Queen's Park	464	East Stirling	453	Queen's Park	534	Arbroath	520
Stenhousemuir	422	Stenhousemuir	404	Brechin City	457	Brechin City	439
Berwick Rang	380	Meadowbank	312	East Stirling	452	Berwick Rang	418
East Stirling	329	Cowdenbeath	309	Alloa Ath	450	Alloa Ath	393
Albion Rovers	269	Albion Rovers	292	Albion Rovers	312	Albion Rovers	385
				Cowdenbeath	311	East Stirling	345
				Meadowbank	294	Cowdenbeath	236

1996-97		1997-98		1998-99		1999-2000	
Rangers	48118	Rangers	49357	Celtic	59271	Celtic	53887
Celtic	47504	Celtic	48532	Rangers	49011	Rangers	48107
Aberdeen	12459	Hearts	15337	Hearts	14233	Hearts	14246
Hearts	12349	Aberdeen	13339	Aberdeen	12580	Aberdeen	12894
Hibernian	10480	Hibernian	12029	Kilmarnock	11533	Hibernian	12070
Dundee Utd	9339	Kilmarnock	9987	Hibernian	10220	Kilmarnock	9419
Kilmarnock	9125	Dundee Utd	9069	Dundee Utd	9392	Dundee Utd	8187
Dunfermline	8819	Dunfermline	8167	Motherwell	8747	Motherwell	7143
Motherwell	7256	Motherwell	7306	Dunfermline	7595	Dundee	6943
Raith Rovers	5890	St Johnstone	6703	Dundee	7082	St Johnstone	6125
St Johnstone	4468	Dundee	3869	St Johnstone	7077	Dunfermline	5066
St Mirren	3451	Raith Rovers	3406	Falkirk	3629	St Mirren	4956
Falkirk	2802	Falkirk	3172	St Mirren	2819	Livingston	3384
Dundee	2797	Partick Thistle	3087	Ayr Utd	2649	Falkirk	3342
Morton	2787	St Mirren	2981	Livingston	2498	Raith Rovers	3123
Partick Thistle	2620	Morton	2576	Raith Rovers	2488	Ross County	2363
Inverness	2495	Ayr Utd	2194	Airdrieonians	2465	Inverness	2281
Livingston	2183	Inverness	1762	Morton	2266	Partick Thistle	2278
Ayr Utd	2016	Airdrieonians	1728	Inverness	2168	Ayr Utd	2180
Airdrieonians	1823	Stirling Albion	1693	Partick Thistle	2083	Airdrieonians	1872
Ross County	1789	Livingston	1336	Ross County	1727	Morton	1348
Stirling Albion	1453	Ross County	1330	Hamilton Acad	1253	QoS	1153
QoS	1214	QoS	1264	QoS	1217	Clyde	1151
East Fife	1148	Hamilton Acad	1260	Clyde	1108	Stirling Albion	867
Hamilton Acad	928	Arbroath	810	Stirling Albion	987	Alloa Ath	825
Clyde	806	Clyde	730	East Fife	913	Arbroath	811
Clydebank	779	East Fife	693	Stranraer	839	Hamilton Acad	695
Dumbarton	627	Stranraer	588	Arbroath	822	Queen's Park	685
Stranraer	601	Alloa Ath	555	Alloa Ath	750	Clydebank	598
Albion Rovers	595	Queen's Park	523	Clydebank	647	Dumbarton	581
Queen's Park	538	Forfar Ath	501	Forfar Ath	589	Stenhousemuir	576
Montrose	523	Stenhousemuir	476	Stenhousemuir	501	Berwick Rang	547
Stenhousemuir	518	Montrose	426	Queen's Park	468	East Fife	533
Forfar Ath	494	Albion Rovers	392	Berwick Rang	393	Stranraer	533
Arbroath	456	Dumbarton	391	Dumbarton	390	Forfar Ath	477
Berwick Rang	456	Berwick Rang	389	Brechin City	374	Montrose	379
Alloa Ath	453	Brechin City	384	Albion Rovers	331	Cowdenbeath	354
Brechin City	378	Clydebank	370	Montrose	312	Brechin City	325
East Stirling	331	East Stirling	351	East Stirling	264	Albion Rovers	320
Cowdenbeath	233	Cowdenbeath	227	Cowdenbeath	224	East Stirling	272

2000-01		2001-02		2002-03		2003-04	
Celtic	59370	Celtic	58587	Celtic	57614	Celtic	58516
Rangers	47532	Rangers	47895	Rangers	48814	Rangers	48992
Hearts	12771	Aberdeen	13923	Hearts	12058	Hearts	11961
Aberdeen	12403	Hearts	12080	Aberdeen	11746	Aberdeen	10389
Hibernian	10793	Hibernian	11588	Hibernian	10157	Hibernian	9127
Kilmarnock	8224	Dundee Utd	8007	Dundee Utd	7666	Dundee Utd	7739
Dundee	8042	Dundee	7958	Kilmarnock	7565	Dundee	7090
Dundee Utd	7830	Kilmarnock	7621	Dundee	7399	Kilmarnock	6966
Dunfermline	6404	Livingston	7478	Livingston	6828	Dunfermline	6236
Motherwell	6209	Dunfermline	6423	Dunfermline	6127	Motherwell	6225
St Mirren	5838	Motherwell	5879	Motherwell	6067	Partick Thistle	4711
St Johnstone	5438	St Johnstone	4581	Partick Thistle	5658	Livingston	4551
Livingston	3567	Partick Thistle	4434	Falkirk	4158	Ross County	3173
Partick Thistle	2917	St Mirren	3578	St Mirren	2717	Morton	2966
Ross County	2788	Ross County	2688	Ross County	2678	St Mirren	2773
Falkirk	2653	Falkirk	2483	St Johnstone	2577	St Johnstone	2622
Ayr Utd	2415	Ayr Utd	2476	Morton	2334	Falkirk	2585
Inverness	2133	Inverness	2019	Inverness	2182	Inverness	2372
Raith Rovers	1791	Airdrieonians	2003	QoS	2146	QoS	2360
Airdrieonians	1676	Hamilton Acad	2003	Raith Rovers	1924	Raith Rovers	2190
Clyde	1472	Raith Rovers	1905	Ayr Utd	1897	Airdrie Utd	1861
Morton	1290	QoS	1891	Airdrie Utd	1442	Ayr Utd	1706
QoS	1271	Clyde	1454	Clyde	1314	Clyde	1652
Queen's Park	1137	Morton	1250	Hamilton Acad	1285	Hamilton Acad	1407
Alloa Ath	933	Arbroath	960	Dumbarton	957	Dumbarton	1050
Arbroath	809	Dumbarton	844	Arbroath	833	Brechin City	809
Stirling Albion	790	Alloa Ath	632	Alloa Ath	828	Stirling Albion	753
Elgin City	671	Peterhead	614	East Fife	799	East Fife	712
Dumbarton	625	Elgin	595	Queen's Park	719	Forfar Ath	663
Forfar Ath	624	Brechin City	547	Peterhead	703	Arbroath	625
Berwick Rang	611	Queen's Park	546	Stirling Albion	653	Stenhousemuir	600
Peterhead	609	Berwick Rang	513	Brechin City	620	Alloa Ath	589
Cowdenbeath	563	Forfar Ath	507	Forfar Ath	589	Peterhead	579
Stranraer	534	Stirling Albion	470	Stenhousemuir	552	Elgin City	527
Stenhousemuir	512	Stenhousemuir	448	Berwick Rang	523	Berwick Rang	521
Hamilton Acad	506	Stranraer	446	Cowdenbeath	497	Queen's Park	515
East Fife	470	Montrose	433	Elgin City	492	Stranraer	503
Brechin City	435	East Fife	384	Albion Rovers	491	Gretna	461
Montrose	393	Cowdenbeath	368	Stranraer	478	Montrose	355
Albion Rovers	360	Albion Rovers	348	Gretna	408	Albion Rovers	349
Clydebank	329	Clydebank	342	Montrose	365	Cowdenbeath	305
East Stirling	264	East Stirling	247	East Stirling	324	East Stirling	278

2004-05*

Celtic	57800
Rangers	48700
Aberdeen	13300
Hearts	12100
Hibernian	12100
Dundee Utd	7700
Dundee	6750
Motherwell	6600
Kilmarnock	6000
Dunfermline	5850
Livingston	4700
Inverness	4000
Falkirk	3800
Partick Thistle	3600
St Mirren	3200
Morton	2620
St Johnstone	2330
Ross County	2300
Hamilton Acad	2140
Airdrie Utd	2100
QoS	1880
Clyde	1620
Raith Rovers	1600
Ayr Utd	1300
Gretna	840
Dumbarton	820
Stirling Albion	810
Peterhead	640
Brechin City	630
Stranraer	590
Arbroath	560
Forfar Ath	560
Alloa Ath	550
Queen's Park	520
East Fife	480
Elgin City	440
Stenhousemuir	420
Berwick Rang	400
Montrose	360
Albion Rovers	300
East Stirling	300
Cowdenbeath	250

* provisional figures

The Early Years
1890-91

Celtic	5580
Rangers	5050
Third Lanark	4556
Dumbarton	3556
Hearts	3388
St Mirren	3333
Abercorn	2850
Vale of Leven	2500
Cambuslang	2444
Renton*	2000
Cowlairs	1611

*Renton expelled after five games
three away v Abercorn, Celtic, Rangers;
two home v St Mirren, Vale of Leven.
The figures have been included here for historical record.

1891-92 / 1892-93

1891-92		1892-93	
Celtic	7636	Celtic	9111
Rangers	5123	Rangers	6444
Third Lanark	4556	St Mirren	4444
Leith Ath	4182	Hearts	3611
Clyde	3909	Clyde	3611
St Mirren	3722	Third Lanark	3600
Hearts	3681	Leith Ath	3056
Abercorn	2773	Abercorn	3000
Renton	2722	Dumbarton	3000
Dumbarton	2545	Renton	2833
Vale of Leven	1586		
Cambuslang	1427		

Seasonal averages since 1961

Season	Division One	Division Two	Overall
1961-62	11147	1686	6154
1962-63	9946	1726	5608
1963-64	9680	1457	5340
1964-65	9505	1026	5030
1965-66	8717	1013	4651
1966-67	9270	1068	4717
1967-68	9378	1239	5083
1968-69	10001	979	5239
1969-70	9954	1087	5275
1970-71	9456	1031	5010
1971-72	10236	1416	5581
1972-73	9203	1368	5068
1973-74	8015	1319	4481
1974-75	8737	1173	4547

Season	Premier/SPL	1st Division	2nd Division	3rd Division	Overall
1975-76	13460	2479	771		5541
1976-77	11844	2331	765		4101
1977-78	13091	2894	985		4704
1978-79	12916	1973	915		4288
1979-80	12365	2198	753		4175
1980-81	9777	2202	609		3481
1981-82	9467	1876	556		3262
1982-83	10333	1739	515		3410
1983-84	11222	1179	572		3440
1984-85	10832	1344	690		3450
1985-86	12588	1288	827		3909
1986-87	11721	1524	662		4591
1987-88	13949	1339	745		5293
1988-89	15708	2455	504		5007
1989-90	15576	2064	761		4924
1990-91	14424	2370	489		4651
1991-92	11785	2037	515		4731
1992-93	11376	2075	534		4615
1993-94	12351	2056	548		4935
1994-95	14155	2733	893	695	4619
1995-96	14774	3325	809	815	4931
1996-97	17130	2414	973	791	5327
1997-98	17983	2597	811	539	5482
1998-99	18636	2949	1314	498	5849
1999-2000	17902	2815	1125	448	5572
2000-01	15905	2072	953	489	5545
2001-02	15988	2401	840	503	5624
2002-03	15626	2133	887	729	5518
2003-04	15209	2236	1111	464	5408
2004-05*	15500	2460	885	455	5470

* provisonal figures

Ever-optimistic, this band of Scotland supporters are all smiles
as they set out on the road to Wembley

Free Falling: 1960-1975

ONE out of every four people who attended a football match in the early sixties stopped doing so by 1975. That stark figure demonstrates how great the loss of support was in an era which produced some of the most memorable achievements and some of the greatest players of all time.

Many reasons can be cited for this 25% drop, from the increasingly pervasive influence of television with its ready-made Saturday afternoon diet of couch potato sport to the rise of the consumer society and a weekend 'shop-till-you-drop' culture by way of uncompetitive Leagues where the winners were known months in advance, others were effectively relegated before a leaf fell from the trees and the rest appeared content with humdrum, mid-table monotony.

All of which contain grains of truth but also the seeds of a contrary argument.

There's no doubt living standards were rising and that a more affluent working class – the staple of any club's support – was emerging. But that increasing wealth led to the car-owning society and with greater investment in transportation getting to a football match was a lot easier than in the past.

Roads improved as motorways were built and the opening of the Forth Road Bridge slashed journey times in the east of Scotland. In the west the rail lines into Glasgow were electrified. Around 80% of the population of Scotland could reach the great trinity of Glaswegian football citadels inside 90 minutes. The downside to this was that many Old Firm fans whose allegiance had previously been in name only could now attend Ibrox or

Over 100,000 for a friendly? The Scottish footballing public's appetite continued to confound the critics.

Parkhead in person whereas before they had contented themselves with watching their local team.

Some clubs took advantage of technology to install undersoil heating, reducing postponements and abandoned games. But where these did occur the ubiquity of floodlighting meant re-arranged games no longer had to take place in front of three men and a dog on a winter's afternoon.

And while no one required a particular talent for prophecy in order to divine how the season would unfold these were hardly the worst of times on the field.

It's frightening to think how badly attendances might have dropped had there been no great European successes for our clubs, no wonderful Wembleys and World Cup extravaganzas for the national side and no Law, Dalglish, Baxter, Johnstone, White, Bremner et al on the pitch.

But the most influential figure of this period wasn't one of those wonderful players, he was a boss. Jock Stein gave an early glimpse of his managerial talents when he guided Dunfermline Athletic to an historic Scottish Cup victory against his once and future club Celtic in 1961. Stein's first trophy also gave a flavour of the times as the awkward tea-time kick-off meant almost 26,000 fewer people watched his side's 2-0 replay victory as attended the 0-0 draw the previous Saturday. Lack of floodlighting was proving a serious hindrance at Hampden Park and this became stunningly apparent later in 1961 when Scotland faced a crucial World Cup qualifier.

They beat the Czechs to force a play-off in Brussels to determine which team would go to the 1962 World Cup in Chile but they did so in front a woefully-low crowd of 51,591. A month later the Hampden lights were switched on and the difference this made was at once apparent as 104,393 turned up to watch Eintracht Frankfurt beat Rangers 3-2 to mark the occasion.

Over 100,000 for a friendly? The Scottish footballing public's appetite continued to confound the critics. The floodlights gave a new lease of life to a ground which was approaching pensionable age and fully one-third of all the six-figure gates ever recorded in Scotland occurred in the 1960s and early '70s.

The national team lost their play-off in Belgium but an exciting array of stars continued to ensure regular 100,000-plus crowds watched them in action. Some of their best performances were away from home at Wembley or in Spain where Scotland humbled the home side 6-2 but there were plenty of Hampden heroics to keep the home punters coming back in their thousands. 132,441 saw the first home win over England in an official international for 25 years in 1962. Slightly more were there to see Alan Gilzean's goal secure another welcome win against the English two years later and over 100,000 turned up on a November night to watch John Greig's stunning late goal give Scotland a World Cup win over Italy.

These were stirring times for the national side and even their failures were successes of a sort. Three times in succession they fell short in their World Cup bids. But the sides which vanquished them were of the highest pedigree. The Czechs reached the World Cup Final in 1962 and Scotland's other conquerors – Italy and West Germany – were the cream of European football.

A new world record for a floodlit international was created in 1965 when 108,453 saw Scotland exhibit the other side of their footballing nature, losing two late goals after leading for most of the match as Poland snatched a dramatic victory.

Domestically, while the others still challenged in the early 1960s the Old Firm's grip on attendances was increasing. One in every six supporters could be found at an Old Firm ground in 1939 but by now that had risen to one in four. In 1960-61 Hearts were second best in crowds to Rangers. That was the last time any club split the Big Two.

Although gates were falling almost everywhere it was most apparent in the two cities best placed to challenge the Old Firm – Edinburgh and Aberdeen. The Dons especially had seen support slump. In 1959 they had played before 100,000 at Hampden. Less than three years later their crowds were in freefall.

In 1961-62 Aberdeen recorded six League gates of under 5,000 with the worst being just 2,642 against Falkirk. At Easter Road there were four sub-5,000 crowds with 1,508 for St Mirren the worst. Hearts, while still going well, lost over 6,000 per game and dropped to a new post-war low.

Some caution must be expressed here about these figures. 1961-62 is the earliest season for which figures are available for ALL clubs so comparisons aren't that easy to make. However, looking at the pattern for subsequent seasons together with the pre-1961 figures which ARE available suggests the picture portrayed is a reasonably accurate one.

Care also needs to be exercised when looking at specific figures as cited above. Until the early 1970s some clubs did not include season tickets and comps in their returns to the Scottish League and it's not always possible to determine those that did.

It wasn't universal doom and gloom. Dundee won the title in 1962 and their gates averaged almost 16,000

Season tickets were a rarity in the 1960s. Rangers led the way with around 3,000 annually. Celtic and the Edinburgh clubs usually had just over 1,000 and Aberdeen slightly less. Other First Division teams ranged between 400-800. Positing a best-case scenario this still leaves Aberdeen with 3,500 for the Falkirk match, Hibs with less than 3,000 for St Mirren and Hearts with a drop of almost 5,000 a game. Hardly the good old days.

It wasn't universal doom and gloom. Dundee won the title in 1962 and their gates never dropped below 10,000 as they averaged almost 16,000. But while fourteen clubs managed a five-figure average the previous year this slumped to six this season – the Old Firm, Dundee, Hearts, Kilmarnock and St Mirren – and even this latter pair had dropped by almost 2,000 and 3,000 respectively.

In the Second Division five teams posted a sub-1,000 average but bright spots could still be discerned amid the murk. After a decade in the doldrums Morton were beginning to stir and they attracted 10,475 for their match with Clyde – just fourteen fewer than watched the supposed rivals for the tag of– 'Scotland's third-biggest club' – Aberdeen and Hearts – at Pittodrie!

The 1962-63 season was devastated by one of the worst winters of the twentieth century and for six weeks at the start of the year there was precious little football. The impact on attendances was enormous as clubs were forced into playing three times a week to complete their fixtures. Even with an extension to the season, Rangers had to play nine games in three weeks in May and two of these were against Celtic.

**QUARTER MILLION
WATCH CUP FINAL**

The Old Firm clashed in the Scottish Cup
Final for the first time since 1928 and an
incredible 249,790 supporters watched
the two games in which Rangers
emerged triumphant 3-0 after a 1-1
draw.

The result of the 1963 Scottish Cup Final served to confirm
Rangers dominance over their rivals and their crowds were
usually far superior too. Ominously, while Hearts reclaimed third
spot in the crowds table they were now watched by only half as
many as a still-struggling Celtic.

Flagging gates received a boost from a totally unexpected
quarter – Greenock. Led by the flamboyant Hal Stewart, Morton
steamrollered their Second Division opponents in 1963-64,
winning their first 23 games. But it was their performances
against top division sides and the incredible gates they drew
which attracted intense media interest in Cappielow.

They won all six of their sectional League Cup matches
before knocking out Motherwell in the last eight. Their exploits
attracted 18,842 for their home leg against the Steelmen with
21,650 at Fir Park.

Morton fans hadn't seen gates like these since the late 1940s
– and seldom even then. Against Hibs at Ibrox in the semi-final
a crowd of 46,894 watched the teams draw 1-1. It was a record
at this stage of the competition for a game not involving the Old
Firm and remains so today.

Morton won the replay 1-0 in front of 36,092 and helped
create a new record in the Final. Such was the interest in the
Greenock side that the League Cup Final topped the 100,000
mark for the first time. Sadly for Morton that was as good as it
got as Jim Forrest scored four for Rangers in a 5-0 victory
watched by 105,907.

Their consolation was to return to the First Division at the
end of the season after an absence of twelve years. Their
average of 8,339 was better than half the clubs in the top flight.

That Morton's crowds were exceptional can be seen from the experience of Second Division runners-up Clyde. Promoted on four occasions since the war with declining crowds each time, their average this term was a catastrophic 1,766

It was also apparent that the low crowds suffered as a result of the weather the previous season were not an aberration. Almost an additional 200,000 spectators had been lost on top of that bad year and First Division crowds dropped below three million for the first time in thirty years.

Drastic remedies were proposed. Rangers wanted restructuring which would have involved axeing five clubs from the League altogether and a protracted court battle ensued which saw the 'minnows' emerge victorious.

In 1964-65 the League put forward its own proposal based on three divisions of 14-12-12 with the admission of a new club to make up the numbers. Controversially their scheme was based not on playing performances but on attendances.

A closer look at the clubs the League reckoned should form the new elite shows little difference from football in the twenty-first century. Of the fourteen earmarked for the new First Division, ten were in the SPL forty years later. Three of the others – Partick Thistle, St Johnstone and St Mirren – have all been recently relegated from the top flight. Morton are the only one of the fourteen not to have figured in the top division in recent years and of the 'excluded' clubs only Falkirk have featured in the SPL fixture list, and not until season 2005-06.

It was ironic that this proto-SPL should be discussed in a season which saw the Old Firm – so ultra-dominant now – reach their lowest post-war ebb. Strange too to refer to a season as such when they each won a trophy and there was even an Old Firm Hampden Final.

But 1964-65 was undoubtedly their low spot. A quick glance at the record books might suggest otherwise as Rangers – 'treble' winners the year before – beat Celtic in the League Cup Final and the Celts won their first Scottish Cup for eleven years. But the League table tells a different story. Rangers were fifth and Celtic eighth. For the first – and only – time ever neither finished in the top three.

Crowds were hit not just at Ibrox and Parkhead but across the country as fewer 'follow followed' them away or bothered to 'hail hail' a cab at home. Kilmarnock, after knocking at the door for several seasons, were the champions and if anyone, fooled by the big international and Cup Final crowds, still refused to believe attendances were falling, the Rugby Park club's gate book told its own story.

Killie played before the lowest average crowd of any post-war title winners yet only the Old Firm, the Edinburgh pair and Dundee were better supported this season. At 10,476 it was over 1,000 fewer per match than when they were promoted from the 'B' Division in 1954. The lower division could only dream of such figures in 1965. Twelve clubs drew less than 1,000 per game and only two averaged above 2,000.

Killie played before the lowest average crowd of any post-war title winners

Jock Stein had led Celtic to the Scottish Cup within weeks of his appointment as Parkhead boss in 1965 and now took his charges to the first of nine successive titles in 1965-66. Rangers followed closely behind and although the Ibrox side lost to their old rivals in the League Cup Final they gained revenge in the Scottish Cup when Kai Johansen's replay goal settled a Final watched by another massive aggregate attendance – this time of 224,756.

The Old Firm had finished 1-2 in the three major trophies for the first time. Forty years later, despite their increased dominance, this remains the only season they have done so.

Celtic's title success paved the way for their ground-breaking European Cup triumph of 1967 when they became not just the first Scottish winners or even merely the first British winners but the first club to smash the southern European stranglehold of Spain, Italy and Portugal.

Yet gates were by no means spectacular for this all-conquering Celtic side. In the League, while they supplanted Rangers to become the best supported club for the first time in almost half a century, their average was just 31,082. Eleven English clubs – half the First Division – did better that year. And it was a sign of the times that more turned up for the European ties with Vojvodina and Dukla Prague than did for the visit of the Ibrox club.

But, comparatively speaking, Celtic were on the rise. They were up by almost 7,000 per match on Stein's first season which was in turn almost 6,000 more than the year before. Nor did Rangers fall away, as Celtic had done in the inter-war years. This was chiefly because the Gers weren't that far behind Stein's Celtic. At any other time their points total would have walked away with the title and in individual matches they often came off best against Celts. They finished second six times in the nine-in-a-row era, usually just a few points behind. And if this wasn't enough to satisfy the Ibrox legions it was sufficient to stop them turning their backs on the team in large numbers. In four of their nine years in purgatory, Rangers were Scotland's best supported team.

It was the failure of Hearts, Hibs and Aberdeen – the clubs from which a challenge was most expected – that contributed most to falling gates

In 1967 they matched Celtic by reaching a European Final but while the Bhoys beat Inter Milan to win the European Cup, Rangers lost out in the Cup-Winners Cup to Bayern Munich in extra time.

Scotland's other clubs did well too. Kilmarnock reached the last four of the Fairs Cup, Dundee United recorded a double victory over Barcelona on their European debut and Dunfermline were only ousted from the Fairs Cup by eventual winners Dynamo Zagreb on the new away goals rule.

But while these clubs had a successful period with Kilmarnock and Dunfermline in particular keeping the Old Firm on their toes, it was the failure of the clubs from which a challenge was most expected that contributed most to falling gates. Hearts, Hibs and Aberdeen were all going through a rough patch and while still the best supported outside of Glasgow these three teams combined average was only just the equivalent of one typical game at an Old Firm ground – and some years not even that.

Scotland's victory at Wembley in 1967 capped a memorable season – one in which our game's stock in Europe reached a peak. But Scottish football's annus mirabilis contained a touch of the horribilus as well.

This was the year when Third Lanark – founder members of both the SFA and the Scottish League – expired after 95 years. Theirs was a strange death. In 1959 they had reached the

League Cup Final and two years later were third in the League and scored 100 goals. Their attendances were a healthy five-figure average.

Yet by the summer of 1967 they had vanished from the scene – a testimony as to how individual control of a club can render that club subject to the whims of one person. It's often been asked what happened to the alleged 10,000 Thirds fans when their club folded. Theories abound about their dissipation among the ranks of the other Glasgow clubs or even the Juniors. The sad truth is there weren't 10,000 Thirds fans anymore.

Their gates had fallen to under 3,000 in their last season in the First Division and, shorn of the lifeline of visits from the Old Firm, Thistle and Clyde, shrank even further until they averaged just 703 in their final season. Their biggest League crowd that season was 1,276 for the visit of Queen's Park.

Third Lanark's was a strange death

It's a sentimental myth but myth nonetheless that a successful Thirds side could have pulled in big crowds. In the same season as they went under, Clyde couldn't attract as many as 5,000 to Shawfield – the Old Firm apart – and Clyde were third in the First Division and reached the semi-finals of the Scottish Cup.

Thirds couldn't have done any better than that. What they could have done though and what they should have done was survive. For the sake of the price of a decent player – their debt was around £40,000 – one of Scottish football's oldest institutions disappeared.

It needn't have happened but the fan power which has saved the day for several clubs in the past few years was a non-existent concept back then. For all that the decade was supposedly one of liberation and empowerment there was still too ready a tendency to bend the knee when the voice of authority spoke.

Stein's Celtic continued to carry virtually all before them domestically. One of their rare losses was at home to Dunfermline in the Scottish Cup in 1968. The Pars marched on to the Final where their opponents were Hearts who had despatched the other half of the Old Firm from the competition.

In the run-up to the Final as much speculation centred on the game's attendance as on its outcome. This was the first Final without an Old Firm presence since 1959 and the 1968 game was watched by only just over half as many as had attended then. At 56,366 it was the lowest since the debacle of 1921 yet it hadn't dropped to the levels feared by many within the game.

The writing had been on the wall since the semi-finals. At Hampden, Hearts, the 'third force' in the Scottish game, had clashed with Morton, who just a few years previously, were packing grounds wherever they played. Only 22,556 saw them in action and their replay was watched by just 11,565.

One area where Scottish football seemed impervious to falling crowds was the international scene

The one area where Scottish football seemed impervious to falling crowds was the international scene. True, the occasional end-of-season friendly failed to entice many along but overall the situation was healthy. Even in 1968 130,711 turned up to see the England game played months earlier than usual, in February, when Scotland drew 1-1 and thus missed out on qualifying for the last eight of the European Championship.

The 1970 World Cup qualifiers opened with 80,858 to see Austria beaten 2-1 thanks to goals from Denis Law and Billy Bremner. Then 97,628 saw the Scots rescue a point with a late Bobby Murdoch equaliser in 1-1 draw with West Germany.

But the next game proved to be a true shocker.

In one of the earliest examples of TV calling the shots the International Championship calendar was altered to be played within a week at the end of the season with all matches televised live. For Scotland fans this meant a midweek match with Northern Ireland sandwiched in between visits to Wales and Wembley with a World Cup match at home against Cyprus a week after that. If something had to give financially (and for many it did) then the midweek match was always going to suffer.

Add to that live TV and a Glaswegian 'double whammy' of vile weather and transport strikes and the recipe for a disastrous turnout is evident.

Only 7,455 hardy souls braved the elements on a truly appalling night to see a 1-1 draw. It wasn't that the match was particularly unattractive – the few there could see the talents of

Billy Bremner, Bobby Murdoch, Colin Stein and Denis Law on display for the home side while their opponents included Pat Jennings, Derek Dougan and the incomparable George Best. This match just happened to be played at the wrong time. To this day it remains the lowest attendance for a Scotland match at Hampden Park.

Less than twelve months later the ground was visited by the second-biggest crowd of the post-war era when 137,284 assembled to wish Bobby Moore and the England team a happy and successful trip to Mexico in defence of the World Cup. Or maybe the 284 did. The other 137,000 were fervently praying for Scotland to give England a right royal gubbing and vindication of the Scottish claim to be 'moral' world champions established at Wembley in 1967.

CELTIC MOVE TO HAMPDEN

Parkhead just wasn't big enough to cope with the crowd expected for Celtic's 1970 European Cup semi-final with Leeds United. As they had done before and would do so again, Celtic moved the match to Hampden where 136,505 squeezed in to watch as the Celts, 1-0 up from the first leg, came back from losing the first goal to win 2-1 on the night and reach their second European Cup Final. It was, and still is, the biggest attendance for any European club competition.

Both sides could take some honour from the first 0-0 draw between them since the opening game in the series 98 years earlier.

Here though, in the space of just ten days in April 1970, both Celtic and Scotland gave the sharpest of rejoinders to those who bemoaned the state of attendances. In the near quarter of a century since football's post-war restart only the Rangers-Hibs game in 1948 had drawn a larger crowd.

Except that another part of Glasgow told a different story that same month when Partick Thistle said goodbye to 68 continuous years in the top flight, watched by just 1,146 against Morton. It was also, though unknown to any at the time, the beginning of the end of the days of 100,000 crowds. A tragic event across the city less than a year later saw to that.

The Old Firm went into their 1971 New Year game at Ibrox much as any other of the time. The crowd of 80,453 was big but not unusually so by the standards of the fixture. In fact the last three League games between the pair at Ibrox had drawn bigger gates and 94,168 had attended a 1967 League Cup match there.

The tensions between the rival sets of supporters were no higher than usual either. If anything less so as Rangers were out of the title race and the match had been moved to January 2nd in a bid to reduce the drink-fuelled violence associated with Ne'erday itself. Only two arrests were made at the match, both for drunkenness.

That's not to say the game was watched pacifically by a soporific crowd. It wasn't. The tackles were as fierce as ever on the field and the passions ran as high as before on the terraces. But what happened at the end of the match had nothing to do with sectarianism, alcohol or any of the associated paraphernalia so familiar to these clubs.

The 1971 Ibrox tragedy could have happened at any packed football ground at the time

The game was heading for a 0-0 draw when Jimmy Johnstone scored for Celtic. Thousands of Rangers supporters headed for the exits but with fifteen seconds to go Colin Stein grabbed a dramatic equaliser.

Many making their way out turned round when they heard the roar accompanying Stein's goal and headed back up the fateful Stairway 13. As they did they met with thousands more streaming out at the final whistle. The two sets collided, some fans fell and in the ensuing chaos that followed sixty-six spectators lost their lives and over a hundred more were injured.

That's the version of events which has long been accepted by supporters although an official inquiry found that the carnage occurred after the match was over when spectators stumbled on the way out. There had been deaths at Scottish football matches before as a result of barriers giving way under pressure from the crowd but these had been small-scale in number, if no less traumatic for the loved ones of those lost. But not since the same venue in 1902 had there been any large-scale loss of life.

It was sheer, horrible chance that it happened again at Ibrox. The awful truth is that a tragedy of this kind could have happened at any packed football ground at the time. Antiquated stadia with no regular checks undertaken on stairs or barriers, no crowd segregation, little if any stewarding, a police force unschooled in crowd control and often showing greater interest in making easy arrests, drunken and often violent fans. All the ingredients for a nightmare were in place long before January 1971.

Nor did the size of the venue matter. Any supporter who undertook the experience can recall how equally frightening it could be to caught up among 25,000 at Somerset Park or Muirton as 100,000 at Ibrox or Hampden.

That there hadn't been similar disasters elsewhere over the years was due more to luck than anything else.

January 2nd 1971 was the day Scottish football stopped getting lucky.

The Ibrox disaster was the focal point for change in the ensuing years as clubs contemplated introducing more seats and began to take measures to keep rival fans apart – even though the introduction of either would have made no difference to the tragedy of Ibrox. But it was going to take another Old Firm game – one in which the fans WERE the cause of the problem, allied to further loss of life in Bradford and at Hillsborough in Sheffield in the 1980s before football finally made a serious attempt to put its house in order.

Antiquated stadia with no regular checks undertaken on stairs or barriers, no crowd segregation, little if any stewarding, a police force unschooled in crowd control and often showing greater interest in making easy arrests, drunken and often violent fans. All the ingredients for a nightmare were in place long before January 1971.

The most obvious immediate effect of Ibrox was to establish a form of licensing for football grounds which involved local authorities, the police and the fire brigade having a greater say in setting crowd limits. The days of almost unrestrained capacities based on estimates of how many bodies could be accommodated if packed together shoulder to shoulder and tighter than the proverbial sardines were over.

In the short term the game made efforts to help the families of the deceased. A benefit match was played at Hampden at the end of January between a Scotland XI and Old Firm Select augmented by stars from south of the border. 81,405 saw the Scots win 2-1.

That was after Rangers returned to Ibrox. Just two weeks after the tragedy they resumed their League campaign with a 1-1 draw against Dundee United watched by 27,776. Incredibly, the disaster had no effect on attendances. Their average attendance for their remaining matches was over 22,000, compared to just over 21,500 for the same period in the previous season.

The club and the media prepared for a supporters backlash which never came. Whether it was intended as a mark of respect for the dead, a belief that the same thing couldn't happen again, or just that plain bloody-minded obstinacy which many show in the face of tragedy no one can say for certain. Though there were some so traumatised by the events of that day that it was a long time, if ever, before they set foot in Ibrox again.

Ibrox crowds were in the news again the following season though not on this occasion for their tremendous loyalty. Before Rangers met Moscow Dynamo in the European Cup-Winners Cup Final they concluded their domestic programme with two abysmally low attendances. Officially they were watched by 6,021 against Dunfermline and by 5,869 versus Ayr United – bad enough at any time but actually much worse than they appear. For Rangers added ALL their season ticket holders to the attendance – whether present or not. As Rangers had far and away the largest number of season book holders this only served to increase their already dominant position in the attendance table.

This sleight-of-hand was usually practised only by the lower orders where the likes of Clydebank would routinely add 600 or 800 to their attendances.

For Dunfermline, 1,632 adults paid for admission along with 999 juveniles. For Ayr it was even lower at 1,485 adults and 994 juveniles. It was only the inclusion of 3,390 season book holders and complimentaries which brought the figures to even semi-respectability. Of course some season ticket holders were present at these games but it's on a par with believing Lord Lucan will ride Shergar in the Derby – but only because Elvis can't make the weight – to think that twice as many season ticket holders as cash-at-the-turnstile fans turned up at these games.

Some of the missing 20,000 regulars turned up in Barcelona to join the crowd of 24,701 inside the Camp Nou as Rangers beat the Russians 3-2 to give manager **Willie Waddell** a European trophy to cap his tenure at Ibrox. Sadly the achievement was overshadowed by running battles between Rangers fans and the Spanish police and ended with the trophy being presented to skipper John Greig indoors and Rangers banned from Europe, initially for two years, reduced after a personal appeal by Waddell to one.

Europe was proving a popular cause with Scottish crowds

even if the heady days of 1967 couldn't be repeated. The Old Firm led the way with full houses for visits from continental giants on too many occasions to list here but Scotland's other clubs did well both on the field and at the gate. Dundee, Dunfermline, Hibs and Kilmarnock all reached the semi-finals of a European tournament watched by big crowds along the way.

Dundee's best was 38,232 against Anderlecht as they won through to the last four of the European Cup. And even though they were 5-1 down from the first leg, they drew 35,169 to Dens Park to see a 1-0 second leg home win against AC Milan in the semi-final. 24,049 saw Dunfermline fail narrowly against Ujpest Dosza in the last eight of the Cup-inners Cup and there were 22,073 at the same stage of the same competition seven years later as they drew with West Bromwich Albion prior to pulling off a sensational victory at The Hawthorns.

Hibs matched their European Cup achievement by reaching the semi-finals of the Fairs Cup in 1961 cheered along the way by 45,000 as they beat Barcelona . And later during this period there were several crowds of over 30,000 at Easter Road. As late as 1973-74 there were 36,051 on hand to see them beaten only on penalty kicks by English champions-elect Leeds United after two 0-0 draws.

A gate of 24,831 saw another 0-0 Leeds draw, this time at Rugby Park in the Fairs Cup semi-finals and 24,325 had to rub their eyes in disbelief as they watched Kilmarnock take on – and hold – Real Madrid in the European Cup.

If others didn't do quite as well then they still had magic memories and bumper gates to recall. Dundee United's first European tie was a Tannadice record gate as they ousted holders Barcelona from the Fairs Cup. 30,000 saw Aberdeen draw with the then-mighty Tottenham Hotspur at Pittodrie and 29,409 saw the Dons do the same against Juventus. Hearts drew 29,500 to see them in European Cup action against Benfica, losing 2-1.

European football returned to Firhill too. Partick Thistle's stunning display in one of Scottish football's greatest all-time upsets when 62,736 saw them beat Celtic 4-1 in the 1971-72 League Cup Final was rewarded with a UEFA Cup place. But a hopeful 16,513 saw Thistle fail to overturn a 1-0 away leg defeat as Hungarians Honved won 3-0 at Firhill.

If 1972 was Rangers year in Europe then domestically it marked the high point in attendances by their temporary replacement as chief challengers to Stein's Celtic – Aberdeen. The Dons had emerged from a decade in the doldrums by winning the Scottish Cup in 1970 and pushing Celtic to the wire in the 1971 league race. Second again in 1972, though further behind, their average of 17,993 was the best outside the Old Firm since Hearts' glory days and the highest from the Dons since 1955-56 – when they had the bonus of being defending champions.

It is also an average which no 'third' club has beaten since (though the Dons themselves came close under Alex Ferguson) and given current capacities looks set to remain unchallenged for some years yet.

Aberdeen's lowest that season was 8,936 against Ayr United. That was higher than their average not that many seasons beforehand. The highs came against the Old Firm – 34,546 v Rangers and 33,695 v Celtic – but they had four other gates in excess of 20,000 with 25,385 v Hibernian leading the way.

It was a welcome, if temporary, reversal of the downward trend. But while it was joy for Rangers, Thistle and Aberdeen (and of course for Celtic who won a seventh successive title, the Scottish Cup and reached the last for of the European Cup) it was less so for Scotland in 1972.

They lost 1-0 to England at Hampden in front of 119,415. Defeat was bad enough. Losing to a goal from Alan Ball even worse. But it was compounded by the knowledge that this would be the last time a crowd of 100,000 saw a Scotland game. There had been 37 such internationals since 1906 and 29 times England had been the visitors when the magic figure was reached.

New limits were due to come into force in 1973-74 and none of Scotland's scheduled fixtures for 1972-73 were likely to draw big gates. Even though one of them was against the English! This was to mark the SFA's Centenary and it was staged on a freezing February night, guaranteed to deter all but the most hardened Scotland fan.

A good job too because Hampden was no place for the

easily upset that night as England staged their own version of the St Valentine's Day massacre, winning 5-0 in front of 48,470 thoroughly miserable fans.

Worries about what would happen to the 'Hampden Roar' in reduced circumstances proved to be groundless. An encouraging 78,089 attended the SFA's other Centenary match on the unseasonal date of June 30th to see world champions Brazil beat Scotland 1-0 in the 100th international to be staged at Hampden.

The next big test was against the Czechs. As in 1961 they stood between Scotland and a place in the World Cup Finals. Scotland went into a match they needed to win under a manager – Willie Ormond – yet to win a game and having lost their last three Hampden games.

There were 89,028 inside Hampden but the noise they generated was greater than that of many a 130,000 crowd. Even when the Czechs took the lead they still roared the team forward. And they received their just reward when goals from Jim Holton and Joe Jordan made it a night never to be forgotten by those who were there as Scotland secured their place in the World Cup Finals after an absence of sixteen years.

It was the start of an exciting era for the national side and it would be twenty more years before a World Cup took place without a Scotland presence.

Crowds even higher than the Czech game were recorded twice in 1974 as England were beaten 2-0 with 94,487 looking on and almost as many – 94,331 – were in place when Spain won a European Championship qualifier 2-1. That large crowd was helped by post-World Cup euphoria as Scotland returned from West Germany as the only unbeaten team in the tournament – 'moral' world champions once again! But the poor qualifying campaign led to a rapid loss of support and only 11,676 saw the 1-1 draw with Romania in December 1975 which marked its end.

By then Scotland had a new domestic league set-up.

Celtic had won their eighth successive title in 1973 but even though they had been pushed all the way by Rangers, taking the title by a single point, the excitement of the race failed to enthuse the fans. Rangers gates rose only marginally compared to 1972 when they had been sixteen points behind in third and Celtic's fell by over 4,500 a match. Aberdeen's failure to sustain their challenge of the previous two years led to a sharp drop at Pittodrie too. Hearts were still a modest outfit and of the leading clubs only Hibs – League Cup winners this term – showed an increase, taking their average to 16,100 – their best since 1960.

The Scottish Cup Final helped mask the situation when the Old Firm clashed for the fifth time in a decade. There were 122,714 present at Hampden as Rangers won their first Scottish Cup for seven years, 3-2. The turnout was indicative of the pulling power the Old Firm still had when the two clubs were on a par with each other but it was the 96th and last occasion a Scottish ground held a crowd of over 100,000. It was also the last time anywhere in the UK that an attendance in excess of that number was recorded.

Of those 96 occasions 92 had been at Hampden and four at Ibrox. Rangers had featured in more than any other team, 39 times to Scotland's 37 and Celtic shared third place with England on 29. Only the Scotland-England fixture drew more 100,000 gates than the Old Firm who had shared the honours 13 times.

The best proof of the Big Two's ever-growing hold on the game is demonstrated by the fact that of the eleven times they shared the Hampden pitch in front of such a gate (two of their 100,000 crowds were at Ibrox), nine had been in the past ten years – the very time when the drop in crowds was exercising most concern.

When other clubs took the Hampden stage though, the gaps in the terracing gaped even wider than before. Industrial disputes among power workers and miners led to energy rationing with evening kick-offs changed to afternoons. A new generation discovered the lost art of burying grandmothers over and over again in order to attend games.

But Hampden was exempt from the restrictions on account of it possessing its own generator so evening games continued to be played there. Exempt status didn't extend as far as weather conditions and the Dundee v Kilmarnock League Cup semi-final was postponed twice before taking place on a freezing cold

Monday evening in December. Many supporters, having
travelled twice previously only to have to turn back, gave up on
the fixture and only 4,682 bodies were dotted around the vast
bowl as Dundee won 1-0. This was a 20th century record low
for a major cup semi-final.

Two days later the Old Firm also met at Hampden in the last
four and nearly 70,000 of the Scottish Cup Final crowd decided
to sit this one out. A crowd of 54,966 was all they could muster
to see a Harry Hood hat-trick give Celtic a 3-1 victory.

Ten days on Dundee beat Celtic, watched by just 28,058 –
the lowest League Cup Final crowd to that point. Many sought to
blame the disputes and the then-current three-day working week
for the low gate. Others pointed to the absurdity of scheduling a
major Cup Final ten days before Christmas.

It took some time for the Scottish League to learn the lesson
as several other December finals were played before common
sense finally took hold and the game was moved back in the
calendar.

Celtic won a ninth successive title but crowds kept falling.
The Division One average of just over 8,000 was the worst for
forty years. The Old Firm had dropped again and Aberdeen had
slumped to just 8,657. The Dons had lost more than half their
support inside just two years. Oddly enough Celtic's figure of
24,762 was actually a few hundred higher than when they had
won the first of their nine titles in 1966.

Over the nine seasons they averaged 29,638, closely
followed by Rangers on 28,924. The Ibrox side generally drew
bigger crowds for knockout competitions and when the Scottish
Cup, League Cup and European ties are taken into consideration
the gap between the two narrows, with an overall average of
34,427 for Celtic and 34,078 for Rangers.

Combined, they played to an audience in excess of sixteen
million over these nine seasons – and that was just for home
games!

1974-75 was an exciting season with the top league cutting
off its membership after the top ten and becoming renamed the
Premier Division. In a radical effort to boost crowds, the bottom
eight joined the top six in Division Two to form the new First

Division and the remainder comprised the new Second.

But the effect on gates was minimal. Division Two, weighed down by the addition of new members Meadowbank Thistle, actually lost support. First Division gates rose by 220,000 but there are lies damned lies and statistics. The two promoted sides drew 60,000 more in total than the clubs they replaced and gates at Ibrox were up by 170,000 as Rangers ended Celtic's hopes of a tenth successive title by sweeping to their first championship since 1964.

No complex calculations are required to show that these figures account for more than the stated increase. For the rest it was 'as you were' or even a slight drop. Even the threat of effective relegation for eight clubs couldn't encourage greater support.

When the batting order for the three new divisions was

finally drawn up it bore a marked similarity to that proposed a decade earlier based on attendances.

Only two of the top ten best supported sides didn't make the cut and this pair – Kilmarnock (seventh best supported) and Partick Thistle (ninth) – wouldn't stay out for long. The two who made it in were Ayr United (eleventh best supported) and St Johnstone (fifteenth in the attendance league).

The middle division was even clearer cut. Based on attendances this would run down to 24th place. Only Raith Rovers (24th in attendances) missed out and the only inclusion below 24th was Montrose (25th).

Considering that Killie, Thistle and Raith all moved up within 12 months and St Johnstone went in the opposite direction, maybe it would have been easier to draw up the leagues according to crowds after all!

Fewer fans – but equal fervour – at Hampden when Queen's Park play at home

All-time low? The 1980 Scottish Cup Final witnessed
some of the ugliesst scenes in the game's history

Simply the Worst: 1975-1994

SCOTTISH football entered uncharted waters in 1975-76 and conditions over the next two decades proved to be a lot more turbulent than the game's authorities had hoped. The return of mass unemployment saw the spectre of the great depression revisit the game. Allied to continued and increasing violence among spectators, crowds plummeted to new lows and clubs sought salvation in part-time status.

The game did recover. But not until after the violence which haunted it was finally tackled and the horrors of the Ibrox disaster were tragically repeated in England. All that lay a long way off as the new three-division set-up came into being on August 30th 1975. Officials studied the attendance returns from the first set of games and were convinced they had mapped out a path to football's sunny uplands.

Using the first day of 1974-75 as the benchmark it looked indeed as if the optimism was justified. On that occasion 95,750 watched the nineteen fixtures for an average of 5,039. The First Division drew 81,742, averaging 9,082. Top crowd was 26,482 for Celtic v Kilmarnock and the lowest the 3,084 who saw Airdrie v Dundee. In the Second Division 14,008 saw the programme – an average of 1,401. Best in that sphere was 2,538 for St Mirren v Stirling Albion with a low of 376 for Berwick v Brechin.

The new format opened in spectacular style as 70,964 saw the Old Firm clash at Ibrox – a figure unsurpassed in thirty years since. That tally contained 3,062 season ticket holders though it's safe to say that on this occasion almost all of these were present.

All told 109,132 attended the five Premier matches for an average of 21,826.

But behind the headlines lay another tale. The Premier Division was deliberately designed to get off to the best possible start with derby – or as close to derby as possible – matches lined up on opening day. In addition to the Old Firm there were 23,646 at Easter Road to see Hibs take on Hearts. The three other games that day fared less well at the gate. Only 5,515 saw Motherwell and Ayr United at Fir Park and the total of 6,067 at Dens for Dundee and Aberdeen would have been regarded as poor at any time.

Worst of all though was at Muirton where a meagre 3,340 saw St Johnstone and Dundee United. If these were the crowds on the opening day, how bad would they get as the season progressed and supporters adapted to one of the most controversial aspects of the change – the fact that teams now met each other FOUR TIMES during the season? Everyone was aware of what familiarity is supposed to breed.

The picture elsewhere was just as gloomy. In the new First Division just 16,213 attended the seven matches – an average of 2,316. Best gate was at Rugby Park where Kilmarnock entertained Hamilton in front of 3,917 and the worst at Shawfield where just 1,256 saw Clyde and Dumbarton.

In the Second Division only 5,312 were counted at seven games for an average of 759. Raith had 1,575 for Stranraer's visit while the 332 for Berwick v East Stirlingshire was the worst.

Bad as these figures are they may even be worse as Raith Rovers counted 440 seasons and comps for every game and Clydebank (official opening day crowd 1,390) added 600 likewise. Berwick Rangers also added a fixed number to all games but in their case it was a more realistic thirty per game while other Second Division clubs added the actual number attending. But the dire state of the game at this level can be seen by the number of fully paying adults at some games.

Albion Rovers, for instance, saw just 46 adults pay for admission v Brechin City. Just 40 of the 310 for East Stirling v Stranraer were paying adults as this club added 250 to each match. Meadowbank were finding attracting support in

Edinburgh as difficult as the sceptics had predicted. Only 36 adults and 44 juveniles paid for admission when they met Stranraer. Nor were they a big attraction on their travels as witnessed when they visited Ochilview and only 41 adults contributed to Stenhousemuir's receipts.

It was the Warriors who hit the low point of the League season when a mere 30 adults paid to get in to their game with Brechin City though even this tally was 'beaten' by East Stirlingshire when just 28 adults and 13 juveniles paid at their Spring Cup match against Montrose.

By the season's end only the most blasé of apologists for the change could herald a success. Only three of the Second Division clubs averaged over 1,000 and two of these – Clydebank and Stirling Albion – were heavily dependent on the assumption that hundreds of season ticket holders attended every game to reach that mark.

By the 1975-76 season's end only the most blasé of apologists for the change could herald a success

In the First, every single one of the eight ex-Division One teams lost support though that was to be expected now that they had lost their lucrative home games against the Old Firm. What was more surprising was that three of the former six Division Two sides also showed a drop in gates. It had been assumed that meeting Thistle, Killie and Dunfermline instead of Brechin, Forfar and Meadowbank would mean an automatic rise in crowd levels for these clubs. It was a shock to find this not so.

Superficially, the Premier, with an average of 13,460, looked healthy. But it wasn't necessary to dig too deep to uncover the truth. Champions Rangers dropped by over 2,200 per game and it was probably worse as they added an additional 350 to the list of season ticket 'ever-presents'. Considering they not only retained the title but also won the 'treble' and now had two massive gates against Celtic to be taken into account this was a big blow to not only the Ibrox club but the new set-up as a whole.

They recorded four gates of under 20,000 compared to none the previous season. They couldn't even blame the 'familiarity factor' for these figures as three of the sub-20,000 crowds came in the FIRST meeting of the season.

While most recorded higher averages this was simply

because they now had two games against the Old Firm plus, usually, another local derby as replacements for visits from Arbroath, Clyde, Dumbarton etc.

The only clubs that could be satisfied with the new order were Celtic – up over 5,000 – and Motherwell who leapt from 5,833 to 9,575 – the biggest proportionate rise of all. This wasn't because the Fir Parkers were particularly delighted to see everybody twice but entirely due to the fact that they had an exciting team to watch which topped the League for a while and eventually finished fourth – 'Well's best for many seasons.

Overall, gates were down though the Premier apologists said this was on account of the fewer games played at the lower levels. They got the answer to that the next season. There were 78 more League games played in 1976-77 than in the last year of the old structure yet over 140,000 fewer fans watched League football.

The big clubs couldn't even blame the 'minnows' for the drop. The Premier Division, with exactly the same number of games as the previous season, lost almost 300,000 supporters. The big boys had wanted to have things all their own way. In their rush to exclude their 'lesser' brethren, they had forgotten a few simple facts.

Chief among these was that ninth place in the old set-up signified mid-table but in the Premier it spelled doom. There was no comfort zone in a league which relegated 20% of its membership. Perhaps club officials were just ludicrously over-optimistic when they so enthusiastically embraced the new order. Maybe they simply thought it couldn't happen to THEIR club. Whatever, the one thing they didn't do was look at the record books.

If they had they would have discovered that the Old Firm, Aberdeen and Hearts had never been relegated. That Dundee, Hibs and Motherwell had suffered that fate just once, spending no more than two seasons 'downstairs'. With Dundee United having progressed to at least the level of this latter three that meant there were eight clubs that considered themselves virtually immune from relegation.

Of course finishing any lower than eighth now turned that

dread prospect into reality. That either every other club would fail to establish themselves in the top flight or that virtual immunity would be lost seemed not to have occurred to the clubs in question, all of whom (with the exception of Dundee United) heartily welcomed the changes.

What actually happened was even worse – an amalgam of promoted clubs failing to make the grade alongside the relegation of famous names. In its first few seasons the Premier Division lost Hearts (three times), Dundee (twice), Hibs and Motherwell. Over the course of time all of these save Hearts have been relegated again and Dundee United have suffered the same fate also. Aberdeen have been involved in play-offs and on other occasions been saved from the drop by reconstruction or the failure of clubs in the First Division to meet ground requirements – as have others.

Only two clubs were permanently safe from relegation. It was an act of sheer grandiosity for any other club to think they were in the same bracket as the Old Firm.

While relegation may be temporary its effects can be long-lasting and Dundee United can trace their progress to becoming top dog on Tayside to the day in 1976 when goal difference kept them (and Aberdeen) up and sent Dundee down. As their neighbours oscillated between the divisions, Jim McLean's United seized their chance to establish themselves as the city's number one side. It's a rare season now in which Dundee draw more fans than United yet for over eighty years they were the undisputed masters of the Tay.

Not even the prospect of silverware seemed to motivate supporters anymore. Hearts met Dumbarton in a Scottish Cup semi-final at Hampden in front of just 16,067 fans. The replay was even worse at 11,273. Yet the chance for the treble enticed enough Rangers supporters out for the Final to bring the attendance to 83,982 – the last above the 80,000 mark – as they easily disposed of the Jambos to secure the prize.

Few if any in the crowd that day would have believed that Rangers wouldn't average 30,000 in a season again until the arrival a decade later of a permed and moustachioed saviour who had never kicked a ball (or a man) in Scottish football.

But if gates were bad for the Old Firm they were truly abysmal for the rest. When two of Scotland's biggest clubs – Hibs and Aberdeen – met to contest a place in the Scottish Cup Final in 1979 a pitiful 9,384 watched them. In the same season just TEN adults paid to watch an East Stirlingshire v Meadowbank Thistle league game. Such was the state of Scottish football at the end of the 1970s.

It wasn't helped that particular season by another dreadful winter which forced postponements on a massive scale but there was a feeling that, barring the odd League Cup upset, no one stood a chance against the Old Firm. The League hadn't gone elsewhere since Kilmarnock's 1965 triumph and the Scottish Cup had been an Old Firm possession since Aberdeen's 1970 victory. The sorry tale of the 1979 Scottish Cup Final shows the level of disillusion within the support. 53,615 watched Rangers and Hibs draw 0-0. That wasn't too bad as an Old Firm Final two years previously had drawn just a few hundred more at 54,037. But the match was so awful that the replay gate fell to 32,853. That was also a dreadful 0-0 draw. After 210 minutes neither side had scored a goal so when the second replay came round, just 27,556 were in attendance.

Hibs and Aberdeen – met to contest a place in the Scottish Cup Final in 1979 watched by a pitiful 9,384

Fortunately they saw a better game as Rangers won 3-2 but such figures would have been unthinkable even in the Celtic nine-in-a-row era when many blithely assumed crowds couldn't get any worse.

Later that year Dundee United and Aberdeen fought out another 0-0 draw watched by just 27,156 in another December League Cup Final. Fortunately common sense intervened to prevent the teams from returning to Hampden for the replay which was instead awarded to Dens Park. The 28,894 present wasn't a much bigger crowd but it as an atmosphere-creating capacity gate which enhanced proceedings as United won their first major trophy, 3-0.

The fear of relegation still haunted supposedly 'big' teams though and often they resorted to desperate measures to avoid the drop. That was certainly the case with Hibs in 1979-80. In the past few years it has been common to speculate as to the identity of the best non-Scottish player to grace our game. Rangers supporters are often divided between Brian Laudrup and Paul Gascoigne while Celtic fans are virtually all agreed that it's Henrik Larsson. They're wasting their breath. The finest non-Scot, and arguably the greatest ever to play in our game, was George Best who signed for Hibs this season and whose impact on attendances was as electrifying as his performances on the pitch. 13,670 turned up at Love Street to see one of the greatest talents in world football make his Scottish debut as Hibs took on St Mirren. At 34, Best was well past his peak and his lifestyle hardly lent itself to fitness but he still possessed his natural talent to twist, turn, beat men and score goals. He did so that day, notching Hibs' counter in a 2-1 defeat.

At Easter Road the following week there were 20,622 in attendance to see the living legend in the flesh as Hibs beat Partick Thistle 2-1. But Hibs were a woeful team this season and it would have taken half a dozen Bests to prevent their relegation. The erratic Best's much-publicised problems persisted during his time at Easter Road and his appearance couldn't always be guaranteed. Nevertheless, for a fleeting moment Best brought glamour to a badly flagging game and proved that fans would still turn out in force to see genuine talent.

Running battles took place on the field between the rival sets of fans and mounted police

Hibs went down as two significant developments took place which altered the face of Scottish football. The Scottish Cup Final of 1980 was another Old Firm affair watched by 70,314 and memorable not for the crowd or for George McCluskey's goal which gave victory to Celtic but for what happened afterwards as running battles took place on the field between the rival sets of fans and mounted police.

This ruination of Scottish football's showpiece day finally forced the authorities into action and legislation was introduced outlawing alcohol at matches as well as enforcing tougher action against offenders. Its impact wasn't immediately apparent but gradually the game began to change as the worst excesses of the 1970s began to disappear from the terraces and many who had given up on the game returned to the fold.

The other significant development was Aberdeen's League championship triumph when they came from behind to topple Celtic. Alex Ferguson was fashioning a team which was ready not just for the occasional victory as had been the case with other non-Old Firm sides in the past, but which was capable of dominating the Scottish game in exactly the same manner as the Old Firm had over the years.

Ferguson's side travelled to Firhill for the last game of the season to complete the formality of their success. They needed to avoid a ten-goal defeat to claim the flag and an upset of that magnitude was never likely. Here was a chance for Celtic fans to turn up to applaud the victors. It was also an occasion for Rangers supporters to pay their respects to a team capable of doing what their own could not.

Allied to the game's well-publicised crowd troubles, economic recession was beginning to bite

And for a few Thistle and Dons fans to enjoy the occasion too. Yet the turnout was a depressingly low 6,463. That was all the mighty footballing city of Glasgow could muster to pay tribute to Scotland's new champions. Confirmation, if it were needed, that for Old Firm fans the game begins and ends with their own team.

But the mould had been broken and for the next few seasons Scottish football was an open and entertaining game with close-fought title races keeping fans in suspense up until the last kick of the season. It was a time in which our teams did well in Europe too. It was also the time when attendances hit an all-time low.

Aberdeen's average attendance in 1979-80 was just 12,944, actually over 1,000 down on the previous season and they lost another 600 the next year despite having the title to defend. Those were still the best figures other than the Old Firm and Aberdeen's decline was far from the worst in the League.

What was happening was that, allied to the game's well-publicised crowd troubles, economic recession was beginning to bite. Unemployment was soaring and soon to reach the three million mark in the UK as a whole. As the centre of the oil industry Aberdeen was better protected than most but not immune to the chill blast from the dole queues.

Nor was central government sympathetic as ministers sought to blame football for much of society's ills and developed schemes for ID cards and one club chairman even advocated electrifying segregation fences while pro-football Cabinet members bit their tongues.

The depression was deep and long-lasting and its effects were felt hardest at different times in different places. The First Division's worst season was 1983-84 and the Second's was in 1990-91. Nor was it solely a Scottish phenomenon. In England the worst season was 1985-86 after the Bradford and Heysel tragedies claimed massive loss of life. The revival stalled in England too, after another 96 fans died at Hillsborough in 1989 and there were times in the 1980s when only Man Utd and Liverpool averaged more than 30,000.

In the Premier Division it hit early and it hit hard. When faced with house repossession, impending eviction or the impossible task of feeding a family from an empty wallet, football looms less important in the life of the average supporter.

Almost half the League clubs were now watched by fewer than 1,000 fans each week

What compounded the problem for clubs was that, unlike the 1920s, the recession bit into an already small and declining base support. Almost half the League clubs were now watched by fewer than 1,000 fans each week. By 1981-82 support was at its lowest level since 1918 when there were only eighteen teams and one division. In real terms crowds hadn't been lower since the Edwardian era.

While this was the worst season for the Premier and the League as a whole it would be wrong to think of the next few years as being a recovery. One of the most commonly heard statements from Rangers supporters about this period is that gates were rising before Graeme Souness took over. Until 1985-86 it would be truer to say that Rangers crowds weren't quite as awful as before but were pretty dire nonetheless. It was only in that last pre-Souness season they rose substantially.

A look at some average gates in the first part of the 1980s shows how bad the situation was. For three successive seasons Rangers were below the 20,000 mark with 16,400 in 1981-82 worst of all and their lowest since 1924. Two seasons later Celtic averaged 18,390, back to the bad old pre-Stein days.

Aberdeen's array of trophies allied to their more favourable economic climate helped them buck the trend. They reached 17,138 in 1984 but even they had to rise from a low of 11,360 two years previously. Hearts, in the First Division, recorded 5,157 in 1982. Hibs had 4,460 at the same level twelve months earlier.

Like Aberdeen, Dundee United proved an exception, aided by playing success and the return of Dundee to the Premier Division, guaranteeing regular derby matches. They reached 11,133 when they won the title in 1983 but that was lower than the 12,830 they achieved in 1989 when they were only fourth.

The attendance tables in this book reveal the dry statistics – Dunfermline 1,090, Kilmarnock 1,351, St Johnstone 957, Airdrie 1,096, Morton 1,256 – as Scotland's mid-ranking clubs were hit the hardest. Clubs in the Premier still had the Old Firm as insulation against the cold. Even if Old Firm fans were travelling in fewer numbers than before they still – local derbies excepted – provided the biggest crowds of the season. Those teams with Premier aspirations or recently relegated, like the ones mentioned above were the clubs which faced the full impact of this catastrophic decline.

Yet other than the mid-1960s, Scottish football was, in terms of playing quality, at its peak. Domestically, competition was good with Aberdeen winning three titles and Dundee United's championship being achieved on a day when three teams could have claimed the title. The end of this period saw the marvellous race of 1985-86 as Hearts blew the championship by losing two goals at Dens Park in the final seven minutes of the season.

The Dons ended the Old Firm control of the Scottish Cup with a treble success of their own and a fourth triumph in 1986 as Hearts ended up double runners-up. True, Rangers were in the doldrums but their plight evoked little sympathy outside the confines of their own supporters.

In Europe our clubs performed with distinction. Aberdeen defeated Real Madrid to win the Cup-Winners Cup and reached the last four in its defence while Dundee United advanced to the same stage of the European Cup only to be undone by some distinctly dodgy officialdom in Rome as a 2-0 Tannadice lead was wiped out.

In 1979 and 1980, both Rangers and Celtic reached the last eight of the European Cup and Aberdeen did likewise in 1986.

Whatever was wrong with Scottish football had nothing to do with the talent on display on the pitch or the level of competition – the two most common charges cited nowadays.

Nor was it down to any failures on the part of the national side. It was the twin strikers of poverty and unemployment that ripped through the Scottish defence with ease in the 1980s just as they had done two generations previously.

If the national team couldn't be held responsible for declining gates in the 1980s they were certainly thought to have an impact in the late 1970s. The disappointing performance in the 1978 World Cup was held to be a factor in the growing disillusionment with football.

Over a quarter of a century later here too, perhaps a 'revisionist' argument can be made. After the fine performances of 1974 there was a growing belief that Scotland could do well in the 1978 World Cup in Argentina. That feeling grew when European champions Czechoslovakia were again defeated at Hampden with Joe Jordan again scoring one of the goals – Asa Hartford and Kenny Dalglish claimed the others – in a 3-1 win watched by 83,679 and when Jordan again featured in the 'Hand of Jord' incident as Scotland defeated Wales to qualify for the Finals that optimism intensified.

Some foolhardy folk even thought Scotland could win it. Only the gullible allowed themselves to be caught up with this. No European team, not then, not now, perhaps not ever, has won a World Cup outside of Europe. No rational, sensible, thinking person thought Scotland could achieve what England, Italy, West Germany and Spain had failed to do.

But rational, sensible, thinking fitba'-loving Scots were in short supply in 1978. If they hadn't been they would surely have observed that opponents Peru had reached the last eight in Mexico in 1970 and had a few decent players in their side. They would have reckoned that in European terms it was the equivalent of meeting Yugoslavia or Czechoslovakia on neutral turf and a 50/50 call, not an easy bit of shooting practice on the way to the Final.

However not even the most rational, sensible and thoughtful person can come to any conclusion about Scotland's draw with Iran other than to say it was a dreadful performance and an unmitigated disaster.

Manager Ally McLeod took much of the stick for his pre-tournament super-optimism but the feeling persists that if McLeod had said, 'Look, we're a wee country. We're delighted to be here and we'll give it our best shot. It's asking a lot of us to make the next stage but if we get a couple of breaks we could just sneak through. Win it? Don't make me laugh,' he would have been hounded by the same media – who made his life such a misery – for being too pessimistic.

Yet, in essence, that was the message from McLeod's successor, Jock Stein. The Celtic legend was keen to dispel the 'wha's like us' mentality and to a large extent he succeeded. His side did no better nor any worse than Willie Ormond's or Ally McLeod's, yet he received none of the adulation with which Ormond was feted nor any of the opprobrium heaped on McLeod.

Stein was on the point of leading Scotland to the World Cup for the second time when, tragically, he collapsed and died at the end of a qualifier in Wales. Scotland lost more than a manager that night. Jock Stein's achievements in the game will be remembered as long as football is played.

In 1986 another famous name announced his arrival in the management hot-seat when Graeme Souness was introduced as the new Rangers player-manager. Souness had never played League football in his native land until then but during his five years in charge he not only awakened the sleeping giant of Ibrox Park he galvanised their long-suffering and mainly dormant support and challenged head-on the hidebound Rangers 'traditions' so dear to so many of their fans.

Apart from a brief flowering under Waddell and Wallace, Rangers had done little since the early 1960s to justify their status as one of the two giants of the Scottish game. Ferguson's Dons won as many titles in five seasons as Rangers had in over twenty. By their own standards League results had been dreadful, culminating in losing more than they won in 1985-86.

But the latent potential of Rangers was never hidden too deeply beneath the surface and in May 1986 Souness saw for himself just how committed the support COULD be when a crowd of 40,741 turned up to see an **Ally McCoist** hat-trick defeat Celtic 3-2 in the Glasgow Cup Final. When so many turned out for a tournament which had been decreasing in importance for half a century, it was a sign that the behemoth was stirring.

Souness took advantage of the ban imposed on English clubs playing in European competition after Heysel in 1985 by persuading top players to come to Scotland, reversing the trend of over a century. The signings of Chris Woods, Terry Butcher and Graham Roberts helped Souness lead the side to their first title in nine years.

It was the longest season ever as two clubs had been added to the Premier without any going down and both the top and the First Division now consisted of twelve clubs playing each other four times for a total of 44 League games.

Despite the fact that there were two extra games to play against promoted Falkirk and Hamilton, Rangers gates soared by an amazing 11,000 per game to 36,152 – their best since 1956 and their (at the time) fifth highest ever. Their total for the season was 795,343, up from 452,634.

Decades of underachievement had created a yearning for success which Souness tapped into. With his expensive transfer signings, the manager indicated that he was prepared to do whatever it took not just to take Rangers back to the top but to keep them there. Rangers fans were not only excited by the prospect, they knew there could be no going back to the past and that helped inspire this quite incredible upsurge at the turnstiles.

The Souness revolution didn't just ignite Ibrox, it sparked off a Celtic revival too as the Parkhead club determined not to be left behind in their centenary season of 1987-88 and Celtic's gates rose to 33,199 as they celebrated their 100th birthday with a League and Cup double. Overall, gates burst through the four million barrier for the first time in almost thirty years.

It shows how much the game has changed in such a short period of time that Celtic's average that year looks woefully low now. At the time it was Celtic's third best ever. The next season – 1988-89 – was the start of Rangers riposte to Celtic's nine successive titles and the effects of what must now be described as a boom were being felt across the game as Old Firm fans started attending away games in greater numbers, boosting crowds wherever they played. Of the ten teams in the Premier Division only Hamilton averaged below 5,000.

And, for the first time ever, that century-long Old Firm boast of being as big as any club in Britain didn't ring hollow. At 39,189, League crowds at Ibrox averaged more than any club in England. It was a feat they were to equal in 1993, 1995 and 1996 with Celtic also doing so in 1999.

Yet League gates fell by 600,000 this season after six successive increases and the first instinct on seeing such a figure would be to conclude the boom was over. It was in fact a statistical anomaly. The Premier reverted to ten clubs. There were 75 fewer League games in total and the Old Firm each played just 18 home games instead of 22. The Premier average rose to its best to that point – 15,708 and with well supported clubs like Falkirk and Dunfermline dropping into the First Division while two clubs of similar stature – Ayr United and St Johnstone – joined it from below, the middle section nearly doubled its average from 1,339 to 2,455.

The century-long Old Firm boast of being as big as any club in Britain didn't ring hollow

Only the Second Division showed a drop and crowd levels there were so low that it didn't take much to cause a massive impact. All it needed was one reasonably well supported side to drop down to that level to make huge changes to gates.

Which is what happened in 1989-90 when Kilmarnock spent a season in the bottom flight. Killie averaged 3,247 – still the best for that division since its inception in 1975 and only a couple of hundred less than the Ayrshire team had played before in the Premier in the early 1980s.

The next few years showed a dip in gates before rising again. Much of this was due to Ibrox reaching saturation point and to clubs preparing to implement the Taylor Report issued after the Hillsborough disaster in 1989 when 96 Liverpool supporters lost their lives in a crush at an FA Cup semi-final match with Nottingham Forest. As pressure built up at the Leppings Lane end of the ground supporters were unable to escape onto the pitch thanks to the fencing erected to prevent pitch invasions.

Chief among Taylor's many provisions was a requirement for the top two divisions in England and the Scottish Premier to provide all-seated, all-covered grounds within five years or within five years of promotion if then playing below that level.

Rangers had been one of the leaders in seating. Aberdeen got there first turning Pittodrie into a 24,000 all-seater and Clydebank – with bench seating – also claimed an all-seated ground but Ibrox was a state-of-the-art facility. The process had begun in 1973 and by 1981 they had built 35,800 seats with standing room for another 9,500 at a total cost of over £10million. But while that seemed ideal – generous in fact for the attendances of the time – it was too small for the modern Rangers. They embarked on a programme of further expansion, eventually filling in the corners with seating.

Aberdeen too had to make improvements to their existing seating and with Tynecastle, Easter Road, Tannadice and elsewhere all busily converting to all-seated status, sections of these grounds were closed as work was carried out, lowering capacity in the interim. For example, Hearts' drop from 13,317 in 1991-92 to 9,829 the following year was chiefly due to such structural alterations.

Graeme Souness didn't stick around to see the completed Ibrox, handing over to Walter Smith, as he took charge at Liverpool near the end of the 1990-91 season, a year when Aberdeen went to Ibrox needing a draw on the last day of the season to win the title. A crowd of 37,652 roared Rangers on to victory and no club outside the Old Firm has come as close to the flag ever again.

Celtic, at that time, didn't look likely challengers either. They failed to build on their centenary season triumphs and lagged badly behind Rangers in playing ability, stadium facilities and finances. By 1993-94 their average of 22,637 while still almost twice that of any other club was itself just over half of what Rangers – on 43,345 – were attracting.

They needed their own Souness figure but when he arrived he couldn't have looked less inspiring if he tried. A small, bespectacled bunnet-wearing guy with a Canadian accent but a tight-fisted, dour mentality in keeping with the image of the cartoon Scot arrived on the scene pledging to build a 60,000 all-seater ground and get out with a handsome return on his investment inside five years.

> The Taylor Report required the top two divisions in England and the Scottish Premier to provide all-seated, all-covered grounds

Many inside the game laughed. In the past five years Celtic had done nothing as their rivals' domination grew with each passing season. It had been five years since their last piece of silverware – the Scottish Cup – adorned the Parkhead boardroom.

In the eight years since the arrival of Graeme Souness the domestic game had changed rapidly and mainly for the better and if many mourned the passing of the terraces, they weren't quite as nostalgic for the old conditions. Some of the change had been occasioned by circumstances beyond anyone's control, like Hillsborough, but much had come from within – arguably one of the most significant in playing terms was the signing of Maurice Johnston – ex-Celtic player and Roman Catholic – by Souness in 1989.

Rangers manager was on record as saying that ability was his only criterion for judging a player but the signing of someone who had not only played for their chief rivals but had even been photographed shortly beforehand in a Celtic strip as he looked likely to return to Parkhead created a media storm.

In retrospect Souness played a blinder. By signing such a high-profile player as Johnston and with full knowledge of his background Souness was laying down the law to the recidivists in the Rangers support. If he could make Maurice Johnston a Rangers player, he could make anybody a Rangers player and instead of a protracted period waiting to see which young lad would make the breakthrough, he presented the support with a fait accompli and handed the difficult job of being the club's first high-profile overtly Catholic player to a man who revelled in the controversy and relished the task in front of him.

At the same time he stole a top class striker from right under Celtic's nose, thus giving his own support a chance to gloat rather than complain about the transfer and to discomfit the Celtic support while neutralising their grounds for complaint. After all, for decades Celtic had pointed to the lack of Catholics in the Rangers ranks. How could they now complain because Souness had signed Johnston?

But it was an approach which ran the risk of alienating sections of the fans. Souness may have calculated that plenty more would take their place and that the sort of supporter who put bigotry before the team would be no great loss anyway.

At the time the furore it caused was a source of bafflement to the rest of the UK as Rangers supporters were seen on national TV threatening to send back season tickets and rip up scarves if the Johnston transfer went through. Embarrassed Scots resident in England and Wales had to explain the whole sorry Old Firm history to friends, workmates and neighbours. Seeing one's countrymen act this way near the close of the 20th century hardly made the Scottish chest swell with pride.

Johnston made his League debut at the start of 1989-90 against St Mirren with a crowd of 39,951 in attendance. Reports that the game would be boycotted were unfounded. The crowd was more or less what was expected

Johnston was also one of the star performers in the national side as Scotland reached a fifth successive World Cup Finals, largely on the back of successful home performances such as that against France when the striker, still at the time with Nantes, notched both goals in a 2-0 win in front of an enthusiastic crowd of 57,292. An even larger crowd – 60,708 – saw England win 2-0 at Hampden to bring down the curtain on the annual clash between the countries in 1989.

Although the Scots made their customary early exit from the World Cup Finals they compensated to some extent by reaching the European Championship Finals for the first time in 1992. Once again they failed to make it past the group stage but this was the only time a Scotland side ever reached the last eight of a major competition.

But the team was growing old together and a dismal qualifying campaign – which saw Scotland forced to forsake their traditional Hampden fortress as the old ground underwent modernisation – ended with the Scots failing to make the 1994 finals in the USA. It was the first such failure in 24 years.

Little solace could be found in European competition. After the great days of the early and mid 1980s our clubs fell back in the rankings. But only after Dundee United blazed a trail across the continent to become the first Scottish club to reach the UEFA Cup Final in 1987.

Once again they beat Barcelona home and away and 21,322

thrilled to the Tannadice triumph. Victory in Munchengladbach took them to a two-legged Final against Gothenburg but despite the vociferous backing of a 20,911 gate at home they couldn't overcome a 1-0 deficit, drawing 1-1. This was the culmination of several good years on the continent for United but it was a peak from which they declined rapidly, never again threatening the European elite.

Hearts had been Scotland's great under-performers in Europe but they took up the UEFA Cup cudgels in 1989, reaching the last eight where a crowd of 26,294 saw them beat the mighty Bayern Munich 1-0 before losing the return 2-0.

And Rangers matched Celtic's 1970 achievement by knocking English champions Leeds United out of the European Cup in 1992-93. The Ibrox side came within 90 minutes of a place in the new-fangled Champions League Final. Like Dundee United this was a peak from which they quickly fell.

This entire period was marked by four watershed years. Those of 1975 and 1994 at either end and 1980 and 1986 in between. 1986 saw the arrival of Souness and Scotland coach Andy Roxburgh – the men who did most to shape the years ahead – and the departure of Alex Ferguson, the dominant personality in the early 1980s, to Manchester United. But that year also saw the Junior Cup Final played at Hampden for the last time. While the Junior game remained healthy, its showpiece match was no longer the great occasion it once was. The days when it pulled in more than the League Cup Final – and even some Scotland games – had long gone.

Crowds had steadily declined to the point when even a Glasgow-Ayrshire clash between two of the biggest outfits in the game – Pollok and Auchinleck Talbot – failed to attract a five-figure gate. Their meeting drew just 7,659 to see Talbot win 3-2 and the SJFA – which had staged some early 1980s Finals at club grounds – withdrew from Hampden for good.

An era which begun with a move to three divisions ended with an extension to four. The latest attempt to find Scottish football's Holy Grail of reconstruction was the decision to move to four divisions of ten at the start of 1994-95 with clubs playing each other four times. Scotland would also belatedly introduce three points for a win.

1993-94 had more than a touch of déjà vu about it as almost half of one division feared relegation while half of another sought promotion and new admissions to the League caused controversy.

Other aspects of this term were oddly familiar with the past. Take the idea of establishing divisions based on crowd figures. The Premier Division was back at twelve members and three had to go. The relegated clubs – St Johnstone, Dundee and Raith Rovers – were also the worst supported.

Nor had clubs learned anything about simple arithmetic. Raith were playing in the top flight for the first time since 1970 yet they voted for three to go down, meaning they would have to finish ninth or higher to stay up. They'd last done so in 1958.

By the time the dust settled there were some surprising outcomes. Stranraer were in the First Division and League football finally arrived in the Highlands as not one but two clubs were accepted into the new Third Division though the Highland League lost three as a messy and often bitter merger was concluded between Caledonian and Thistle.

Clyde, who had been forced to leave Shawfield in 1986 and had shared at Firhill and Hamilton in the interim, moved to a new home in a new town as Cumbernauld joined Inverness and Dingwall on the travel roster. Meadowbank Thistle thought about making a similar move, to Livingston.

And the wee guy with the bunnet settled into his seat at Celtic Park.

The lowest crowd for an international at Hampden was the 7,455 who saw Scotland draw 1-1 with Northern Ireland in May 1969

Stands and Deliver: 1994-present

WHEN TV commentator and erstwhile Celtic Chief Executive **Jock Brown** said that when the history of Celtic came to be written in fifty years time the two names which would feature as the most important in the club's history would be **Jock Stein** and **Fergus McCann**, he was met with a chorus of guffaws from sports desks across the country.

Not that Scotland's football writers were disputing his assessment of Stein's position in the pantheon of Celtic greats. It was the idea that 'The Bunnet' could even be mentioned in the same breath that was considered risible. There aren't too many laughing now.

Celtic had been on the verge of receivership when McCann – a Celtic fan since boyhood – took over, pledging to stay for just five years as Parkhead was redeveloped and the club's finances re-organised. The new Celtic chief would never win any popularity contests and when rules, regulations and contracts barred his way he took no notice of them, ploughing on regardless. But he did precisely what he said he would do. After five years he left the club with a ground transformed from a crumbling hulk to one with 60,000 shiny new seats. The level of debt, it not eradicated, was manageable.

He also walked away with a substantial profit on his investment. But then so could anyone else if they'd been prepared to take the same risks McCann did. It should not have been beyond the wit of the old Celtic board to raise the £9m McCann invested.

But the dynasties that had ruled Celtic for a century feared fresh investment would mean relinquishing control. McCann proved it was possible to bring in new money while retaining an iron grip on the club. He did this by welcoming the clubs' supporters – or at least their cash – as he raised the money needed for rebuilding through a series of share issues. This brought in not just large institutions or wealthy individuals but tens of thousands of regular Celtic supporters anxious to provide the wherewithal for the future and proud to have a stake in the ownership of the club.

These supporters were a vast, untapped market. Celtic could attract upwards of 60,000 for big games but their usual support was under half that figure. McCann's genius was to convince the casual Celtic supporter that it was necessary to subscribe to EVERY game in order to see the important ones.

> **McCann's genius was to convince the casual Celtic supporter that it was necessary to subscribe to EVERY game in order to see the important ones.**

It wasn't an original approach. David Murray had pioneered the concept at Rangers but it had been easier to do so there when the club was winning everything in sight, the stadium held around 40,000 and was full to capacity every home game. McCann sold the same idea to success-starved Celtic supporters. He convinced them that despite an average gate of only 22,637 when he took over that the only way to guarantee their place in the 60,000 seater Celtic Park of the future was to buy a season ticket.

It was a gamble. According to Tom Campbell and Pat Woods in 'A Celtic A-Z' the club's League average over the entire post-war period was only around 27,000. A safer option would have been to rebuild Celtic Park to the same capacity as Ibrox or smaller. Decreasing the supply would have stimulated demand but McCann reckoned Celtic fans would respond to an appeal to outdo their rivals and he was right.

In his first season crowds improved by 2,000 despite the fact that Celtic played all their home games at Hampden as Celtic Park began to be rebuilt. By 1997 even though the rebuild wasn't complete Celtic recorded an average of 47,504 – the biggest in their history. McCann promptly sacked his manager Tommy Burns. Huge gates were insufficient compensation for failure to prevent Rangers from equalling Celtic's nine successive titles that season.

Wim Jansen, who replaced Burns, stopped Walter Smith's ageing Rangers team from going one better than nine championships in a row when Celtic won the League in 1998. The next season was the last of McCann's five years and if he harboured any doubts about his decision to go these were surely dispelled on the opening day when the League flag was proudly unfurled at Celtic Park for the first time in a decade and the first time ever at the new 60,000 seater ground.

The transformation in just four years had been remarkable and it should have been a proud moment for McCann. But he had parted company with the title-winning Jansen – the third boss to leave during McCann's time in charge – and the supporters left him in no doubt as to whom they reckoned had been most responsible for Celtic's success. As the flag was raised in full view of the 59,220 spectators in the ground, McCann was met by a chorus of boos from the crowd.

Despite his ruthless, flint-hearted image, he must have been deeply hurt at receiving this kind of treatment from the Celtic support. True to his word, he walked away at the end of the season, with his wallet bulging but also with a legacy which will long endure. 'The Bunnet' has received a kinder press in the years since and even amongst the Celtic support there is now a grudging acceptance of the major role he played in saving their club.

Although he was the most important figure to emerge in 1994, McCann wasn't the only new arrival on the scene nor was Celtic Park the only ground to undergo radical transformation.

Of the 42 clubs playing SPL or Scottish League football in 2005-06, 37 were in the Scottish League at the time of its centenary in 1990. Fifteen of these clubs have rebuilt their grounds as all-seater stadia and another eight have moved to entirely new locations in the intervening period in the biggest and fastest transformation of conditions for spectators since organised football began.

Inverness and Dingwall proved to be worthy League locations as Inverness Caledonian Thistle reached the SPL and Ross County the First Division. Even in their early days they showed their potential as the Third Division drew bigger gates than the Second! Ross County in particular enjoyed excellent attendances, rising to 3,173 in 2003-04 – a figure that meant they were the best supported side outside the SPL and an

Since 1990 fifteen senior clubs have rebuilt their grounds as all-seater stadia and another eight have moved to entirely new locations

astonishing achievement for a town the size of Dingwall.

These clubs' success paved the way for the admission of Peterhead and Elgin City in 2000 as the Scottish League compensated for having overlooked the Highland League for so long. And when Gretna joined in 2002 it gave League football its widest geographical coverage ever.

All was far from rosy however. Gretna owed their place to the problems of Airdrie and Clydebank. The former went bust over debts involved in building their new stadium. An audacious bid to replace Airdrieonians with a new club called Airdrie United, starting out in the Third Division, was rejected and Gretna elected instead.

Undaunted, Airdrie United simply took over Clydebank and moved that homeless club to the ground that had been the source of so much trouble and changed their name so that the Airdrie United rejected for membership of the Third Division started out in the Second. It was a breathtaking act of piracy which left a nasty after-taste as Clydebank lost League football yet again and were re-formed in the Junior ranks they had departed in 1964.

The Bankies had been struggling for years after losing their Kilbowie home and lived a peripatetic existence, wandering from Boghead to Cappielow in search of a permanent base. Their fans grew so fed up with the failure to find a home that they boycotted the club's League Cup game against East Stirlingshire in 1999, leading to that competition's all-time record low attendance of just 69 spectators.

If Clydebank's supporters had no great love for the League Cup the same couldn't be said of Raith Rovers whose spectacular penalty kicks victory over Celtic in the 1994-95 Final brought European football to Stark's Park.

At least it did when playing Faroese and Icelandic opposition. When drawn against Bayern Munich, Rovers forsook home advantage for a larger crowd, moving the game to Easter Road where 12,818 attended. Raith were beaten but not disgraced by the Bundesliga giants and when the Fife team led at half-time in Munich's Olympic Stadium it was one of the better moments in European campaigns of the recent past.

There hasn't been a great deal of success for Scottish clubs in Europe and at times fans have baulked at the admission prices for these games and there have been occasions when more supporters have watched Rangers play lower league clubs in domestic cups than have attended Champions League games.

Raith Rovers weren't the only side other than the Old Firm to get their hands on silverware in the 1990s. Aberdeen's League Cup triumph the next year was one of a number of false Dons dawns as the Pittodrie club struggled to recreate the heady days of the 1980s. Kilmarnock and Hearts both won the Scottish Cup and enjoyed a boost to their gates both domestically and in Europe. Killie in particular enjoyed a few good seasons and their average of 11,533 in 1998-99 was better than when they won the League in 1965.

Hearts faced an uncertain future over the fate of their Tynecastle home which failed to meet new UEFA regulations and in 2004-05 took their European ties to Murrayfield. They were rewarded with gates of 27,272 and 26,182 for the visits of Schalke 04 and Ferencvaros, the third and fourth best European crowds in their history and their largest since 1960. Proof that supporters would still turn out in impressive numbers if the occasion warranted it.

But the best European performance of the past decade was Celtic's march to the UEFA Cup Final in 2003. Apart from a game against Lithuanian unknowns Suduva, their gates never dropped below 53,000. Of course the modern UEFA Cup is nowhere near the standard of the competition when Dundee United reached the Final as the teams United beat then would be in the Champions League now. But it was still an impressive achievement for Martin O'Neill's side as they defeated clubs from England (twice), Spain, Germany and Portugal before losing to Porto in Seville where the number of Celtic fans present was estimated to be anywhere from 20,000 to half of Glasgow, depending on whose version is most believable.

But the team that lined up for the Final contained only two Scots. This was a trend which had been developing for many years. 1994 was the last year in which either Rangers or Celtic fielded a starting line-up consisting of all Scottish or Scots-qualified players. Since then the number of Scots in the line-up has fallen consistently with no more than a seemingly token presence being maintained at times.

Supporters of the Old Firm didn't mind where their players came from as long as their team kept winning. Often though the imports failed to justify their price tags and their salaries. For every Laudrup and Larsson there were countless Daniel Prodans. The mass importation of players also led to problems in selecting the national side, particularly as a similar process was under way in England.

There, the number of Scots in the top division declined from over 100 in the 1960s to around twenty by the start of the twenty-first century. Many of these were youth signings and where Scots did hold down regular spots in the English Premiership it was invariably in a struggling side.

The effect of this took some time to become apparent and Craig Brown's Scotland enjoyed a good period of success. Brown led the Scots through an impressive qualifying campaign for the 1996 European Championships even though home games were confined to the still unfinished Hampden and gates were down on previous efforts. The best crowd was 35,505 for a 1-0 win over Finland although every qualifier bar the one against the Faeroes drew over 30,000.

With the Finals being staged in England, qualification was a must, as Scotland had no wish to repeat the experience of 1966 of a major competition taking place on the doorstep without Scottish involvement. Brown's team acquitted themselves well but – as in all previous trips – failed to make the latter stages. With Hampden undergoing the final phase of its renovation Scotland's 1998 World Cup qualifiers were played at different venues. There was an excellent crowd of 46,738 at Ibrox to see a 1-0 win over Sweden and 17,996 saw Estonia beaten 2-0 at Rugby Park. Celtic Park was the venue for the 2-0 victory over Austria with 43,295 in attendance and 20,160 saw Belarus beaten 4-1 at Pittodrie.

The gates at Kilmarnock and Aberdeen may seem a lot smaller than the others but this was actually a sensible move of the SFA's to take these ties to grounds where crowds which would look lost in Glasgow were actually close to capacity elsewhere.

47,613 were at Celtic Park as Scotland beat Latvia 2-0 to secure their place at France 1998. The tournament itself ended in disappointment again but Scotland picked themselves up to try and reach a third successive European Championships.

Tynecastle and Pittodrie were the venues as 16,930 and 18,517 saw victories over Estonia and the Faeroes but the narrow nature of the triumphs – 3-2 and 2-1– over traditionally weak countries was the first indication that all was not well with the national side.

The Czechs gained revenge for previous defeats when they won 2-1 at Celtic Park in front of 44,513. They won every match in the group, beating Scotland in Prague after being two goals down, and the Scots trailed in a poor second. This affected gates for the remaining qualifiers as just 30,574 saw Bosnia beaten 1-0 at Ibrox and 22,059 were at Hampden for the 3-0 win over Lithuania.

Scotland were forced into a play-off with England and the all-seated Hampden welcomed a crowd of 50,132 as two **Paul Scholes** goals gave the English a seemingly insurmountable advantage. But **Don Hutchison's** goal at Wembley won Scotland the match if not the tie as they sat out a major competition for the first time since 1994.

The qualifying campaign for the 2002 World Cup was poor even if Scotland lost just one match in their group. A series of draws, particularly at home where ten-man Belgium came back from 2-0 down and Croatia joined Scotland in a 0-0 bore, denied the Scots even a play-off place. 47,384 had turned out for the Croatia match but when just 23,228 bothered to attend the final game against Latvia, which Scotland rather luckily won 2-1, Craig Brown stepped down after over eight years in the job.

The new manager was German legend Berti Vogts and a series of bad results in friendlies put him at a disadvantage with much of the media before any of his teams played on Scottish soil. When they did the friendly results were no better but Scotland came good again at home in the European qualifiers, winning very match bar a 1-1 draw with World Cup Finalists Germany.

Support was superb. The lowest gate was 37,548 for

Iceland. Somehow a crowd of 40,109 was enticed along to see the Faeroes and there were 48,047 for Germany. The best was reserved for last as 50,343 saw Darren Fletcher score the goal against Lithuania which won Scotland a play-off place.

When James McFadden scored the only goal of the game against the Netherlands in front of 50,670 in the first leg of the play-off all looked well with the world but a horrendous 6-0 battering in the return dispelled any illusion that Scotland were back on track.

When the 2006 World Cup campaign opened with a 0-0 draw with Slovenia before a crowd of 38,278 Vogts' time was fast running out. A month later Scotland were beaten 1-0 by Norway despite the encouragement of most of the 48,882 present. After an insipid draw in Moldova and with the qualification campaign in tatters, Vogts departed the scene to be replaced by Walter Smith who took over with Scotland at their lowest ever level internationally and little prospect of any great improvement in the years ahead.

For seven successive seasons total League attendances in Scotland have been over four million.

After 130 years the well from which the Gallachers, McPhails, McGrorys, Laws, Baxters, Bremners, Johnstones, Sounesses, Dalglishes, McCoists and so many others had sprung appeared to have run dry.

Yet supporters seem undeterred. In an attempt to understand the present position and to foresee the future the author asked two respected experts in the field for their assessment.

Here's what **Doctor Pangloss** had to say.

In its first season the SPL average crowd was 18,636, a figure bettered in 115 years of League football as a top flight average only by the peak post-war boom seasons of 1948-49 and 1949-50.

And while crowds have fluctuated since, the lowest SPL average of 15,209 is still better than every season bar four of the 23 years of the Premier Division which preceded it. In 2001-02 total attendances in the SPL and the Scottish League came to over 4,300,000 – a figure unequalled for the period for which full records are available and almost twice as many as the low point of 1982.

For seven successive seasons total League attendances in Scotland have been over four million. Barring the boom years after both World Wars this is the longest sustained period at such a high level.

With a population approximately one eleventh that of England & Wales, Scotland attracts one seventh of the total League figures south of the border. The Premiership comparison is even better with the SPL attracting more than one quarter of the numbers in the English Premiership. Expressed as a percentage of population SPL attendances are around 70%, the English Premiership just over 25%

Additionally the SPL consistently records the sixth or seventh highest average gates in Europe and easily outstrips any country of comparable size as well as many far larger ones.

The League has a TV deal in place which is working and augurs well for the future. Clubs are beginning to exploit the internet as a source of revenue and this will only serve to increase their financial well-being in the years ahead. The worst of the financial crisis is over and the SPL has survived intact.

Scottish clubs are starting to produce their own talent again and the next few years will see the national team return to a respectable position in the world game as the SPL goes from strength to strength. The Old Firm will continue to be the standard bearers but Hearts' European crowds in 2004-05 shows what is possible for the others. With the requirement for SPL membership reduced to 6,000 seats the Scottish League will return to being an exciting and vibrant competition in which all its members can aspire to SPL status.

Cassandra saw things differently:

The SPL is an ugly boil on the backside of Scottish football which needs to be lanced as a matter of urgency. Since its inception its clubs have become encumbered with massive debts which will take decades to repay.

One quarter of its membership was in administration in

> The SPL is an ugly boil on the backside of Scottish football which needs to be lanced as a matter of urgency.

2003 thanks to paying ludicrous wages to average players which could never be met by gate money or TV rights and the people to blame for this are the same people who brought us the SPL. If they can't run their own clubs properly, why should we trust them with an entire League?

The top two clubs in the SPL don't even want to be in it. They'd sooner end over a century of tradition and possibly destroy Scotland's status within UEFA and FIFA in pursuit of a quick buck in the English Premiership.

If it ever happens they'll kill the game in Scotland. The Scottish game may be dying anyway. Outside of the Old Firm no one has a chance. The others finish 30 points or more behind each season and the chances of winning one of the cups are just as remote. These days for every twenty domestic trophies the Old Firm pick up, only one goes elsewhere.

If their fans ever get fed up then they're deep in trouble. Clubs whose historic attendances are around the 30,000 mark shouldn't be budgeting on the basis of selling season tickets way in excess of that number. All it would take is for a few gaps to begin to appear in the stands and season ticket sales would slump as supporters began to pick and choose their matches once again.

Our teams' performances in Europe are a disgrace. If they're not scraping past sides from Liechtenstein on goal difference they're losing to outfits from Latvia and Iceland. No Scottish side apart from the Old Firm has reached the last eight in Europe since the 1980s.

The national team is a laughing stock and it doesn't matter who is in charge. We're at the lowest of the low and it will be years, if ever, before we improve. Chances of reaching a major finals in the next decade are zero.

Below the SPL it's just as bad. A team can finish bottom of the Scottish League year in, year out, miles behind the rest without fear of losing their place.

Attendances only look good because of the Old Firm's season ticket holders. The gap between them and the rest is getting wider. Sixty years ago one spectator in every six could be found at either Ibrox or Parkhead. Forty years ago it was one in four and twenty years ago it was one in three. Now, it's one in two. Soon there'll be nobody watching the other teams at all.

Looking at it another way, fifty years ago it took the worst supported club an entire season to match one average crowd of the best supported club. Today it would take the worst supported club **twelve years** to do the same. When the SPL was set up it took the third best supported club three games to match the attendance at one of the best supported club's matches. Now it takes five.

And the SPL is a cartel. The old Premier Division had the highest relegation ratio in Europe at 20% of clubs each season. The SPL has the lowest at 8.33% and it doesn't even necessarily implement that. In its first six years just four teams were relegated. We were told this was because of the 10,000 seats rule which was sacrosanct and backed by all the clubs whether they were in the SPL or not.

Until they changed it overnight. Just as they changed their opposition to ground-sharing. OK, these were sensible moves but why deceive us in the first place? And not every rule change has been positive. What happened to the winter break? And the Under-21 League which was going to give the youth a chance?

As for TV coverage, hardly anyone watches the channel it's on and we know from the experience of boxing what happens to a sport when no one gets to see it anymore. It withers at the grass roots as the next generation loses all interest in it.

Woe, woe and thrice woe. The game's a bogey.

Our prognosticating pair may be wide of the mark but they represent the two extremes of thought concerning the future. But predictions are a risky business. Twenty years ago few people would have foreseen all-seater stadia and regular gates of over 40,000 and 50,000 for routine League matches.

Rather than forecast the future this section will draw to a close by outlining what the author thinks SHOULD be the first steps on the way ahead.

This would start with a unified governing body to replace the three which currently exist on the same floor at Hampden Park. It would oversee an integrated League structure which involved a pyramid system including the Juniors with automatic promotion and relegation, augmented by a play-off system designed to keep interest going to the end of the season. Supporters Trusts would exist at every club with directly elected representatives in every boardroom.

This could be done in short order and at no expense if the will was there and clubs were prepared to set aside special interests for the greater good. There is, therefore, very little likelihood of it ever happening.

The only thing that can be said with any confidence is that the future will belong – as it must – to the supporters. Irrespective of TV audiences, internet broadcasts or any other means clubs devise to maximise their income, there's no show without Punch.

The 'good old days' of the immediate post-war era won't be back and we can only hope the same can be said about the early 1980s. If support remains around the same levels as for most of the past fifteen years or so with most clubs slightly up one year, a little down the next but never deviating too far from the long-term norm then there's every chance that this most fascinating of games will continue to enthral future generations as it has our own and those of the past 130 years.

But if it goes down the path it has hinted at in recent times of living way beyond its means and serving up an inferior product on the pitch the game needs to fear for its future. In the era of multi-channel TV and 24/7 internet access there are alternatives aplenty to football and the game cannot blithely assume it will always remain the most popular mass spectator sport in the world.

The next few years will determine which road is travelled.

Five grounds – Broadwood (pictured), the
Caledonian Stadium, the Falkirk Stadium,
New Douglas Park and Raydale Park – set
new records in the 2004-05 season

ABERDEEN

v Hearts, Scottish Cup Quarter-Final,
March 13th 1954
Attendance: 45,061

Aberdeen: Martin, Mitchell, Caldwell,
Allister, Young, Glen, Leggat, Hamilton,
Buckley, O'Neil, Hather

Aberdeen in the 1950s had a team
which brought silverware to Pittodrie.
Scottish Cup winners in the first post-
war tournament, Aberdeen narrowly lost
the 1953 Final to Rangers after a replay.
The following year the Dons were on the
march to Hampden once again.

Hearts travelled north on March 13th
1954 in fine fettle. They too were striving
for honours. It had been almost half a
century since they had last won a trophy
but they arrived at Pittodrie top of the
league and dreaming of the double.

The clash was keenly anticipated and
Pittodrie's previous best of 44,414, set
against Rangers in the league in April
1948 had been under threat for some
time. Visits from both Edinburgh clubs
had attracted over 40,000 since then and
when the last spectator squeezed
through the turnstile a grand total of

45,061 were in attendance.

And it was the home support which
enjoyed the proceedings as Aberdeen
controlled the match from the kick-off.
By the interval the Dons had forced
eleven corners to Hearts' paltry two. Yet
all they had to show for their dominance
was a solitary goal from **Joe O'Neill.**

One of the biggest films of 1954 was 'A
Star Is Born' and that phrase must have
been on the lips of thousands of Dons
fans in the second half as they
applauded a virtuoso performance by
one of their own. **Graham Leggat** was
Aberdeen born and bred. He'd joined the
Dons from junior side Banks O' Dee and
this was his first home cup tie. The 19-
year-old right winger mesmerised
supporters, team-mates and opposition
alike with his dazzling runs, unerring
crosses and incisive passing.

Older hands stood in awe of the
youngster as he single-handedly bossed
the game. Leggat himself added a
second and veteran **George Hamilton** a
third as Aberdeen ran out easy 3-0
winners. They had, as one pressman put
it, 'played Hearts off the park.'

The Dons astonished the whole of

Scotland in the semi-finals by thrashing Rangers 6-0. And while they lost the Final to a Jock Stein-inspired Celtic, they were soon back for more.

The following season saw Aberdeen win the big one as the Championship came to Pittodrie for the first time. This fine Aberdeen side won the League Cup the next season.

But the size of the crowd that day proved the magic of the Scottish Cup. No league game between Aberdeen and Hearts at Pittodrie has ever topped 28,000. Indeed just seven days later the teams met again and even though both still had a chance of the flag, there were just 17,000 in attendance.

Pittodrie held a few more 40,000-plus gates before its capacity was reduced, first to 38,000 then, as Aberdeen pioneered all-seated grounds, to 24,000. Currently, the stadium's 21,474 seats is less than half the number who attended that record-breaking game. Even so, it is the largest ground in Scotland outside Glasgow.

As for the star of the show, the local boy most certainly 'done good'. Graham Leggat went on to have a successful career on both sides of the border and also with Scotland. He emigrated to Canada in 1971 and after a spell coaching began a second career as a sports broadcaster.

AIRDRIEONIANS

v Hearts, Scottish Cup Quarter-Final, March 8th 1952
Attendance: 26,000*

Airdrieonians: Fraser, T Brown, John Murray, Cairns, Rodger, Shankland, W Brown, McMillan, Lennox, Welsh, McCulloch

Airdrie's greatest era in terms of playing

success was in the 1920s but, like so many other clubs, it was the immediate post-war boom that produced the biggest crowds. They found it difficult to survive in the 16-team top division and were in the midst of their customary relegation struggle when this Scottish Cup tie provided a welcome distraction.

Cup success was way overdue. It had been twenty years since the Diamonds had last reached the semi-finals.

So it was that a crowd of 26,000 descended on their Broomfield ground and, for the home support at least, it made for pleasant watching. Airdrie took the game to their more-fancied opponents and a **David Shankland** free kick from all of thirty yards opened the scoring after 17 minutes.

Excitement reached fever pitch after half an hour when **Ian McMillan** scored from close in to put Airdrie two up at half-time.

Hearts looked a beaten side but a goal from **Willie Bauld** not only restored hope, it prompted a pitch invasion by their supporters. Once order was restored Airdrie set about defending their lead. They hung on with grim tenacity until, with ten minutes on the clock, **Alfie Conn** equalised. It finished 2-2, leaving the Hearts fans relieved and the home contingent dismayed that a game their side had controlled for so long had slipped away.

Those Airdrie supporters among the 40,528 present at the Tynecastle replay could scarcely believe their eyes as their heroes again squandered a two-goal lead. **Ian McMillan's** twin strikes looked to have settled the tie but Hearts came storming back to win by an incredible 6-4.

For Airdrie it was back to the bread-and-butter of the league. Their next home game – against Partick Thistle – drew just

12,000. An amazing figure nowadays but routine back in 1952.

Broomfield saw its capacity challenged on other occasions, especially when the Old Firm came to town or in big cup ties but it's unlikely that it ever accommodated quite as many fans ever again. Indeed, by the time Airdrie said goodbye to the ground in 1994, after residing there for more than a century, its capacity stood at little over 10,000.

After a few seasons ground-sharing with Clyde, Airdrie moved to their shiny new, 10,000-seater stadium, only to find they had been lumbered with playing at the ludicrously entitled Shyberry Excelsior Stadium.

The new ground's record was set just two weeks after opening. In just their second appearance in their new home, Airdrie shocked champions Celtic 1-0 in the League Cup on August 19th 1998. The crowd was 8,762.

The best attendance so far to see the newly formed Airdrie United at the more sensibly renamed New Broomfield is the 5,704 who saw them celebrate winning the Second Division title with a 2-0 win over Morton on May 15th 2004.

*The crowd for this match has been estimated variously at between 24,000-26,000 and while similar figures have been cited for other games, the author has been unable to find any proof of a higher attendance for any other fixture.

ALBION ROVERS

v Rangers, Scottish Cup Second Round, February 8th 1936
Attendance: 27,381

Albion Rovers: Gourlay, Waddell, Beath, Anderson, Bruce, McFarlane, Grant, Lyon, Rice, Browning, Dudley

Picture, if you will, the scene at a regular Albion Rovers match in the twenty-first

century. There are a few hundred diehards, some huddled together in the open air, defying the elements to do their worst. Others, of a more delicate disposition, seek the security and dubious 'comfort' of the stand.

Even the most dedicated of Rovers fans would scarcely argue with a description of Cliftonhill as ramshackle, limited, as it is, to a capacity of just over 1,000.

Now think what this ground would look like bursting at the seams almost 70 years ago. That's what it looked like that day in 1936 when Rangers came to Coatbridge on Scottish Cup business.

Rovers were enjoying one of their periodic, if often all too brief, spells in Division One. Rangers, as usual, were near the top of the table. Chances of an upset seemed remote.

But in the first few minutes play the giant-killing odds reduced sharply. With just five minutes gone, Rangers' centre-half **Jimmy Simpson** suffered a split nose. In time-honoured fashion the father of Lisbon Lion Ronnie Simpson soldiered on but as a 'passenger' stuck out on the wing purely as nuisance value.

Three minutes later the disorganised Rangers defence conceded a penalty. The vast crowd hushed as **Willie Bruce** stepped up to take the kick, only to fire his effort wide of the goal.

Lacking their lynchpin, Rangers were forced into hasty tackling and gave away a free kick just outside the penalty area ten minutes from the break. **Bruce** made amends by lofting the ball over the defensive wall for **James Rice** to head past **Jerry Dawson** in goal and put Rovers ahead.

They held their lead until the interval and stood steadfast for twenty minutes of the second half under the most ferocious of onslaughts before **Jimmy Smith** grabbed the equaliser.

Rovers fought to stay in the tie but Rangers, en route to a third successive Scottish Cup triumph, would not be denied. The blue tide washed over Rovers resistance as **Smith** scored twice more to secure his hat-trick and a 3-1 win for the men from Ibrox.

Remarkably, given the size of the crowd and the fact that it took so long for Rangers to break down Rovers, there was no trouble. No fighting and no crushing even though the crowd was said to be '400 more than previous best.'

The receipts of £1,096 were a record too and even though Celtic, Aberdeen and Dundee all had home ties the same day, the largest crowd in Scotland that afternoon was recorded at Cliftonhill.

Difficult as it is for the modern spectator to imagine Cliftonhill with so many spectators inside, visualising the next match played there is a lot easier. Barely 1,000 bothered to turn out to see Rovers take on Hibs in the league.

ALLOA ATHLETIC

V Celtic, Scottish Cup Fifth Round, February 5th 1955
Attendance: 15,467

Alloa Athletic: McInnes, Farrell, Kerr, A Miller, Wilson, Lynch, McKinstray, Kiernan, Wishart, G Miller, Davidson

Most record books list Alloa's record attendance as 13,000 against Dunfermline in a 1939 Scottish Cup tie. This match, which drew substantially more, has somehow been overlooked.

It shouldn't have been. Celtic were reigning holders of the 'Double' and in the running for the title. The Wasps lay third from bottom of the 'B' division. Nor

should the round fool the reader. The Scottish Cup has changed its format many times in the course of over 130 years and although this was a fifth round tie, the competition had only reached the last 32.

This was Celtic's first game in defence of the trophy. It should have been no contest.

Celtic certainly didn't seem prepared for the way Alloa came at them in the opening stages. The Celts were 'completely knocked out of their stride by the quick-tackling Alloa team,' as one newspaper put it. After 25 minutes a poor passback led to a Wasps corner and **Billy Lynch** grabbing the opener.

Alloa were still well on top when Celtic were awarded a 'soft' penalty. Justice was done when the spot-kick was blasted wide. But just on the stroke of half-time came a second award and this time **Mike Haughney** made no mistake. The teams left the field level at the interval.

Ten minutes into the second period, **Jimmy Walsh** fired Celtic in front and their support relaxed, thinking the tie was over. Alloa had other ideas. Four minutes later the home fans erupted with joy as the veteran **Tom Kiernan** rose above the entire Celtic defence to head home the equaliser. This was the 36-year-old's final season and this goal against one of his former clubs was his first in the Scottish Cup since 1938!

Now the press remarked that 'Alloa played as if defeat was out of the question.' Sadly for the Wasps it wasn't. With fifteen minutes remaining **Bertie Peacock** edged Celtic ahead. But the tie was still in doubt with Alloa furiously battling for an equaliser until **Walsh** scored again three minutes from time.

Alloa had lost 4-2 but they had given the

mighty Celtic a fight. It was an occasion well worthy of their biggest crowd. Like many other record gates it is a crowd that will never be seen at the venue again. Today, Recreation Park can hold a mere 3,100.

Alloa's next home game was another high-scoring affair which they also lost – 6-4 to fellow strugglers Brechin City. But that was watched by a comparatively poor 2,000 supporters.

ARBROATH

v Rangers, Scottish Cup Third Round, February 23rd 1952
Attendance: 13,510

Arbroath: Dorward, Stirling, Malcolm, Grant, Gray, Till, McBain, Box, Gallagher, Murray, Rennett

Mention Arbroath and the Scottish Cup and the most common association is with their world-record 36-0 thrashing of Bon Accord back in 1885. Yet a few months earlier great controversy attended the visit of Rangers in a Scottish Cup tie. The Red Lichties defeated the Glaswegian side 4-3 only for Rangers to complain about the size of the pitch, protesting they had been 'beaten on a back green.' The SFA upheld the complaint and Rangers won the re-arranged tie 8-1.

That decision still rankled. So much so that Arbroath always seemed to pull out something extra when the Gers came calling. In four league visits to Gayfield the spoils had been divided on every occasion and while Arbroath had lost several times at Ibrox in the Cup, no Rangers side had visited Arbroath in knockout competition since that fateful day almost 70 years beforehand.

Few gave Arbroath much hope of preserving their proud record against the Glasgow giants. The Red Lichties languished at the foot of the 'B' Division. Rangers had their troubles too but they were of a different magnitude entirely. They trailed well behind Hibs in the league and the Scottish Cup represented their only hope of avoiding a second successive trophyless season for the first time since 1917.

Five-figure crowds were a rarity at Gayfield. 12,092 had attended a Second Division promotion encounter with Dundee United and the Red Lichties arrival in the top flight led to a 12,800 gate when Aberdeen were the visitors but there had never been such a gathering for a Scottish Cup tie.

The gate numbered 13,510 in total, producing receipts of £1,140. Latecomers missed the first significant action when **Willie Thornton** scored for Rangers after just three minutes. Gers supporters sat back and waited for the expected goal deluge. And waited. And waited. For Arbroath had found a resilience lacking in the league. Not only did they prevent Rangers from adding to their lead, the Red Lichties actually began to dictate play. Unfortunately for them while their defence was firm and their midfield inventive, their forwards were poor. Despite controlling much of the action they rarely threatened the Rangers goal and the 'A' Division team reached the interval with their narrow advantage intact.

The second half threatened to follow the same pattern until **Thornton** popped up again to score a second seven minutes after the restart.

There was no further scoring and Rangers supporters were relieved rather than overjoyed to hear the final whistle signify their team's first-ever Gayfield victory. They had travelled in anticipation of an easy victory but had watched their team scramble to a flattering scoreline. 'Thornton Saves Shaky Rangers' was the headline verdict the next day.

For Arbroath this performance was the sole shaft of light in a dark, grim season. Their next home game was their last of the season and just 2,600 saw them lose to Stenhousemuir. They finished bottom and ended up indebted to Rangers reserve side. By winning their section of the 'C' Division (and with Dundee's second string doing likewise in theirs) they ensured there would be no relegation (as reserve teams were not allowed to be promoted), thus sparing Arbroath from the ignominy of joining local rivals Brechin and Montrose in Scottish football's phantom zone.

The Red Lichties have never again drawn a crowd anywhere near the figure they enjoyed that day. With the capacity now reduced to just 4,165 such heady days can never return.

AYR UNITED

v Rangers, Scottish League Division One, September 13th 1969
Attendance: 25,225

Ayr United: Stewart, Malone, Murphy, Fleming, Quinn, Mitchell, Young, Ferguson, Ingram, McCulloch, Rough

Somerset Park hasn't changed a great deal since this match took place. Which makes it all the harder to comprehend how such a vast crowd fitted into such a small space. Today the crumbling wreck is limited to just over 10,000 yet in days gone by Ayr United's ground was no stranger to 20,000-plus. And not just against the usual suspects like the Old Firm and Ayrshire rivals Kilmarnock either. Visits from the likes of Morton and Motherwell also brought big attendances in the post-war boom.

By 1969 those days lay long in the past and Ayr looked to the future under manager **Ally McLeod**. The man who would later convince much of Scotland that he would return from Argentina with a World Cup to declare at Customs first honed his own special brand of Panglossian wisdom at Somerset Park.

He told the unbelieving fans he would win them promotion. And he did. Then he told them his team feared nobody. And they didn't. Next, he proclaimed they had the beating of the mighty Rangers. And they had.

On this day his newly-promoted side took on a Rangers team that had yet to concede a league goal let alone lose a game. But it wasn't just the original Super Ally's patter which sparked the vast interest in this match. Ayr had started the season well. Promoted sides tended to struggle badly but a 3-0 home win over Hibs, a draw away to Dunfermline and the narrowest of losses at Dundee led many to believe McLeod was building the finest United team for many years – if not ever.

As for Rangers, their unbeaten start fired up hopes. Scotland's most expensive player – Colin Stein – was enjoying his first full season at Ibrox and the supporters were further enthused by the return of the prodigal son. After an absence of four years the peerless Jim Baxter was a Rangers player once again.

Even though a big crowd was anticipated, no one, not McLeod, Rangers nor the police, reckoned just HOW big. At ten minutes to three, the gates were hurriedly closed and turnstiles locked as thousands of angry latecomers were turned away. The swelling mass inside forced hundreds of schoolchildren over the terracing wall while others shinnied their way on to turnstile roofs or climbed up floodlight pylons, not simply to obtain a view of the pitch but to escape the dangerous crush.

Eventually the game got under way five minutes later than scheduled with hundreds of kids still sitting around the ground less than two yards from the pitch. There they stayed for the 90 minutes.

Somehow, by some miracle, 25,225 bodies had crammed into Somerset Park. By even greater good fortune they managed to leave all in one piece.

It was the home team that gave the masses most to shout about. After just seven minutes **Quinton 'Cutty' Young** sparked off celebrations among the home support and stunned silence from the Rangers legions when his shot from around twenty yards turned into the first goal Rangers conceded in the league.

The Ayr fans were still singing and dancing when, just six minutes later, **Young** turned provider. His cross was met by **Jacky Ferguson's** header and the homesters were two goals ahead.

The crowd could scarcely believe it. Nor could the Rangers support. In those days of unsegregated crowds fighting was liable to break out between rival fans and the police had their work cut out to restore order.

None of this affected the teams. Ayr stayed in command throughout the game. It finished 2-1 to Ayr. Amid all the tumult it had escaped the attention of many that Baxter had even been on the pitch – an indication that the finest talent of his day had burned out too soon.

Ayr didn't have long to enjoy their famous triumph. Seven days later they were thrashed at Rugby Park and there were many Ayr supporters who would have gladly have swapped success against Rangers for victory at Kilmarnock.

The crowd of 7,431 for Ayr's next home game – a 1-0 win over Morton – may have looked small by comparison with their record but it was significantly greater than the few hundred regulars who attended just a few years beforehand.

BERWICK RANGERS

v Rangers, Scottish Cup First Round, January 30th 1960
Attendance: 16,000

Berwick Rangers: McQueen, Fleming, Beecham, McLeod, Rugg, Campbell, Foulis, Kennedy, Purvis, McKenna, Whitelaw

It's common knowledge that the biggest crowd to watch a Berwick Rangers match did so when their Glasgow namesakes came to town. Less well-known is the fact that this happened seven years BEFORE Berwick's famous victory over their illustrious opponents.

Although they had competed in the Scottish Cup since the 1920s Scottish football's English 'lodger' had a less than successful history in the tournament. On many occasions they failed to qualify for the competition proper.

Soon after joining the 'C' Division of the Scottish League in the early 1950s their fortunes improved dramatically. They made a name for themselves as 'giant-killers'. Alloa Athletic, Dundee United, Ayr United – all from a higher sphere – bowed to Berwick in the Scottish Cup.

Most famously of all there was a 3-0 thrashing of Dundee which took them into the last eight and a visit to Ibrox. They were well beaten but their heroics that season prompted a massive turnout of 60,245 to see the 'wee' Rangers take on the big boys. Now, five years later, came the chance to test themselves at home against the Glasgow side.

Their Shielfield ground was tested to the limit. The previous ground record was under 10,000 but that was easily overtaken as 9,000 Rangers supporters converged on the ground. They were joined by almost as many sporting the colours of the Northumberland team as Berwick's usual crowd of 1,500 was augmented for the day by many just keen to catch a glimpse of the visitors' famous names such as **Eric Caldow, Alex Scott, Ian McMillan** and **Davie Wilson**.

And they saw a belter of a match. Berwick belied their status as underdogs by taking the game to their opponents as often as they could. As one match reporter saw it, 'they fought, challenged and tackled for every ball – AND USUALLY REACHED IT FIRST.'

But once **Davie Wilson** put the visitors ahead after 35 minutes most onlookers expected the game to take an all too predictable course with the First Division team winning easily.

Berwick hadn't received the memo. Five minutes later Shielfield exploded into riotous celebration as **Ian Whitelaw** equalised. The teams left the field just as they had entered it 45 minutes previously – all square.

Berwick kept battling away in the second half but eventually superior skill and fitness began to tell and **Wilson** put the Glaswegians ahead once more, after 62 minutes. The game remained in the balance though and it was only when **Wilson** secured his hat-trick with just three minutes left that the vast army of travelling fans could breathe a sigh of relief.

It ended Berwick Rangers 1 Glasgow Rangers 3 but the visitors knew they had been in a battle. The end of 90 minutes

saw an invasion of the pitch – not from Berwick fans keen to show their appreciation, but from Glasgow Rangers supporters delighted to have escaped a major upset!

Glasgow Rangers marched all the way to Hampden for their first Scottish Cup win for seven years. For Berwick it was back to league duty. Their next home game brought two welcome points from a 2-0 victory over East Fife. Sadly, their cup heroics did little to convince many of their new guests to make a return visit to Shielfield. The usual hardy band of around 1,000 stalwarts watched the league match.

Of course it wasn't the end of the wars of the Rangers. Seven years later the two teams did battle once more and in the greatest feat of 'giant-killing' in Scottish Cup history, Berwick – led by goalkeeper-manager **Jock Wallace** – defeated their Glasgow rivals 1-0. Shielfield was packed once more, but crowd restrictions reduced the attendance that day to 13,283.

BRECHIN CITY

v Aberdeen, Scottish Cup Third Round, February 3rd 1973
Attendance: 8,123

Brechin City: McEwan, Kidd, Gillespie, Donnelly, Milne, Clark, Millar (Britton), Coutts, Reid, Cunningham, Dow.

Not even the most rabid of Glebe Park aficionados would describe Brechin City's Scottish Cup history as glorious. In 65 years in the competition prior to this game their greatest moment had been eliminating top-flight Kilmarnock at Rugby Park. And that was before World War II. More recently, they had given Aberdeen a big fright in the Cup in 1960, drawing at Pittodrie and taking the replay to extra time before succumbing 6-3.

The contrasts between the clubs could scarcely be greater. Aberdeen in the early 1970s were constantly challenging at the top of the Scottish game. They had internationalists aplenty and had pulled off one of the greatest coups of the era in signing the Hungarian genius **Zoltan Varga.**

Varga was one of those rare players whose name on the team-sheet was by itself guaranteed to bump up the crowd. Poor old Brechin, however, were in the depressingly familiar position of propping up the Second Division table.

Yet such was the interest in this tie that there were more people inside Glebe Park at kick-off than lived in the whole of Brechin!

The town's population is under 8,000 and 8,123 managed to pack tightly into Glebe Park's confines, beating the previous record – set against Dundee in a 1964 Scottish Cup match – by a hundred. The receipts came to a new record of £2,436.

But before a ball was kicked, trouble broke out on the terracing. Scottish football in the 1970s was plagued by violence at football matches. With unsegregated grounds and a popular culture which extolled the 'virtues' of constant and heavy drinking, booze-fuelled 'bovver' was as much a part of the football scene as pies and Bovril.

Yet no one expected an outbreak here, in the douce, trim settings of homely Glebe Park. With turnstiles quaintly secreted inside surrounding hedges, Brechin's home was the most unlikely of venues in which to witness a passable imitation of Custer's last stand.

Whatever the reasons, it was a sad opening to Brechin's record day as supporters were ejected from the ground by police prior to the match kicking off.

At least the fighting didn't seem to have any effect on the City team as they matched their opponents' ball for ball and man for man for the opening fifteen minutes.

But when **Barrie Mitchell** fired Aberdeen ahead the writing was on the wall. Brechin continued to fight but when **Drew Jarvie** added a second and **Mitchell** scored again before the interval the tie was effectively over.

Three down at half-time and with the cause lost Brechin relaxed in the second half as did Aberdeen, allowing the Angus side to make a decent fist of it. Goals from **Ronnie Miller** and a **Doug Clark** penalty put a better gloss on the outcome. The final scoreline of 4-2 to the Dons may suggest a tougher struggle than was actually the case but nor was this match the one-sided slaughter the teams' respective league positions might have suggested.

Brechin returned to attempting to hoist themselves off the bottom of the table. Here too, they experienced little joy. Their next game saw the Glebe Park attendance return to its usual level as 565 saw them lose to Stirling Albion. Of the 13 league games played after Aberdeen's visit, City drew two and lost eleven, finishing bottom of the league.

Brechin City have enjoyed greater success in the intervening years but with its present capacity of 3,060, Glebe Park will never again be able to boast that it held more people than the whole of Brechin.

CELTIC

v Rangers, Scottish League Division One,
January 1st 1938
Attendance: 83,500

Celtic: Kennaway, Hogg, Morrison,
Lynch, Lyon, Paterson, Carruth,
McDonald, Crum, Divers, Murphy

Pick up any football reference book you
care to mention and you'll find Celtic's
biggest gate was on January 1st 1938.
Almost every single one of them will
also state the crowd was 92,000.

And thereby hangs a tale.

For the figure of 92,000 as a Celtic
record appeared long before this match
was actually played. As far back as 1930
the Athletic News Football Annual made
this claim – though without specifying a
particular match and/or date. It is only in
post-war publications that this date was
tagged onto an existing figure.

Contemporary reports give a figure of
between 82,000-83,500 in attendance
with the latter generally accepted as
correct. The Glasgow Herald reported
that around 10,000 were turned away
with the gates closed and even more
intriguingly that the total was 'short of
the ground record of 88,000'.

Maybe the 92,000 refers to the number
who INTENDED to watch the game. At
any rate it appears clear that Celtic Park
never contained a crowd of that size.
And an exhaustive trail through match
reports not just for Old Firm games but
for other big Celtic matches, Scottish
Cup Finals and semi-finals and
internationals staged at the ground has
failed to unearth a crowd of 88,000
either.

But there was good reason for over
90,000 fans to TRY to see this game. For
much of the inter-war period Celtic had
played second fiddle (and a poorly

played fiddle at that) to Rangers. In the
years approaching this game that began
to change as Celts lifted their first title in
a decade in 1936 and followed up with
the Scottish Cup the next year.

And as the bells rung in the New Year
both Old Firm clubs glanced
apprehensively around them as, for
once, the traditional two-horse
Championship chase threatened to
develop into a more open competition.

Celtic approached the match perched on
top of the table, ahead of Hearts only on
goal average with Rangers a point behind
but with a game in hand.

Yet history was against them. They had
enjoyed a Ne'erday triumph over
Rangers just twice since the outbreak of
the Great War. Only one of these
victories had been at Parkhead and that
was ten years previously!

Celtic's forward trio of **Malky
MacDonald, Johnny Crum** and **John
Divers** were the revelation of the Scottish
season and it was they who took the
game to Rangers from the kick-off.
Rangers were, it was said, 'lamentably
lax and stereotyped in movement'. They
certainly appeared to have no answer to
Celtic's fluidity and the only great
surprise was that a solitary **John Divers**
goal was all they had to show for their
efforts by the interval.

The celebrations sparked off by that goal
led to a barrier collapsing in the crush
and fifty fans had to be treated for
injuries. It was an indication that huge
crowds and spectator safety didn't
always walk hand in hand.

Six minutes into the second half a **Malky
MacDonald** penalty gave Celtic a two-
goal cushion and they began to put on a
show for the massive crowd. They
strolled through the rest of the game
imperiously, adding a third with twenty

minutes remaining when **Divers** shrugged aside several challenges to power home a fine individual effort.

But although **Divers** and **MacDonald** were the names on the scoresheet just about everyone in the ground agreed that **Johnny Crum's** display had been the finest on the field.

The seething cauldron of the Ne'erday game was replaced in their next home game against Aberdeen by a more genteel atmosphere as huge gaps opened up on the terraces. Only around 20,000 bothered to turn up to salute the conquerors of Rangers.

Maybe supporters were more careful with their cash in the 1930s? Or perhaps they were just more discriminating in their choice of match?

Celtic beat the Dons 5-2 and lost just once more in the league, eventually taking the title by three points from Hearts.

Today of course Celtic Park can never hold as many people. It does though have one claim it could never have made back in the 1930s. Then, large as the ground was, it was a poor third in capacity behind Hampden and Ibrox. Now, transformed into an all-seated capable of accommodating 60,355 it is by far the biggest in Scotland, lording it over its two chief rivals by almost 10,000 seats.

And while the Millennium Stadium in Cardiff (and the rebuilt Wembley when it is completed) can both claim to hold more, these grounds are only used occasionally for football.

The only purpose-built football stadium in the UK which outstrips the modern Parkhead is Old Trafford.

CLYDE

v Rangers, Scottish Cup Second Round, February 10th 1912
Attendance: 48,000

Clyde: Grant, Gilligan, Blair, Walker, McAndrew, Collins, Hamilton, Jackson, Morrison, Carmichael, Stevens

Clyde's record attendance at their former Shawfield stadium is a bit like claimants to the throne of France. There are plenty of contenders, all of dubious legitimacy, none with rock-solid proof and seeking a title that no longer exists.

The record books are agreed that Clyde's biggest attendance was 52,000 and that the match in question was a league game against Rangers on November 21st 1908. The record books are wrong!

Clyde did play Rangers at Shawfield on that day, losing 1-0 but contemporary reports place the attendance at no higher than 18,000. Newspapers can, of course, be wrong but it's stretching credibility too far to imagine that they were all wrong and by so much.

Gates of that level weren't unknown at that time but they were rare. Usually it was only big Cup matches and internationals that could hope to attract so many. Even Old Firm meetings rarely topped the 50,000 mark.

Admittedly the introduction of greyhound racing in the 1930s impacted on capacity but even so all the evidence points to only one conclusion. There were not 52,000 supporters at Shawfield on November 21st 1908.

Quite why this date ever found its way into the records is another mystery. The first reference to a figure of 52,000 in print appears to be the Athletic News Football Annual for 1921-22 but no date is given. That doesn't appear until the Athletic News's successor publication the Sunday Chronicle Football Annual mentions it in its 1947-48 edition. Nearly forty years after the event!

All of which, while ruling out the 'official' record still leaves open the question as to when exactly Clyde's biggest gate was. To confuse matters even more there is a game against Rangers which favours a 'Bourbon restoration' and an 'Orleanist' upstart featuring Celtic.

By 1912 Clyde had emerged as one of the best teams in the land and their Scottish Cup tie against Rangers was an eagerly anticipated contest though none could have guessed what a controversial affair it turned out to be.

They saw a determined 'Bully Wee' dominate from the start. Just eight minutes had lapsed when a Morrison header put Clyde in front. Five minutes later the same player made it two and Clyde were coasting to victory. It really was a one-sided affair as Clyde hit the bar and left-winger Stevens missed an open goal before a long-range Carmichael effort found the net to make the half-time score a barely believable Clyde 3 Rangers 0.

At last Rangers woke up and tried to claw their way back into contention, scoring five minutes after the restart. But with 74 minutes played and no further change in the scoreline the Gers supporters decided to intervene. Hundreds, frustrated by their team's inability to make any impact on the game, rushed onto the pitch in an attempt to get the game abandoned and force a replay. It was a tactic repeated several times over the years and one which never brought success.

The referee had no option but to blow his whistle and lead the teams off. Clyde, understandably, were incensed at this attempt to deny them a famous victory

and immediately claimed the tie, insisting they would scratch from the competition rather than replay. This placed Rangers in an awkward position as the Ibrox club would have looked like bad sportsmen if they pleaded for a replay for a game they were clearly going to lose. Rangers recognised this and withdrew from the competition, thus allowing the result to stand.

Clyde marched on in the Cup all the way to the Final where they lost to Celtic. It was 1939 before the Bully Wee finally got their hands on the Scottish Cup.

Two years later Clyde met Celtic in another second round tie and after a 0-0 draw at Shawfield, lost at Celtic Park in the replay.

This is the other contender for the record crowd. In its round-up of the weekend's matches the Glasgow Herald gave the crowd as slightly less than that of 1912 at 46,000 with takings of £1,037. But in its match report the same paper, while making the crowd even smaller, at 45,000, also said this had been Clyde's 'largest gate and the poorest game'. More intriguingly the match report mentions receipts of £1,300 – 'the exact sum as appeared in the Athletic News Football Annual as having been paid by the mythical 52,000 of 1908.

So while the 1912 match appears to have been Clyde's biggest home gate no one can say so with absolute certainty. Fortunately the record for their present Broadwood stadium is not in dispute

To return to the analogy, while the aristos who fled the French Revolution headed for London or Vienna, Clyde flitted to Cumbernauld via Maryhill and Hamilton! After ground-sharing with Partick Thistle and Hamilton Accies upon departure from Shawfield, the 'Bully Wee' set up shop in their new surroundings in 1994.

Their new ground's capacity was tested to its limits by a visit from Celtic on February 27th 2005 when a full house of 8,200 saw the visitors win a Scottish Cup tie 5-0.

COWDENBEATH

v Rangers, Scottish League Cup Quarter-Final, second leg, September 21st 1949
Attendance: 25,586

Cowdenbeath: Moodie, Hamilton, Cameron, Menzies, Holland, Durie, McGurn, Mackie, Armstrong, Reid, Dick

Cowdenbeath are one of those teams and Central Park another of those grounds where it is difficult, if not impossible, for the twenty-first century mind to envisage such massive attendances.

Today they are generally regarded as the smallest of Fife's four professional clubs but that wasn't always the case. During the inter-war period Cowdenbeath spent a decade in the top flight and for long stretches were Fife's only representative in Division One.

But by the time of this fixture they were in a position more familiar to Scottish supporters – close to the bottom of the league and performing poorly. Yet somehow they had – for the first time – reached the last eight of the League Cup.

By the time they travelled for the first leg they were third bottom of the 'B' Division with just one win from six games. Rangers, by comparison, were unbeaten in their six 'A' Division matches and had eliminated Celtic, Aberdeen and St Mirren in their League Cup section.

None of this deterred 1,000 diehards from making the journey to Glasgow for the first leg where they were outnumbered 28-1. What they witnessed was nothing short of sensational. Their

side rallied after losing a goal to equalise then had the audacity to take the lead. Even after Rangers pulled level Cowdenbeath didn't fold. Instead they stunned the home supporters by taking a 3-2 lead and defended it resolutely for over twenty minutes until the final whistle.

It was Rangers first ever home defeat by a lower division side and it set the scene for a superb encounter in the return leg.

The match programme hailed the achievement of the first game, saying football experts thought 'Cowdenbeath would return from the game three or four goals down.' They were way off the mark. Most 'experts' thought Cowden would do well to keep the score in single figures.

Interest in the game set all Fife alight and with a large contingent arriving from Glasgow, Central Park was bursting at the seams as it admitted a grand total of 25,586 through its portals.

It was the Fifers who had most to cheer in the first half as first Cowdenbeath set out to repel the relentless Rangers onslaught, then, with that job done, to take the offensive themselves. When an **Alec Menzies** thunderbolt flew into the net there was pandemonium on the terraces. Now Cowden were two goals ahead on aggregate. A foul on winger **Willie 'Girnie' McGurn** brought anguished appeals for the penalty which might have killed off the tie.

At length Rangers began to see more of the ball and they spent the last twenty minutes of the first half virtually encamped in their opponents half though making little headway. Half-time arrived with Cowdenbeath still ahead.

Just five minutes into the second half a Sammy Cox effort levelled proceedings on the day and reduced Cowden's advantage to a single goal.

The Rangers pressure was intense. **Billy Williamson** hit the post then saw a shot actually cross over the line only to be ruled out. Keeper **Bob Moodie** had to be on the very top of his game to repel other efforts.

Cowdenbeath needed respite and they got it when they resumed the attack with **Armstrong, Reid** and **Menzies** all going close. But with two minutes to go Rangers again had the ball in the net only for the linesman to tell the referee it was offside.

The glorious morning newspaper headlines were floating in front of the eyes of the Cowdenbeath fans. There were just fifteen seconds remaining when their dreams were dashed as Rangers scored to go 2-1 ahead and make it 4-4 on aggregate.

Cowdenbeath steeled themselves for extra time but to have victory so cruelly denied took its toll on morale. Rangers were in charge for the extra half hour and a **Sammy Cox** shot after twelve minutes put them ahead overall.

Still the game Fifers refused to buckle. Part-time they may have been but their effort was as fully professional as their foes. The game stayed on a knife-edge till the end of the 120 minutes brought relief to Rangers and despondency to gallant Cowdenbeath as the game finished in almost total darkness

The Kingdom claimed revenge though as East Fife eliminated Rangers in the semi-finals. Cowdenbeath returned to the task of attempting to pull away from the foot of the table. Without, it has to be said, any great success. They lost their next home game 3-2 to Dundee United, watched by just 2,500. Such an attendance would bring a warm glow to the club treasurer today but this was, in those boom years for crowds, a pretty poor reward for all Cowden's efforts.

Today Central Park is so reduced that only a fraction of that massive crowd would be admitted. Current capacity is a mere 4,370. In 1949 Cowdenbeath played before an AVERAGE in excess of that figure.

DUMBARTON

v Raith Rovers, Scottish Cup Quarter-Final, March 2nd 1957
Attendance: 18,001

Dumbarton: O'Donnell, McKay, Rollo, Cairns, Craig, McCall, Brown, Gibson, Hugh Gallacher, John Gallacher, Heaney

Dumbarton are one of the oldest clubs in Scotland yet their record gate came 85 years into their existence and even more surprisingly their biggest crowd wasn't against one of the giants of the game but the more modest outfit from Kirkcaldy.

The Sons attendances heyday came a decade or so after most clubs. The immediate post-war boom passed them by as Dumbarton struggled near the bottom of the table and made little impact in the knockout tournaments. In 1954 they even suffered the ignominy of dropping into the 'C' Division where they spent a season playing against reserve sides from the west of Scotland.

So when they returned to the 'B' Division in 1955 and began to flirt with the promotion positions, gates at Boghead increased dramatically. In 1957 in the Scottish Cup they were the shock team of the tournament, eliminating two First Division sides in Queen of the South and Motherwell to reach the last eight.

These factors combined to produce a Boghead crowd which was unexpected, unprecedented and unrepeated as the Sons strove to grasp a semi-final spot for the first time in the twentieth century.

By the time the teams kicked off 18,001 supporters crammed into Boghead, paying record receipts of £1,347.

The Sons enjoyed good possession at the start of the match but they had taken a gamble by fielding striker **Hugh Gallacher** who was clearly unfit. It was inside-forward **Bob Gibson** – appropriately enough an art teacher by profession – who provided most of the artistry in the home team.

After twenty minutes though, they fell behind and were left chasing the game. At half-time Raith still clung on to their narrow advantage. The Sons had chances to level after the break, notably when **John Gallacher** set off on a mazy run, only to hit the bar.

That was as close as Dumbarton got. A knee-high volley from Raith's **Copland** put the Fife team two ahead after 64 minutes and silenced the hitherto raucous Boghead crowd. Three minutes later Raith put the issue beyond doubt by scoring a third. Rovers were reduced to ten men when **Hugh Gallacher** caught keeper Drummond with a boot. **Drummond** had to go off, requiring five stitches above his left eye and left-back **Bain** took over in goal.

It made no difference. Ten-man Raith strolled through the remainder of the game and even added another goal to their tally to run out 4-0 winners.

The Sons were quickly back in Boghead action, beating Arbroath 3-1 four days later. The crowd of 3,000 was below average but a fair figure for a midweek game coming off the back of a heavy defeat.

Dumbarton had never been noted for large attendances. They spent fifty years outside the top division following relegation in 1922 and in all that time never once played host to a five-figure crowd in a league game.

Although they hosted the occasional big crowd against the Old Firm in the few seasons they spent in the top flight in the 1970s and 1980s they never experienced anything close to the number who turned up back in 1957.

Boghead had many critics in the nineteenth century, even more in the twentieth and was clearly inadequate for the twenty-first, so – Sons diehards apart – their move to a new stadium in 2000 was welcomed by Scottish fans.

It was no great surprise that the initial capacity of the new Strathclyde Homes Stadium was set at a modest 2,020, though with room for expansion should performances justify it and costs can be met.

So far ther best attendance at their new home was 2011 on January 3rd 2004 when the Sons beat high-flying Morton 1-0 in a Second Division match. It will be a long time, if ever, before a Dumbarton side enjoys the vocal backing of 18,000 fans.

DUNDEE

v Rangers, Scottish Cup Second Round, February 7th 1953
Attendance: 43,024

Dundee: Brown, Follon, Cowan, Gallacher, Cowie, Boyd, Burrell, Toner, Flavell, Steel, Christie

Unlike many record-setting matches, the size of the crowd here came as no great surprise for Dundee had enjoyed a few epic battles with Rangers in the preceding years and competed more often than not on equal terms. The Dens Parkers were also no stranger to 40,000-plus crowds on their home turf. Visits from Aberdeen and Raith Rovers had produced such mammoth gates in the previous two seasons. Indeed, Dundee usually AVERAGED over 20,000 in the league at this time.

It wasn't simply the post-war boom which fuelled these huge Dens Park gates. The manner in which Dundee had battled back from adversity to emerge as contenders for ALL the game's top honours had brought the Tayside public out in great numbers.

Within three seasons Dundee had emerged from the ignominy of the 'B' Division to the brink of the title. Leading on the final day of the season in 1949 they lost at Falkirk, allowing Rangers in to snatch the flag.

They were a resilient lot, this Dundee side though and in 1951-52 they won the League Cup and reached the Scottish Cup Final where they lost to Motherwell. In this season – 1952-53 – they had already retained the League Cup trophy and were set on adding the Scottish Cup to their collection of silverware.

The game watched by this huge crowd wasn't of a vintage standard but it was entertaining enough for the first hour with both teams having chances but with both fine defences on top.

Then sixty short seconds changed everything. With 59 minutes played Rangers' **Johnny Hubbard** nipped past defender **Gerry Follon** on his blind side and flashed in a shot to give Rangers the lead.

A minute later it was Dundee keeper **Bill Brown's** error which helped tumble his side out of the Scottish Cup. Arbroath-born **Brown** is widely regarded as Scotland's finest goalkeeper of the past sixty years, having played with distinction for Dundee, Tottenham Hotspur and Scotland in a medal-strewn career. But on this day he was playing in

only his second game of the season and his rustiness showed.

A harmless-looking cross-cum-shot was sent over by Gers' **Derek Grierson** which, to the horror of both himself and his team-mates, **Brown** fumbled. The Dundee fans in the crowd watched dumbstruck as the ball dropped gently over the line.

At 2-0 there was no way back against Rangers famed 'Iron Curtain' defence and all the tricks and wiles of **Billy Steel** and his talented team-mate **Bobby Flavell** came to nothing. Dundee were out, beaten in front of their biggest ever gate.

Rangers went on to win the Scottish Cup that season. Dundee returned to Dens Park seven days later for a vital league game against. . . Rangers!

This time there were 'only' 24,000 in attendance, still an excellent turnout. And they saw a fighting performance from the home side which helped them to a 1-1 draw, part of a sequence of four successive draws followed by three straight wins which helped the Dens Parkers pull away from the foot of the table.

Although moves to a new purpose-built stadium which they would share with neighbours Dundee United have been mooted, Dundee remain at Dens Park, their home for over a century. The ground is now a modern all-seater, capable of holding just 11,506.

DUNDEE UNITED

v Barcelona, Inter-Cities Fairs Cup
Second Round Second Leg, November
16th 1966
Attendance: 28,000

Dundee United: Davie, Millar, Briggs,
Neilson, Smith, Wing, Seemann, Hainey,
Mitchell, Gillespie, Persson

Today, Dundee United are usually the
more popular of the two clubs in the city
but that wasn't always the case. For
decades United (and in their previous
incarnation as Dundee Hibernian) lagged
well behind Dundee.

The arrival of **Jerry Kerr** as manager was
the beginning of the transformation.
Kerr's achievements were built on by his
successor **Jim McLean** as Dundee United
rose from obscurity to winning trophies
and European glory.

Kerr was the Bill Shankly to McLean's
Bob Paisley – although their
personalities suggest it should have been
the other way round.

Jerry Kerr took United into the top league
at the first time of asking, in 1959-60
and, more importantly, kept them there.
Success was incremental rather than
spectacular. United won no prizes but
they maintained a steady progress.

In 1965-66 United finished in a giddy
fifth. In those days that was good
enough to qualify for Europe so they
took their place in the draw for the Inter
Cities Fairs Cup – the forerunner of the
UEFA Cup.

Excitement at the prospect of jousting
with continental giants was tempered
somewhat when they received a bye in
the first round but their second round
opponents couldn't have offered a
tougher baptism. Barcelona, then as
now, were titans of the European scene
and Fairs Cup holders as well.

At least, thought the cynics, Dundee
United would make a few bob out of
what looked like an extremely short
introduction to European football. And
who could gainsay the critics? While
Barca were as accomplished a side as
any in continental competition, United's
experience amounted to a risible 14
appearances in total.

Scottish football began to lose some of
its introversion in the 1960s and United
were one of a number of clubs to
introduce Scandinavian imports into the
domestic game. Their 'Vikings' as they
were wearily but inevitably daubed by
the press all had some grounding in
continental competition. Left-winger
Orjan Persson had played twice
previously and left-half **Lennart Wing**
once. Given that these had been for the
Oergryte team beaten by Dunfermline
Athletic a year previously it was difficult
to see how that would help United
overcome Barcelona. **Finn Seemann**, on
the right wing, with seven outings, was
the only player in the team with any real
knowledge of this level.

Of the eight Scots in the side, seven
were continental 'virgins.' Only **Billy
Hainey**, with four previous Fairs Cup
games for Partick Thistle, had played in
Europe before.

Safe to assume therefore that little was
expected of United when they entered
the forbidding Camp Nou. Their
appearance hardly excited the Catalan
fans either. A miserly 22,459 bothered to
turn out to watch the expected ritual
slaughter.

Someone forgot to send Jerry Kerr's side
the script. **Hainey** and **Seemann** – the
continental 'old boys' of the team –
stunned the Barcelona 'socios' into
silence. Hainey netted in the thirteenth
minute and Seemann converted a
penalty close to the hour mark. Although

Barcelona pulled a goal back late in the game, United held on to record a famous 2-1 victory and set the scene for a Tannadice night never to be forgotten.

Even though the second leg was more than three weeks after the first that did little to quell the mounting excitement on Tayside. Every possible vantage point had been taken well before kick-off as a full capacity crowd of 28,000 gathered to roar on their heroes.

Barcelona needed to score first if they were to get back into it and a more experienced team might have set their stall out to prevent this from happening by man-marking and playing four or five at the back.

But in their glorious naivety Dundee United played the game in the traditional way. They were the home team. Home teams attacked and away sides defended. So it was that at every available opportunity United spread the ball wide to **Persson** and the Swede's trickery did the rest. Quite simply, in an era when such awards were uncommon, Persson was easily the Man of the Match.

But it was **Ian Mitchell** who hammered the first nail into the Catalans coffin, scoring in the 17th minute. United kept the pressure on and reached the safety of the interval one up on the night and two ahead on aggregate.

Three minutes into the second half and any lingering hope of a Barcelona revival was snuffed out thanks to a goal from **Hainey**. All that was left now was for United to play out time.

2-0 on the night and 4-1 on aggregate, not only had Dundee United knocked out the holders in their first European tie, they became the first team apart from the mighty Real Madrid to defeat Barcelona in both legs. It was, as another pressman opined, 'A VICTORY THAT WILL RING ROUND EUROPE.'

But before they could savour the prospect of the continent's biggest names trembling at the prospect of visiting Tannadice, United had domestic matters to attend to. Their next home game was against Aberdeen which they lost 3-1 in front of just 9,860.

United's European campaign didn't resume until February 1967 when their next opponents were almost as mouth-watering a proposition as Barcelona. Juventus too were one of the biggest names in football in the 1960s but their notoriously fickle fans weren't any keener than the Catalans to turn out in great numbers. Just 6,800 watched as United lost 3-0 in Turin.

Hope sprung eternal in the Tannadice breast and United followed up their record crowd by providing their second biggest ever for the visit of the Italians. There were 27,245 present to watch United gain a 1-0 victory on the night, courtesy of a goal from another of their imports, **Finn Dossing**, but lose 3-1 on aggregate.

United went on to great achievements both at home and in Europe in the decades ahead though never again hosting crowds like those that saw Barcelona and Juventus both beaten at Tannadice. But with an all-seated capacity of 14,223 Tannadice, which was once capable of holding only two-thirds as many as its neighbour, has outstripped Dens Park. It is yet another area where United have pulled ahead of their city rivals.

DUNFERMLINE ATHLETIC

v Celtic, Scottish League Division One,
April 30th 1968
Attendance: 27,816

Dunfermline Athletic: Martin, W
Callaghan, Lunn, McGarty, Barry, T
Callaghan, Lister, Paton, Gardner,
Robertson (Mitchell), Edwards

Three days before this game supporters
of both these clubs celebrated in
Glasgow – and one of them wasn't even
playing! Dunfermline Athletic defeated
Hearts in the Scottish Cup Final to take
the trophy for the second time in the
1960s. Their rise from perpetual
struggler to a place in both the Scottish
and European elite was masterminded
by the man now in charge of Celtic –**Jock
Stein**.

Stein, of course, had also transformed
the Parkhead club, turning them from
domestic also-rans into European
champions and Celtic celebrated every
bit as much the day the Pars won the
Scottish Cup. For, on that same
afternoon, Rangers' defeat at home to
Aberdeen, handed Stein and Celtic the
third of what would become nine
successive titles.

Unless, that was, Dunfermline beat Celtic
by 16-0! So this should have been cause
for a double celebration, a joyous
outpouring of all that was good about
Scottish football. Instead, it almost
turned into disaster.

Not for the first time the size of the
crowd took the game's authorities by
surprise. It shouldn't have. Ever since
Dunfermline won their semi-final this
game, originally down for the same day
as the Final, had been earmarked for this
date. It was obvious the title might be at
stake and that a large number of Celtic
supporters would be heading for Fife.

It was equally obvious that there was a

good chance that Dunfermline would
bring home the Scottish Cup and that the
home fans would also be out in force to
celebrate. Yet provision for policing and
stewarding both inside and outside East
End Park was totally inadequate.

There were fans perched on the roof,
walls were scaled, floodlights climbed
and turnstiles smashed by those
desperate to get in. The gates were shut
with at least 3,000 still outside the
ground.

Inside, the game had to be stopped
twice, for a total of 17 minutes in all.
The first time was to get fans off the roof
and the second when crush barriers gave
way and the crowd spilled alarmingly
down the steps. 49 fans required
treatment, fifteen of whom were taken to
hospital and a pensioner died when he
fell off the roof of a nearby garage.

As Celtic supporters poured onto the
pitch, Jock Stein, thinking this was an
over-exuberant pitch invasion, leapt out
of the dugout and onto the field to
remonstrate with them. Police
considered abandoning the game but
fears of the riot such a move might
provoke stayed their hand.

The official attendance was 27,816,
almost 3,500 more than the most East
End Park had previously held. But the
3,000 locked out were matched by at
least a similar number who broke in and
perhaps many more. **Hugh Taylor**, in the
following day's Daily Record
commented, 'I would say that at least
33,000 saw the game – but not in much
comfort for most of them.' Taylor also
claimed that the mayhem surrounding
the match had produced 'the most
terrifying moments Scottish football has
known.' That tragedy did not unfold at
East End Park was down to luck rather
than judgment.

Despite the death and the hospitalisations the toll could have been much greater. Scottish football got lucky that night. It wouldn't stay lucky for long. Tragically, no lessons were learned from this latest flirtation with near-catastrophe and none would be until 66 lives were lost in Glasgow in January 1971.

Nor could the blame for the chaotic scenes in Dunfermline be laid at the door of hooliganism. These two teams had just won the greatest honours in the land. Their supporters wanted to pay tribute to their heroes, not fight with their rivals.

The match itself passed by without major incident. Dunfermline's Cup-winning eleven started the game and after 25 minutes of actual play **Pat Gardner** put the Pars ahead. Shortly before the break **Willie Callaghan** miscued in an attempt to cut out a pass and **Bobby Lennox** capitalised on the error to equalise.

It was **Lennox** who popped up again, in the 72nd minute, to score what proved to be the winner as Celtic ended the game 2-1 to the good.

The Pars' next home match wasn't until August 10th when the new season opened with a visit from Dundee United in the League Cup. Dunfermline won 3-2 before a much more subdued crowd of 7,477.

Today, East End Park has been converted into an all-seated stadium with a capacity of 11,998 – or only around a third of the number who wanted to get in back in April 1968.

EAST FIFE

v Raith Rovers, Scottish League 'A' Division, January 2nd 1950
Attendance: 22,515

East Fife: Niven, Laird, Stewart, Philp, Findlay, G Aitken, Gardiner, R Aitken, Morris, Brown, Duncan

East Fife established themselves as a team to be feared either side of World War II when, first, they won the Scottish Cup while in the Second Division in 1938 then repeated that achievement in the League Cup ten years later. On that latter occasion they ran away with the 'B' Division title as well, giving Fife its first taste of post-war top-flight football.

Raith Rovers followed along in their slipstream twelve months later, losing to Rangers in the League Cup Final but winning promotion by a point.

Rovers joining the Methil team in the 'A' Division ensured Fife of its first top division Ne'erday clash since 1931 so interest in this game was immense. There had always been a strong rivalry between Fife's league clubs and even in the lower division this fixture could attract big crowds with 19,700 turning out at Stark's Park on New Year's Day 1938 for a Second Division game between the clubs.

East Fife's previous best of 20,737 set against Rangers the previous season was smashed when 22,515 Fifers walked through the turnstiles to see the match.

The play was even at first but the home side soon began to exert control. In **Allan Brown** they possessed the most outstanding player on the field and it was the inside-left whose pass set up **Bert Aitken** to head in the opening goal after 25 minutes.

Rovers fought to stay in the game and did well to reach the dressing room just one goal in arrears. Six minutes into the second half and **Brown** doubled the advantage with a shot from 25 yards. East Fife were flying now and on the hour mark a headed cutback from **Ian Gardiner** allowed **Brown** in to claim his second and East Fife's third.

3-0 was the final score, earning the Bayview team full Kingdom bragging rights – for the time being. That East Fife had easily swatted away the Kirkcaldy challenge was incontestable and a look at the Bayview line-up shows why. Five players in East Fife colours that day played for Scotland at some stage of their careers. **George Aitken, Allan Brown, Henry Morris** and **Davie Duncan** were all capped while at Methil while **Ian Gardiner** earned his Scotland call-up after joining Motherwell.

The attendance would never be surpassed at Bayview but on a day when over 280,000 watched the eight 'A' Division games, five matches drew bigger crowds than East Fife.

East Fife's next home game also drew a big crowd when 18,674 attended five days later to see Rangers win 2-0. The Ibrox team also prevented East Fife from achieving further trophy success when they beat them 3-0 in the Scottish Cup Final later that year.

East Fife play before much smaller crowds these days in their 2,000-seater New Bayview Stadium. The new ground has also seen 'full house' signs. East Fife celebrated their centenary in 2003 with promotion from the Third Division and towards the end of that term twice played to a packed stand. They lost 1-0 at home to Morton on April 19th 2003 in front of 1,991 but clinched promotion in the final game of the season on May 10th when 1,996 saw them beat Queen's Park 1-0 thanks to a **Kenny Deuchar** goal.

To give an indication of how big the 1950 crowd was, if East Fife played before capacity crowds for eleven consecutive home games next season, they still wouldn't have appeared in front of as many as their forerunners of more than half a century ago!

EAST STIRLINGSHIRE

v Partick Thistle, Scottish Cup Third Round, February 19th 1921
Attendance: 12,000

East Stirlingshire: Buchanan, Mitchell, Hopewell, Monteith, J Wilson, Johnstone, N Wilson, Mooney, Shearer, McNeilage, Currie

East Stirlingshire were a team with grievances at the time of this tie. They had been admitted into league football before local rivals Falkirk but it was the Bairns who were elected to the top flight and went on to become one of the best teams in the country, winning the Scottish Cup in 1913.

On top of that while the Scottish League continued operating its top division during wartime it shut down the Second Division in 1915. It wasn't until nearly three years after the end of the war that the lower division finally re-started.

For clubs like East Stirlingshire, confined to local leagues, the Scottish Cup was the focus of their discontent – an opportunity to show the game's rulers they deserved a place at the table.

Three factors combined to ensure a record crowd this day. The rare chance to see a Scottish League side in action, the realisation that this might be the last time a Scottish Cup tie was played at 'Shire's Merchiston Park home and the opportunity for East Stirling to reach the quarter-finals of the Scottish Cup for the first time since 1891.

Around 12,000, including a fair number from Glasgow, saw the tie and while Thistle were always in control it was never easy. They led 1-0 at half-time, courtesy of a **Jimmy Kinloch** goal and the same player scored again in the second half. But a goal from right-winger **Neil Wilson** kept local hopes alive until the end. At 2-1 to Thistle it was a brave but eventually doomed bid for glory by 'Shire.

The optimistic 'Shire officials noted that Thistle went on to win the Scottish Cup and mused openly that with a bit of luck it could have been East Stirling's year. That is taking the legendary optimism of the football fan too far.

This match was indeed the last cup tie to be played at Merchiston Park as 'Shire rejoined the Scottish League at their new Firs Park home in August 1921. And they would rue the missed chance to reach the last eight for a long time. Sixty years to be precise. It was 1981 before an East Stirling side appeared in the quarter-finals of the Scottish Cup.

The biggest crowd in the eighty-odd years they've played at Firs Park came in November 1935 when East Stirling met St Mirren in a league match. The attendance was around 10,000 – a big gate by Second Division standards and due to the presence of a large number of Falkirk fans out to cheer their local rivals against the Bairns' chief challengers for the Division Two title.

But the biggest crowd ever to see a home game involving East Stirling wasn't at either Merchiston Park or at Firs Park. It was at New Kilbowie in Clydebank!

In 1964-65 East Stirling departed Firs Park for New Kilbowie and changed their name to ES Clydebank. The move lasted just one season and was bitterly opposed by 'Shire supporters but

nevertheless the players were largely the same ones as had played for 'Shire. East Stirling did not resign membership of either the SFA or the league. No new club called **ES Clydebank** applied for or was admitted to membership of either body. Therefore the only conclusion that can be drawn is that even though they were no longer called East Stirlingshire and didn't even play in Stirlingshire, this was East Stirling in another guise.

They pulled off a 1-1 draw in the Scottish Cup away to Jock Stein's Hibernian and attracted 14,500 supporters to the replay which Hibs won 2-0.

It's doubtful if Firs Park could ever have held such a crowd, even in the days before spectator safety became an important consideration. Today, East Stirling's home is restricted to a capacity of a mere 781.

ELGIN CITY

v Arbroath, Scottish Cup Second Round, February 17th 1968
Attendance: 12,608

Elgin City: Lawtie, Gerrard, Laing, Smith, Grant, Middleton, Dalziel, Graham, Anderson, Thomson, Gilbert Sub: Carroll

Elgin City, then in the Highland League, made a real name for themselves as Scottish Cup 'giant-killers' in the 1960s. Elgin had emerged as the dominant northern club. They won the Highland League eight times in eleven seasons between 1959-60 and 1969-70 inclusive and were runners-up twice, scoring a century of goals on six occasions.

A 5-1 demolition of Forfar in the Scottish Cup announced their arrival on the national scene in 1960 and they put up a tremendous struggle against Celtic in the next round at their Borough Briggs home where, in front of 11,207, Elgin took a first half lead and held it with only seven minutes remaining before two late goals allowed Celtic to scrape through.

They returned to national prominence in 1967 when they knocked out First Division Ayr United 2-0 on their own Somerset Park turf in the first round proper. That earned them a trip to Parkhead in the next round but the team that was on their way to winning the European Cup was hardly likely to trip up against a side from the Highland League and Celtic ran out easy 7-0 winners. Elgin's consolation was their share of the gate money from the 34,000 crowd – the second largest number ever to watch a match involving a Highland League club (the largest also involved Elgin when 36,324 saw Rangers beat them 6-1 in a 1952 cup tie).

Such a drubbing would have discouraged many teams but not Elgin City. Twelve months later they were back for more. They defeated Albion Rovers before assuming an unfamiliar role as the 'big' team in the next round when they played Tarff Rovers of Newton Stewart. Elgin had to fight all the way and they trailed for a long period before finally emerging victorious by 3-2.

That brought Forfar Athletic back to Borough Briggs. It wasn't quite as easy this time for Elgin but a **Bryan Thomson** hat-trick gave them a 3-1 win before an excellent attendance of 6,608 to take them into the last sixteen for the third time in the decade.

Their reward was a home tie against Arbroath – at the time a fine side, challenging for promotion to the First Division. A big crowd was guaranteed but no one expected more people to watch Arbroath than had turned out for Celtic. But on the morning of the match, Aberdeen's tie at Dunfermline was called

off and in a superb display of northern solidarity, dozens of Dons supporters buses turned round and headed for Borough Briggs.

They helped bring the total attendance to 12,608 – the largest number to ever set foot in a Highland League ground. It is a record which remains intact to this day and one which in all probability, given modern restrictions on capacities, will never be broken.

The noise made by the fans as the Highland League's official history so elequently put it twenty five years later, 'crashed down on the pitch like the breakers on Lossiemouth beach in bleakest mid-winter'.

Elgin weathered the early storm and the longer the game progressed the more confident and aggressive they became. The ever-reliable **Bryan Thomson** and partner **Jim Anderson** both scored in the second half to give Elgin a 2-0 win and create a little bit of history.

For the first time a Highland League club had reached the quarter-finals of the Scottish Cup.

And that magnificent crowd boosted the cause of those who reckoned the Scottish League should open its doors to its Highland neighbour. Of the five other cup ties completed that day only the game at Dens Park between Dundee and Rangers attracted more spectators. And two of those ties were all-first division clashes – Airdrie v Hibs and Dundee United v Hearts!

A generation passed after their glory run of 1968 before Elgin City were finally admitted into membership of the Scottish League in 2000.

A 1990 win over Arbroath remains their last Scottish Cup success at Borough Briggs, which now holds just 4,962.

FALKIRK

v Celtic, Scottish Cup Third Round,
February 21st 1953
Attendance: 23,100

Falkirk: McFeat, McDonald, Rae,
Gallacher, McKenzie, Hunter, Delaney,
Dunlop, Weir, Campbell, J Brown

Falkirk had a history of superb Scottish
Cup attendances. Other than a visit from
non-league Newton Stewart they hadn't
dropped below a five-figure attendance
since the war. So when the third round
draw paired them with Celtic there was
every expectation not just of a big gate
but that their 15-year-old record of
22,618, set against Rangers in the league
would be under threat.

That became even more apparent when
the Bairns received 10,000 applications
for just 1,400 stand tickets. Celtic supporters, disgruntled both by their ticket
allocation and their club's distribution
method called for a boycott of the game.

This was an abysmal failure as Celtic
supporters, like those of Falkirk, turned
up at Brockville in their thousands. There
were 23,100 in total, setting a new
record. They were to see a match none
of them would ever forget.

It's very often the case that former
players can return to haunt their old
clubs and that's precisely what happened
here – twice! Falkirk's centre-forward
Jock Weir was a former Celtic player and
he was determined to put one over his
old team. So too was the brilliant **Jimmy
Delaney**. At 38 **Delaney** was in the
autumn of a medal-strewn career which
had begun when he signed provisional
forms for Celtic back in 1933. Delaney
had been the idol of Celtic Park for over
a decade and he was yet another reason
why the boycott failed miserably. It was
like asking today's Celtic supporters to
refuse to go to a game even if they knew

it was the last time they would see
Henrik Larsson play.

Aided and abetted by the skilful half-
back **Jimmy Gallacher** the ex-Celts ran
the show early on and after just five
minutes **Weir** outjumped both keeper
Bonnar and **Jock Stein** to head the
Bairns in front.

After eighteen minutes it got even better
for Falkirk. Inside-left **David Campbell**
found himself offered a free header with
no Celtic player within ten yards of him.
Campbell despatched his header with
aplomb to make it 2-0.

Falkirk reached the break with their two-
goal lead intact and their own goal rarely
threatened. They were heading for an
easy victory until the 53rd minute. What
happened next was burned permanently
into the memory of all who were
present.

Celtic won a corner and coming over to
take it stepped forward one **Charles
Patrick Tully**. **Charlie Tully** was one of the
greatest entertainers of his day and he
was worshipped by the Celtic fans. His
corner kick fooled everyone and flew
straight into the net. The Bhoys joy was
short-lived as the furiously flagging
linesman attracted the referee's attention
and the corner was ordered to be re-
taken.

To the amazement of his team-mates,
the opposition, both benches, and
everyone in the ground save possibly
himself, **Tully** did exactly the same thing
again, scoring directly from the corner,
though there was a suggestion that it
took a glance off a defender en route to
goal. This time the referee had no
hesitation in pointing to the centre circle.

If **Tully** represented the joyous, carefree
face of football then the game's Janus-
like ugly twin bared its fangs just a few
minutes later.

Celtic surged forward and with 59 minutes on the clock **Willie Fernie** equalised. That was the signal for a pitch invasion by Celtic fans. It wasn't a spontaneous outburst of relief that Celtic had unexpectedly found a get-out-of-jail card but more of an ugly, in-your-face gesture of triumphalism by people humiliated at having spent the best part of an hour losing to a side they considered beneath them

Barriers were ripped up and tossed aside by the hordes determined on displaying the Mr Hyde half of their nature. As the supporters swarmed all over the field they left a trail of wreckage in their wake. Fifty fans ended up hospitalised that day.

When the game restarted Falkirk's composure had gone. With 66 minutes played Celtic capped a remarkable comeback with a goal from the unlikeliest of sources. **John McGrory** only scored three times in the league for Celtic in all the years he was with the club. But in the 1952-53 Scottish Cup he was a man inspired. When he put Celts 3-2 up at Brockville it was his eighth strike in the tournament that season.

Any hopes of a Falkirk fightback ended when keeper **Archie McFeat** had to stretchered off the pitch. Defender **Joe McDonald** took over in goal but with the Bairns down to ten men all they could hope for was to prevent Celtic from scoring again. This they managed to do but with Celtic triumphing 3-2 Falkirk were left only with memories of a marvellous match, a new record crowd and receipts of £2,510.

It was April 4th before Falkirk were back in action at Brockville when they met Motherwell. By then they were third bottom of the league, a point clear of relegation but having played more games than their rivals. A battling performance gave them a 2-1 win.

Buoyed by the epic against Celtic and starved of a home match for six weeks a better than expected crowd of 14,000 saw this game.

The Bairns have now departed their ancient home and have finally taken up residence at the new Falkirk Stadium. At the time of writing this book the record for the new ground was 4,491 for a 0-0 draw with St Mirren in a league game on October 23rd 2004.

This though is one record which is sure to be beaten in the near future now that Falkirk are in the SPL and their ground now has 6,100 seats.

FORFAR ATHLETIC

v Rangers, Scottish Cup Second Round, February 7th 1970
Attendance: 10,780

Forfar Athletic: Phillip, McKenzie, Sime, Knox, Milne, Fyfe, Wyles, May, Waddell, Mackle, Stewart

Memories of Rangers debacle at Berwick in 1967 were still fresh when these two teams were pulled out of the draw together and Forfar harboured dreams that lightning may, after all, strike twice.

Rangers had visited Forfar before, notably in the Scottish Cup when they won a hard-fought tie 3-1 in front of the then Station Park record crowd of 9,813.

Rangers may have been living in the shadow of Jock Stein's Celtic but Ibrox legend **Willie Waddell** had taken charge just two months earlier and the new manager's enthusiasm for the task of restoring former glories had rubbed off on his players. Rangers had won eight of their nine games under Waddell's tutelage with the other a draw at Celtic Park. Forfar came into the tie having lost their last three league matches and had reverted to their usual position in the lower reaches of Division Two.

Come the day and a gathering of 10,780 assembled at Station Park, easily the biggest in Forfar's history. It was the first and last time that ground saw a five-figure crowd in attendance.

Forfar set out to frustrate Rangers attacks and they succeeded – for all of eight minutes. That was how long it took for **Alex MacDonald** to get his name on the scoresheet.

But at 1-0 the Loons still had a chance. They repelled Rangers constant forays until the 22nd minute when **Colin Stein** fired the Gers two ahead. After that the floodgates opened. **Andy Penman** added a third six minutes later, **Kai Johansen** scored with a penalty two minutes after that and three minutes from the interval Rangers skipper **John Greig** made it five.

Rangers played the second half at walking pace. **Greig** scored again and **Sandy Jardine** rubbed further salt into Forfar's wounds when he wrapped up the scoring to leave the result 7-0 to the visitors.

Forfar's next home match was three weeks later when they recovered some pride with a 2-0 win against local rivals Brechin City, watched by a more modest crowd of 616.

If Rangers or any other team ever fill Station Park again the numbers needed to do so have been much reduced. Forfar Athletic's home of 120 years now operates with a maximum capacity of 5,177.

GRETNA

v Dundee United, Scottish Cup Third Round, January 17th 2005
Attendance: 3,000

Gretna: Mathieson, Birch (Smith 82), Irons, Aitken, McQuilken, Baldacchino (Prokas 34), McGuffie, Gilfillan, Skelton, Bingham, Deuchar

Gretna had played in English football for over half a century before being elected to the Scottish League in 2002. After a couple of seasons spent adjusting to the Scottish game they took the Third Division by storm in 2004-05. Backed financially by club owner Brooks Mileson, Gretna attracted players of the calibre of David Bingham and Kenny Deuchar to their Raydale Park home.

By the turn of the year promotion was almost a formality and the club turned their attention to the Scottish Cup. A third round pairing with Dundee United had all the ingredients for an upset. Gretna had won every match at home, United had yet to win away. Their under-fire manager Ian McCall was returning to the part of the country he grew up in. Gretna's veteran defender Davie Irons – at 43 the oldest player in British football – had actually gone to school alongside McCall's older brother.

Mileson guaranteed to meet all ticket costs himself so that fans could attend free and Gretna erected a temporary stand to take their capacity to 3,000. But when the great day dawned it did so to atrocious weather as Scotland was gripped by the worst winter storms for many years. The march was postponed.

The weather was still foul but had relented enough to permit the tie to go ahead nine days later and the SPL side were intent on turning Gretna's big occasion into an anti-climax. They scored after just three minutes and added a second four minutes later. With only twenty minutes played, a penalty put United three ahead and the tie appeared to be over.

A second spot-kick award nine minutes from the break gave the Tayside team the chance to further emphasise the gulf in class but when keeper **David Mathieson** dived full-length to keep out **Mark Wilson's** attempt it served instead to inspire a Gretna fightback. They began to carve out chances of their own and when, after 41 minutes, a **Bryan Gilfillan** effort was blocked there was **Kenny Deuchar** – a doctor by profession – prescribing his own medicine for the home support by knocking in the rebound.

Almost immediately a chaotic series of refereeing decisions culminated with Gretna coming right back into the game. **Deuchar** found the net for a second time but whistler Charlie Richmond looked to have given United a free-kick, then signalled a goal before finally pointing to the penalty spot. **Mark Birch** gleefully scored from the spot to make it 3-2 at half-time.

Ten minutes into the second half and a **Stevie Crawford** lob gave United their fourth and once again Gretna looked beaten. But the Third Division team refused to give up. **Gavin Skelton** smashed home a thunderbolt shot after 62 minutes to make it 4-3 and Raydale Park exploded with delight.

It was Gretna, chasing the equaliser, who finished the stronger but the SPL side had just enough experience to keep the home side at bay and narrowly book their passage into the fourth round.

It had been a mighty effort and one well worthy of a record gate. But doubts remain over the size of the crowd. Gretna posted a maximum of 3,000 with the SFA but sceptics pointed out that

with the match being played on a stormy Monday evening and a travelling support diminished both by the timing and their own side's poor performances that a full house seemed unlikely.

The match report in The Scotsman, while accepting the 3,000 figure, said 'It was disappointing to observe that many ticket holders had stayed away, though hardly surprising given the adverse conditions and the unfamiliar scheduling.'

Gretna's previous best was 2,307 against Rochdale in the English FA Cup in 1991 and without the temporary stand their usual capacity is just 2,200 although plans are in place to develop the ground. Until they do so they will remain a statistical oddity – a team whose best gate was in the Scottish Cup and their second best in its English equivalent.

HAMILTON ACADEMICAL

v Hearts, Scottish Cup Third Round, March 3rd 1937
Attendance: 28,690

Hamilton Academical: Morgan, Wallace, Scott, Cox, Thomson, Jarvie, King, Gardiner, Wilson, Harrison, McNee

Anyone who ever visited Hamilton's old Douglas Park ground with around 3-4,000 in it will testify that number made for a good atmosphere. Imagine then the same setting with close to 30,000. It seems impossible that such a number ever crammed in to the ground but that's what happened on a Wednesday afternoon in 1937.

In 1936-37 Hamilton were comfortable in mid-table and this tie with third-placed Hearts represented an attractive prospect with the winners sure to be one of the more fancied sides left in the tournament.

In the pre-floodlit era it was common for midweek matches to be played in the afternoon and often, attendances suffered as a result. But for as keenly anticipated a clash as this, supporters could usually find a reason to escape from work.

The Hearts supporters played their part in boosting the crowd too. Six special trains, packed to standing room only left Edinburgh for Hamilton helping to swell the number present to a record-busting 28,690. The barriers broke in two parts of the ground but fortunately there were only a few minor injuries sustained by supporters.

And it was the Hearts followers who had most to cheer once the game got under way. The visitors were well on top and after a string of near-misses Hearts eventually took the lead in 34 minutes and held it comfortably till half-time.

Hamilton began to come more into things in the second period but were unable to give their star player **David Wilson** any decent chances. **Wilson** was one of the most prolific goalscorers in Scottish football history and was the leading marksman in the country this season.

Midway through the half **Wilson** was the link man in a move which started with inside-right **Gardiner** and ended with left-winger **McNee** scoring the equaliser.

Hamilton were in the ascendancy now and the same trio combined to lethal effect in the 75th minute with move culminating in a glorious rising shot from **McNee** which left the keeper with no chance. 2-1 to the Accies and no further scoring meant celebrations for Accies supporters.

Oddly enough Hamilton's next home game in the league was against Hearts. Fewer travelled from Edinburgh for that game and home fans were none too keen either. Just seventeen days after the cup tie Hamilton demolished Hearts 5-1 with only 6,000 watching.

Hamilton's modern New Douglas Park with its 5,396 all-seated capacity would fall short of holding that size of crowd. The current record is the 3,543 who turned out to see Accies' first match back in the First Division when they lost 1-0 to Partick Thistle on August 21st 2004.

HEART OF MIDLOTHIAN

V Rangers, Scottish Cup Third Round, February 13th 1932
Attendance: 53,396

Hearts: Harkness, Anderson, King, Massie, J Johnston, Bennie, R Johnstone, White, Battles, Smith, Murray

The Great War devastated Hearts. The Edinburgh club lost many players through death or injury and it took many years for them to recover. As a consequence a club that was on the brink of smashing the Old Firm duopoly in 1914 was forced to take a back seat for much of the 1920s.

By the early 1930s Tynecastle was starting to buzz again. The club had purchased the ground and, like many new home owners, set about improving and extending it. The capacity stood at just under 56,000 when this game was played.

It was a vital game for both clubs. It had been 26 years since Hearts had last won the Scottish Cup and this was a wonderful chance to show that they could again rival the Old Firm.

For Rangers, the league title, which had been their private property for the past five seasons, was slipping away and the Scottish Cup represented their only real opportunity for silverware.

So it was a keenly anticipated contest which encouraged a crowd of 53,396 (100 fewer than is sometimes stated) to roll up to Tynecastle. Although theoretically 2,500 below capacity the gates had to be shut before kick-off.

Hearts gave as good as they got for the first quarter of an hour but were left chasing the game when Rangers scored after fifteen minutes. Undeterred, Hearts put Rangers on the rack, forcing them onto the defensive, ultimately winning a penalty.

The usually reliable **Alex Massie** missed the spot-kick but in the crush to see the kick taken, one of the barriers gave way and hundreds of supporters tumbled onto the pitch. One contemporary account claimed, 'From the stands it appeared certain that serious physical damage had been caused to many of the hemmed in spectators.' Although 29 supporters needed medical attention, only two were taken to hospital and their injuries weren't too serious.

The missed penalty seemed to take the sting out of Hearts efforts and matters were compounded in the second half when left-back **Bob King** was sent off.

Rangers held on to their narrow lead and at full-time a number of Hearts fans, angry at King's dismissal, ran onto the field and made a bee-line for the referee. The unfortunate official had to be protected from harm by Hearts manager **Willie McCartney** who shielded him to the safety of the dressing room.

Hearts next home game was two weeks later when champions-elect Motherwell came calling. A 1-0 win gave 'Well two more precious points in their championship chase. There were 23,074 present. A full 30,000 down on the Rangers game but a respectable crowd all the same.

Tynecastle was renovated in the 1990s and with an all-seated capacity of 17,700 can't hold the crowd for the Motherwell match let alone the Rangers game.

Because Tynecastle no longer met UEFA requirements, Hearts took their UEFA Cup campaign in 2004-05 to Murrayfield where they attracted crowds in excess of 25,000, proving that supporters will still turn out in numbers to see a successful Hearts team.

HIBERNIAN

V Hearts, Scottish League Division One, January 2nd 1950
Attendance: 65,850

Hibernian: Younger, Shaw, Cairns, Combe, Paterson, Buchanan, Smith, Johnstone, Reilly, Turnbull, Ormond

It's a familiar story in Scottish football. At New Year in a certain Scottish city the top two teams in the league meet for their traditional derby game before the biggest crowd of the day. As the 1940s gave way to the 1950s it was no different. Except that on January 2nd 1950 the city was Edinburgh and the top two teams were Hibs and Hearts!

Hibernian had emerged during wartime as the chief challengers to Rangers and their championship victory in 1948 was only the second outwith the Old Firm since 1904. Hearts hadn't enjoyed similar success but a victory over Celtic on Hogmanay 1949 saw them sneak ahead of Rangers into second place on goal average, four points behind Hibs.

Edinburgh, which had already benefited from the massive upswing in crowds in the post-war era, prepared itself for the biggest match of the season, basking in its new and hard-won limelight. Hibs, having won every game at Easter Road thus far, were favourites.

New Year revelry soon came to an end though as the 65,850 people shoehorned inside Easter Road struggled to find a decent vantage point. The gates were closed before kick-off. Inside the ground some people struggled for breath as schoolboys were passed down to the bottom of the terraces and then onto the track. As the crowd spilled over onto the pitch mounted policemen drove them back to the jam-packed terraces. More than fifty fans were stretchered out and given emergency treatment in a nearby school. One man collapsed and later died.

When the game got under way Hibs were first to strike, **Gordon Smith** giving them the lead. Such was their dominance that there was general agreement in the press box that the Hi-bees would have been four up in the first half had it not been for the brilliance of **Jimmy Brown** in the visitors goal.

Hearts came more into it after the break with their midfield winning the tackles. With 52 minutes played **Alfie Conn** grabbed the equaliser. Hibs may have boasted the 'Famous Five' of **Gordon Smith, Bobby Johnstone, Lawrie Reilly, Eddie Turnbull** and **Willie Ormond** but Hearts had a reply in the equally talented if outnumbered 'Terrible Trio' of **Alfie Conn, Willie Bauld** and **Jimmy Wardhaugh** and it was the last-named of these who put the Tynecastle team ahead, a lead they never looked like losing.

2-1 it stayed. Their greatest rivals had spoilt Hibs' record-breaking day. The Daily Record claimed Hibs had 'lost at midfield'.

In fact it was an incredible day for crowds. East Fife also set their record gate and over 370,000 watched the 16 league games. The AVERAGE 'A' Division gate was 35,000 and 'B' Division's

average was almost 11,500.

Hibs' next home game saw them return to winning ways with a 4-1 victory over Stirling Albion five days later, watched by an excellent attendance of 27,000.

Easter Road is now an all-seated ground capable of holding 17,458. It would take almost four full houses to equal the record set over half a century ago. Hibs' achievements of that era have not been forgotten though with one of the new stands behind the goal named after the 'Famous Five.'

INVERNESS CALEDONIAN THISTLE

v Celtic, Scottish Premier League, March 16th 2005
Attendance: 7,045

Inverness Caledonian Thistle: Brown, Tokely, Dods, Munro, Golabek, Hart, Duncan (Black 89), McBain, Wilson, Bayne (Fatai 78), Juanjo (Prunty 72)

The Highland League had been established back in 1893 but it was over a century later before any of its clubs were admitted to the Scottish League. And when the opportunity arose, as it did in 1994, there was a price to pay. In order to guarantee a place in the league for the Highland capital, two of Inverness's three clubs decided to merge.

It was a decision which caused much anguish to supporters of both Inverness Caledonian and Inverness Thistle and which still rankles with some to this day. But the die was cast and the new club quickly began to make a name for itself in its new surroundings.

ICT progressed rapidly through the ranks and established themselves as a side to be feared in the knockout tournaments. In the Scottish Cup in 2000 they pulled off one of the biggest shocks in the tournament's history by beating Celtic 3-1 at Parkhead, an event which prompted a famous headline in the Scottish edition of The Sun: 'SuperCaleyGoBallisticCelticAreAtrocious'.

Nor was this success a one-off. ICT have reached the last four of the Scottish Cup twice in recent seasons and have taken the scalps of Hearts (at Tynecastle) and Celtic again (this time at home) for good measure.

In 2003-04 they won the First Division but had to endure an agonising wait before their promotion to the SPL was confirmed. The Highlanders' ground was well short of the 10,000 seats then required for the top flight and it was only after agreeing to use Aberdeen's Pittodrie for their home games that their position among the elite was secured.

With a round trip of over 200 miles in prospect for every 'home' match few gave much for their chances of survival and with just one win in their opening ten games ICT looked certainties for the drop. But gradually the Highlanders found their feet in the big time. They began to pick up points before being hit by another crushing blow when manager John Robertson departed to take over at Hearts.

Undaunted, they appointed **Craig Brewster** as player-manager and the new boss picked up where Robertson left off. Finally they got a break from the authorities in January 2005 when they were permitted to play the remainder of their home fixtures at their Caledonian Stadium. Their twelfth 'home' match was their first in Inverness as top-flight football arrived in the Highlands for the first time. ICT celebrated with victory against Dunfermline and followed that up by beating high-flying Hibs.

Their third game in Inverness was

against defending champions Celtic and despite being played on a Wednesday night in front of live TV cameras Highland fans tuned out in force. Theoretically the ground's capacity was 6,280 – just a couple of hundred above the SPL's revised minimum. In practice supporters found whatever vantage point they could as a total of 7,045 attended, almost 800 more than ICT's previous best of 6,290 set against Aberdeen in the Scottish Cup in 2000.

Caley Thistle had climbed to eighth in the table. With four wins and two draws in their last six (including taking a point at Ibrox) they were Scotland's form side and their confidence was expressed within a minute of kick-off as **Roy McBain** struck a shot from thirty yards to test Rab Douglas in the Celtic goal.

But for most of the first half they were on the back foot. Sorely missing the guile of their injured player-manager they nevertheless put up a splendid rearguard action, restricting Celtic to long-range efforts which rarely troubled keeper **Mark Brown**. It was goalless at the interval as ICT left the field to the cheers of their fans.

Celtic were more dangerous after the break but Caley Thistle held firm until the 63rd minute when Celtic's Aiden McGeady demonstrated some close control inside the penalty area before slipping a pass through to Craig Bellamy whose shot beat Brown at his near post.

Still the game Highlanders battled away with **Barry Wilson** firing just over the bar from twenty yards. But with just six minutes remaining hopes of salvaging a point were dashed when **Ross Tokely** fouled Bellamy inside the area. Alan Thompson sent Brown the wrong way from the penalty spot to seal a 2-0 win for Celtic.

Craig Brewster summed it up post-match

when he said, 'We competed well in the first half but in the second we got a bit of a lesson.' Even so it was a demonstration of how far ICT had progressed that they were disappointed to lose at home to the Scottish champions. The club had done enough in their first season in the top league to suggest that the famous Highland hospitality stopped when the game started. Inverness looked likely to be a tough venue for visitors for many years to come.

Both constituent parts of the merged club had their own proud pasts and their biggest crowds came in the Scottish Cup. For **Inverness Thistle** it was January 30th 1954 when this side, MacFarlane, Christie, Nimmo, Mackintosh, Jack, Hendry, Grant, Mackenzie, Mitchell, Gallacher, Lytham, took on a Hamilton Accies team then in the 'A' Division in a first round tie.

Thistle took the lead on the stroke of half-time but fell behind in the second half. They squared the game at 2-2 only for Accies to go ahead once more. With three minutes remaining the Highlanders equalised once again to secure a famous draw in front of 6,000 fans at their Kingsmills ground. They were defeated 3-1 in the Douglas Park replay but they were indeed as the press noted somewhat patronisingly 'eleven glorious hielan' laddies.'

Inverness Caledonian also had many glorious battles against league sides in cup ties at their Telford Street ground. Sadly their record gate wasn't one of them. A stirring win over Stenhousemuir sent them into the last sixteen in 1958 where they met Motherwell on March 1st.

Robertson, Baillie, Neville, Bolt, McGillivray, Christie, McBeath, Campbell, Clyne, Chisholm and Munro were the men sent to do battle on behalf of the

Highlands and for the first 40 minutes the honours were even before Motherwell snatched two late goals to lead 2-0 at the break. After the interval Motherwell turned the screw, running out 7-0 winners before a crowd of 9,370.

KILMARNOCK

v Rangers, Scottish Cup Quarter-Final, March 10th 1962
Attendance: 35,995

Kilmarnock: McLaughlan, Richmond, Watson, Davidson, Toner, Beattie, Brown, Black, Kerr, Sneddon, McIlroy

The late 1950s and early 1960s had seen the emergence of Kilmarnock as a power in the land. Manager **Willie Waddell's** team were always in the forefront of the chase for honours but never quite managed to win any. A succession of losing finals and second places earned them the title of Scotland's champion runners-up.

Their Scottish Cup campaign of 1962 couldn't have got off to a better – or easier – start. A first round bye followed by a trip to Brechin and a visit from Ross County, then a Highland League side, allowed them to rack up thirteen goals in two games. The feeling was there that if only they could beat Rangers the Scottish Cup would be within their grasp for the first time since 1929.

Interest in the game was immense. Every single one of the 36,500 tickets printed was quickly snapped up including the allocation of 7,000 sent to Ibrox. Of course not everyone who buys a ticket in advance can guarantee getting to the game and by the time this one kicked off there were 505 ticket holders missing, leaving 35,995 inside Rugby Park.

The home fans found their voice first when **Hugh Brown** dispossessed **Jim Baxter** and crossed for **Andy Kerr** to plant a diving header past **Billy Ritchie** in the Rangers goal to give Killie the lead after just eight minutes.

Kerr, one of the most prolific scorers in the game, spurned several opportunities to settle the tie including heading over from close range and settling for a speculative shot when a more productive pass looked on.

Killie playmaker **Davie Sneddon** was the most influential player on the park, outshining even Baxter. But it was a Sneddon tackle on **Ian McMillan** on the edge of the area which saw a penalty awarded just before half-time. Ayrshireman **Eric Caldow** sent McLaughlan the wrong way to take the teams to the dressing rooms at 1-1.

Sixteen minutes into the second half Rangers took the lead with a move in which the ball was touched just four times. Ritchie's clearance found **Ralph Brand** who moved it on to winger **Davie Wilson**. He laid it off to **McMillan** who blasted home from twenty yards.

The Ayrshire team came storming back. With twelve minutes left Sneddon set up **Bertie Black** and the striker fired past Ritchie to equalise.

With just seven minutes remaining and thoughts turning to a replay, **McMillan** demonstrated the full range of trickery in his arsenal, setting off on a solo run, weaving past defenders when he could, going through them when he had to and finishing with an unstoppable shot.

As Killie surged forward in search of another equaliser a Rangers breakaway led to **Brand** scoring two minutes from time to make the final score 4-2 – a result that looked a lot more convincing than it actually was.

Kilmarnock returned to league duty and seven days later Rugby Park was a much quieter place as Killie struggled back from a goal behind to beat bottom club Stirling Albion 2-1. The Scottish Cup hangover didn't just affect their players. They were watched by the lowest crowd of the season. There were just 4,671 present.

Having accumulated nine 'silver medals' in the course of seven years, Kilmarnock finally made the breakthrough in 1964-65 when they won the Scottish League Championship.

It wasn't until 1997 that they finally got their hands on the Scottish Cup again. By then the days of 30,000-plus crowds at Rugby Park lay long in the past and the ground had been transformed into its modern incarnation as an all-seater, holding 18,128.

That's only half of what it used to hold but Rugby Park is the fifth biggest ground in Scotland and the largest outside Glasgow and Aberdeen.

LIVINGSTON

v Celtic, Scottish Premier League, August 18th 2001
Attendance: 10,024

Livingston: Sanchez Broto, Hart, Bollan, Rubio, Andrews, Wilson (Lowndes), Fernandez (Tosh), Bingham, Quino, Xausa (Anderson), Lovell

For twenty years they were the club formerly known as Ferranti Thistle until they became the club formerly known as Meadowbank Thistle. Livingston's league history – no matter their choice of nomenclature – has been a chequered one.

Admitted controversially to the league in 1974, they were viewed as cannon fodder by their opposition. Not to mention resentment by ambitious Highland League clubs who felt that one of their number should have been given the nod.

Despite the sad history of failure of other Edinburgh teams like St Bernard's, Leith Athletic and Edinburgh City to maintain league membership, Meadowbank not only survived but also prospered.

They finished second in the First Division in 1988 but were denied promotion through reconstruction. But their place in the grand scheme of things was put into sharp perspective when supporters were prevented from using the main stand on a freezing winter's day because a cat show taking place under the stand had priority.

Little wonder then that they seized the chance to change names again and also location by moving to Livingston. Even this was controversial as their small but dedicated band of supporters were implacably opposed to the move. The club made its intentions clear by changing name before they even moved out of Edinburgh.

The move brought the success they sought as they moved up the divisions, reaching the SPL in 2001.

While their success had been rapid it wasn't universally welcomed. To many, Livingston, with their name changes, their flit from Edinburgh and their policy of buying in continental players on exorbitant salaries while failing to bring players through from the ranks represented much of what was wrong with Scottish football in the twenty first century.

Neutrals should have loved them. Rising from the third to the top inside five years with Livingston becoming the first new town (as well as the first New Town) in Scotland to welcome top-flight football

since Stirling in 1949 should, in theory, have made them everyone's 'second' team.

Instead there was suspicion as supporters were fearful of what might happen to their own clubs if it was so easy to up sticks and change name and location. This loathing found expression in the commonly used epithet 'Franchise FC' hurled at Livvy.

This day they out up the shutters so effectively that the only item of note – the size of the crowd of 10,024 apart – was that ex-Ranger **Gary Bollan** was sent off as Livingston obtained their second 0-0 draw against the Old Firm within a fortnight.

It wasn't pretty but it was effective. When they returned for the next home game they defeated Dundee United 2-0 before a crowd of 6,107 and recorded their fourth clean sheet in six matches. Though this was only the second of those games they had managed to score in themselves.

This style allowed them to qualify for Europe at the first attempt but their introduction to the continental scene left a lot to be desired as they struggled to an away goals win over a team from Liechtenstein before being drubbed in Austria in the next round.

Livvy have one claim to fame that can never be taken away from them. They were the first side to set their club attendance record at an SPL fixture.

MONTROSE

v Dundee, Scottish Cup Quarter-Final,
March 17th 1973
Attendance: 8,983

Montrose: Whisker, Thomson, Martin, O'Donnell, D'Arcy, Livingstone (Guthrie), Barr, Lowe, Third, Johnston, Cramond

For Montrose FC the 1970s were simply the 'good old days.' The Gable Endies had reached this stage of the Scottish Cup on only two previous occasions.

Hard-fought replay victories over Clyde and Hamilton set up this quarter-final meeting with Dundee. The Dens Parkers were a strong outfit in the early 1970s and it was clear from the moment the draw was made that Montrose's previous best gate of 6,389 – against Celtic in the Scottish Cup in 1939 – would be under threat.

If ever a tie could be described as David v Goliath, this was it. Dundee had a team with international experience. Four of their eleven were Scotland caps and they also fielded ex-Links Parker **Gordon Wallace** – one of the game's top strikers.

Taking on this formidable force were Montrose's collection of part-timers. Builder, electrician, painter, fork lift operator, machine setter, Montrose's eleven worked in various jobs during the day. But they were talented too. Players like **Les Barr** and **Dennis D'Arcy** were respected throughout the game as two of the most resolute defenders in the land. Up front, **Harry Johnston**, **Gordon Cramond**, **Bobby Livingstone** and **Brian Third** formed a potent attack.

Montrose were a well-run club and used the match programme to make a few barbed comments about the state of the game, noting 'we are comfortably off and pay our bills every month' – a statement many clubs wish they could make today. And in a riposte to those who advocated cutting the smaller clubs adrift from the league 'we apologise for our existence and continue to give our thousand or so faithful fans somewhere to go on a Saturday afternoon.'

On this particular Saturday afternoon there were 8,983 in their ground – easily beating the previous best – and although the Gable Endies fought valiantly, the gap in class was both too big and too apparent. **Gordon Wallace** and **Jocky Scott** scored the goals which virtually sealed the tie before the break.

In the second half **Scott** scored again and **John Duncan** bagged one too while a **Les Barr** penalty put a more respectable sheen on the final result as Dundee strolled to a 4-1 victory.

Two weeks later Montrose were back in action at Links Park, defeating Queen of the South 2-1 in the league before a much smaller crowd of 936. With Links Park now reduced to a capacity of 3,292 this is one record that will never be broken.

MORTON

v Celtic, Scottish League Division One,
April 29th 1922
Attendance: 23,500

Morton: Edwards, McIntyre, R Brown, Gourlay, Wright, McGregor, McNab, McKay, French, A Brown, McMinn

It's unusual for any club's last game of the season to pull in its biggest crowd. Rare indeed for that crowd to be the best in all their history. But that's what happened at Cappielow on this day.

Morton were an average league team at the time but in the Scottish Cup they had been inspired. Two weeks before this game they had beaten Rangers to win the trophy for the first, and so far only, time.

The success took the Greenock club aback. Their anticipation of victory was so low that they hadn't even bothered to make arrangements to put the trophy on display in Greenock or to even think about a possible replay and had made a commitment to play a friendly in the north-east of England 48 hours after the Final!

So it was that the famous old Scottish Cup came to be paraded through the streets of Hartlepool, serenaded by the town band as the victorious team marched from the railway station to their hotel.

Not only was this the last fixture of the season, it was their first home Saturday match since their triumph. There was still a carnival atmosphere in the town and their fans were determined to turn out in numbers to show their appreciation of their heroes.

For Celtic the stakes simply couldn't be higher. They led the league by a single point from rivals Rangers. Given the Bhoys far superior goal average they needed a draw to win the championship.

Mix those ingredients together and you have the recipe for a record crowd. All told there were 23,500 inside Cappielow at the kick-off. The Morton team contained ten of the eleven Hampden heroes. Odd man out was centre-forward **Jock Buchanan** who had replaced the injured **George French** in the Final.

French returned for this game to receive the cheers of the fans who knew that without his contribution there would have been no trophy in the Cappielow board room. **French** was Morton's leading scorer with 37 goals, 28 in the league and nine cup, a remarkable tally at a time when there had to be THREE defenders between the forward and the goal in order to be onside.

While Morton were carefree, lackadaisical even, Celtic were a tensed-up, nervous side, acutely aware of what they stood to gain – and lose. The tension spread to the terraces and the gala occasion was marred by fighting amongst the fans which spread to the field of play as battling supporters spilled onto the pitch. The situation was further inflamed by the presence of banners among the Celtic fans in support of Sinn Fein.

There are those who believe football's problems with violence started sometime between the first manned space flight and the introduction of colour television. They're wrong and there are all too many sad examples like this one to prove it.

Players from both teams attempted to quell the rioting fans. Once order was restored and the game restarted, **Alfie Brown** gave Morton the lead after 37 minutes and they retired to the dressing room ahead.

Telephones were a luxury in those days and radio was in its infancy. The quickest and most effective means of communication was carrier pigeon. Whether they heard by word or bird is unclear but news filtered through that Rangers were drawing at half-time against Clyde. If the scores stayed the same Celtic would win the league.

It's dangerous of course to rely on your rivals not to win and Celtic came out with all guns blazing after the break. Morton held firm until, with only six minutes remaining, **Andy McAtee's** header levelled the scores. With Rangers drawing too both Morton and Celtic could leave the field at the final whistle with honour intact and honours unpacked. Celtic went off to pick up the championship while Morton stayed home to polish the Scottish Cup.

Morton's next home game wasn't until the start of the following season when an excellent crowd of 10,000 saw them beat Motherwell 2-0.

In the intervening years Morton have recorded several gates of over 20,000, coming close to but never quite matching the record. Today, the most Cappielow can accommodate is 11,589 and this is yet another example of a club and ground record which will remain in perpetuity.

MOTHERWELL

v Rangers, Scottish Cup Quarter-Final Replay, March 12th 1952
Attendance: 35,632

Motherwell: Johnston, Kilmarnock, Shaw, Cox, Paton, Redpath, Sloan, Humphries, Kelly, Watson, Aitkenhead

If there ever was a 'Golden Age' of Scottish football then surely it was in the first twenty years or so after the restart in 1946. If that term can be further defined and distilled into a single season then there are only two real contenders. One is at the end of this period, 1966-67, with Scottish clubs in the ascendant in Europe and the national team triumphant at Wembley. The other is 1951-52.

Many non-Old Firm fans of a certain vintage will plump for this season. It was the first time that all of the game's three major domestic honours resided elsewhere than Glasgow and gates were still riding high. No fewer than FOUR clubs set their all-time record attendances in the Scottish Cup in 1952 inside just eighteen days. This match saw Motherwell join Arbroath, Queen of the South and Airdrieonians in so doing.

The story of Motherwell and the Scottish Cup over the preceding two decades was one of agonising heartbreak. Four times in all they had travelled with hope and confidence to the Scottish Cup Final and on each and every occasion they had returned defeated.

Another Motherwell campaign seemed destined to end in failure when they trailed 2-0 to Rangers at Ibrox. But the Steelmen fought back to earn a draw and force Rangers to make the trip to Fir Park the following Wednesday afternoon.

Their ground had held over 30,000 on many occasions but the crowd of 35,632 this day exceeded all others. They saw a fiercely-fought match. Motherwell were in control from the start. It was indeed 'one way traffic'. But it was Rangers, very much against the run of play, who took the lead when **Willie Thornton** scored after eleven minutes and despite all Motherwell's pressure that was the way it stayed till half-time.

This Motherwell team weren't going to let a one goal deficit stand in their way. After all if they could come back from two down away from home, what was a mere goal at Fir Park?

Under a stream of constant pressure, Rangers fabled defence wilted when **George Young** handled inside the penalty area. **Johnny Aitkenhead** slotted the spot-kick home to send the home fans wild.

The usually dependable **Young** was at fault again nine minutes from time when his opposite number **Andy Paton**, that rarity in any era – the skilful, ball-playing centre-half – beat him to send off a pass to **Aitkenhead** whose cross was met by **Tommy Sloan**. Sloan sent the ball back into the penalty area where **Wilson Humphries** side-footed it into the net to give Motherwell the lead.

Now it was Rangers' turn to fight like furies and in the dying seconds a goal-bound **Thornton** header was met with a fine save by **Jim Johnstone**. That was the end of the action. Motherwell's record crowd had witnessed a famous triumph.

As chance would have it, Motherwell's next home game in the league was also against Rangers. The Steelmen weren't entirely safe from relegation in what was a highly competitive league. Although the crowd was smaller, the 22,000 present still constituted a perfectly good attendance and they saw 'Well complete a 'double' with another 2-1 win which hoisted the home side towards mid-table and dented Rangers' declining title hopes.

Motherwell's magical run wasn't over yet. They won through in an epic semi-final struggle with Hearts ro reach yet another Scottish Cup Final, Motherwell finally laid their bogey to rest with an emphatic 4-0 win over Dundee in front of 136,495 fans – the largest crowd ever for a game not involving Scotland or one of the Old Firm.

Fir Park has seen some big gates since those days and the Scottish Cup has returned to Motherwell. But as an all-seater ground a full house these days means a more modest tally of something approaching the modern 13,757 capacity.

PARTICK THISTLE

v Rangers, Scottish League Division One, February 18th 1922
Attendance: 49,838

Partick Thistle: Campbell, Struthers, Bulloch, Gibson, Lambie, Harris, Blair, Kinloch, McColl, McMenemy, Salisbury

Partick Thistle are the great survivors of Glasgow football. While Queen's Park remain resolutely amateur, Clyde departed the city for Cumbernauld and Third Lanark vanished altogether, the Jags alone have stayed the course to offer a professional alternative to the Old Firm in Scotland's largest city.

Their position as Glasgow's 'third' club wasn't inevitable nor for a time did it even look possible. For a while Thistle looked like they may go the same way as Cowlairs, Linthouse, Northern and another club named Thistle – all Glaswegian sides whose tenure in the Scottish League proved to be short.

For Thistle struggled to obtain support in Partick. Their last game at their old Meadowside ground drew fewer than 400 supporters. Forced by circumstance to seek pastures new they moved to Maryhill and, while retaining the name of their original residence, it was there that they found success.

Maryhill, in the north-west of Glasgow, was far enough away from the Old Firm's homes to allow Thistle to lay first claim on the hearts and minds of its citizenry. Something that Thirds, Clyde and Queen's, with their closer proximity to the Old Firm, could never do.

Within a few years of taking up residence Thistle were attracting large crowds to their Firhill stadium. In 1912, just three years after moving, they burst through the 40,000 barrier in a Glasgow Cup tie.

1920-21 was, for Thistle, a marvellous season, capped by the club's success in winning the Scottish Cup and the following season gates rose to an average of around 14,500 in the league.

At 49,838 the crowd for this game was a new club and ground record. More than eighty years later only the Old Firm and the Edinburgh duo can claim to have attracted more people to a league match.

Thistle had the better of the exchanges in the first half but were unable to make their superiority count. Rangers came more into it in after the break but they were up against a man inspired in goalkeeper **Kenny Campbell.**

Scottish international Campbell's heroics looked to have earned Thistle a draw until disaster struck with just three minutes remaining. There was a melee in the Jags goalmouth and the keeper was unsighted when **Alan Morton** prodded home the only goal of the game. It was a bitter disappointment for the massive home support.

Thistle bounced back immediately. Seven days later they faced Bathgate in a Scottish Cup tie at Firhill and won 3-0, before a crowd of 16,000.

Alas, their efforts to retain the national trophy came to an end in the semi-finals, beaten once more by Rangers. This time, at the supposedly 'neutral' venue of Ibrox Park!

Although the Jags remained one of the best supported sides in Scotland they never came anywhere close to upsetting the Old Firm supremacy in the city.

Having remoulded Firhill into an SPL-compliant ground with 10,921 seats and battled back from the brink of financial disaster, they can face the future with a confidence which comes from having been through the hardest of times and survived.

That crowd of 49,838 can never be matched nowadays but it has been bettered in the past. Thistle, like Queen's Park, have a club attendance record which is less than that of their stadium.

On February 25th 1928 Scotland met Northern Ireland at Firhill and a massive **54,723** turned out to watch even though there were no Thistle players in the Scotland team. They saw a game in which the Scots dominated from start to finish yet somehow contrived to lose 1-0.

Only Hampden, Ibrox, Parkhead and Easter Road have held larger attendances.

PETERHEAD

v Raith Rovers, Scottish Cup Fourth Round Replay, February 25th 1987
Attendance: 8,643

Peterhead: Buchan, Wilson (Porter), Donaldson, Jopp, Sievwright, Burke, Walker, Bell (Guyan), Loch, Bain, Fraser

Peterhead's Scottish Cup record was hardly inspiring. In nineteen previous meetings with Scottish League sides they had triumphed just once. So when they were drawn against East Stirlingshire at home in 1986-87 few thought progress was possible.

But Peterhead pulled off a shock 1-0 victory and a 3-1 win away to fellow Highland League team Rothes sent them into the last 32 where they were rewarded with a home tie against three-times Scottish Cup winners Clyde.

The First Division team were expected to take care of Peterhead in short order. But it was Clyde who felt the full brunt of a north-east gale force as the battling Buchan team chalked up a famous 2-0 win before 2,196 fans.

Peterhead were now in the last sixteen of the Scottish Cup for the first time and just 90 minutes away from equalling Elgin City's achievement of 1968. Cup fever began to take hold as the Blue Toon met the Lang Toon when the draw sent them to Kirkcaldy to take on Raith Rovers.

Gary Loch's opening goal brought cheers from the 1,200 Peterhead fans in the crowd of 3,259. But it was the locals who had most to cheer for the rest of the first half as Rovers struck back and reached the interval with a 2-1 lead.

In the second period Peterhead won a penalty when **Jim Bain** was pulled down. All looked lost when **Neil Burke's** spot-kick was turned past the post. But from the corner kick **Ally Bell** rose above everybody to head home the equaliser and bring Raith to Buchan for the replay four days later.

With a home tie against St Mirren awaiting the winners excitement in Peterhead and the surrounding area was palpable as the kick-off approached. The previous ground record of 6,310, set when Celtic visited in 1948, was easily beaten as, somehow, 8,643 bodies managed to squeeze their way into position for the start of the match.

They saw a dreadful start by the home team who found themselves two goals down after just six minutes. But the Blue Toon refused to allow their big day to become a stroll in the park for the Rovers and **Kevin Walker** reduced the leeway. It had little effect though as Raith scored again.

The second half belonged to Peterhead as time and again they took the game to their opponents but with little reward. The crowd remained undaunted and continued to roar on their team. There were just fifteen minutes left when **Walker** ignited a fresh spark of hope by scoring again.

Then with ten minutes on the clock, came the moment that set Peterhead alight as **Jim Bain** rammed in the goal which tied the match at 3-3.

It had been an epic cup-tie but it wasn't over yet. The following Monday the teams met at Arbroath but at last the league team's superior fitness began to tell as Rovers won the second replay 3-0 before a gate of around 6,000 which again included a sizeable contingent from Peterhead.

The Blue Toon did eventually reach the last eight of the Scottish Cup. Airdrieonians, their last sixteen opponents in 2000-01 which was Peterhead's first season as a Scottish League side, were expelled from the competition, giving Peterhead a walkover into the quarter-finals.

They went down 3-1 at Livingston but put up a decent enough fight to impress those watching.

Recreation Park is no more and Peterhead now play at the Balmoor Stadium. The new ground can hold 3,150, including 990 seats, so the club record will stand forever. The best attendance at Balmoor is 2,158. That was the number who saw a friendly with Aberdeen on July 6th 2002. But for a competitive match the record is the 1,693 who watched the 0-0 draw with Albion Rovers on May 3rd 2003 as Peterhead narrowly failed to win promotion from the Third Division.

QUEEN OF THE SOUTH

v Heart of Midlothian, Scottish Cup Third Round, February 23rd 1952
Attendance: 26,552

Queen of the South: Henderson, Sharp, Binning, McBain, Aird, Greenock, Houliston, Rothera, Patterson, Neilson, Oakes

Queen of the South had risen rapidly since joining the Third Division in 1923 and by the time of this match were a well-respected top-flight side.

Queens made good progress in the Scottish Cup this season. They put six past Brechin at Glebe Park then drew away to St Johnstone before winning the Palmerston Park replay.

Hearts were a good team. Third in the table they travelled to Dumfries seven days before the cup tie and drew 1-1 – a result which gave both sides confidence for this match.

The attendance demonstrated the allure of the Scottish Cup. While the league game drew a fine crowd of 12,500, more than twice that many took their places a week later. Palmerston was packed with 26,552 in attendance as the teams did battle. The takings were a record £1,715 16/3.

But Queens were lethargic, slow to the ball, second best at everything and penned into their own half of the field as Hearts ran rampant, firing in shots at will. Perhaps the occasion got the better of the Dumfries team? Certainly the Edinburgh side were more used to playing to packed houses and experience is often a telling factor in these conditions.

At any rate all the pressure came from the team in maroon. But as Hearts failed to capitalise on their control, Queens' fans began to harbour thoughts that their team might make it to the interval unscathed. It was just as these thoughts began to be voiced out loud that the roof fell in on Queens.

With 37 minutes gone Hearts finally opened the scoring and three minutes later struck again to send a shell-shocked Queens to their dressing room two goals down.

The second half started much the same way as the first with Hearts cruising towards a seemingly effortless victory. It was time for a local hero to emerge. **Jackie Oakes** had first signed for Queens back in 1937 and after a successful spell south of the border with Blackburn and Man City Oakes had returned this season to end his playing days at Palmerston Park.

Now aged 32 it was Oakes who brought

Queens back into contention with a screaming shot from the edge of the penalty area after 53 minutes. Just a goal in arrears and with plenty of time on the clock it was the signal for an instant role reversal with Queens pushing forward and Hearts looking ragged on the ropes.

Hearts were experienced enough though to weather the storm and after 73 minutes **Alfie Conn** scored a third goal which put the outcome beyond doubt.

Queens returned to the league. Four days later they beat Dundee 1-0 in front of a much smaller crowd of 5,000.

Palmerston Park no longer resounds to the cheers of such massive crowds. It now holds just 6,412, 3,509 of whom can be seated.

QUEEN'S PARK

v Rangers, Scottish Cup First Round, January 18th 1930
Attendance: 95,772

Queen's Park: RGC Peden, K Campbell, W Wiseman, R Grant, R Gillespie, WS King, J Crawford, JM Dodds, D McLelland, JB McAlpine, GD McKenzie.

Only Rangers can claim a record home attendance greater than that of Queen's Park but the Amateurs biggest gate is not the largest their ground has ever held. It's not even close. In fact it's exactly the 100th biggest crowd Hampden Park has ever held.

That's the price to be paid for having a home ground that's synonymous with the Scotland national side and Scottish and League Cup Finals and semi-finals.

The image most people hold of Queen's Park is of a club gamely battling away watched by a sparse crowd of a few hundred dotted around the national stadium. It wasn't always so. Queen's of course were the progenitors of the Scottish game and were the predominant club before the professional era, winning ten of the first twenty Scottish Cups.

But even in the inter-war period Queen's Park were a respectable power in the land.

It was a remarkable achievement for the strictly amateur club in the late 1920s and early 1930s to hold their own with the professional teams around them. In the seasons leading up to this match the Queen's Park renaissance was in full flow. In 1928 they reached the semi-finals of the Scottish Cup and the next year they finished fifth in the league, scoring 100 goals in the process.

They had a good support too with league gates usually averaging 8,000 – 12,000 a season. And in the Scottish Cup that figure could rise substantially, like when over 65,000 turned up to see them beat Partick Thistle on their run to the last four in 1928.

Not really surprising therefore that this game attracted such a huge crowd nor that it eclipsed all others played that day. 95,772 turned up to see the Spiders take on the Gers.

If they were expecting cavalier football they were disappointed. What should have been an open-ended, attacking occasion became bogged down in trench warfare. For turning the game into a war of attrition the Sunday Mail pointed the finger firmly in one direction. It was, said the paper, 'Rangers' safety first tactics' that had turned this tie into such a dull game.

Queen's Park should have taken that as a compliment. Here were the mighty Rangers, the most expensive, most feared, most successful combination in the land content to play the game away from the danger areas, reduced to

rearguard action and petty fouls in a bid to stop Queen's.

The game suffered though, with the Rangers method condemned as 'spoiling' in the Sunday papers. There were quite a few scholars in the ground and the Sunday Mail opined, 'The students with their gay garb and tricks were the brightest feature of this Hampden cup tie.'

The 1930s definition of 'gay garb' probably isn't quite the same as that of the 21st century!

Supporters were counting down the seconds till half-time came along to rescue them from the monotony when Rangers were awarded a free kick thirty yards out. The ex-Queen's Parker **Alan Morton** gained possession and tried his luck with a shot. It looked like it was going harmlessly past the post when **Bob McPhail** nipped in with a header to give Rangers the lead.

Seven days later the Spiders were back at Hampden facing St Johnstone in the league. They won 3-0 against a backdrop of just 4,500 spectators.

Hampden Park has changed greatly from those days. It's now a UEFA-accredited five-star stadium with seats for 52,025. Queen's Park are still there too, striving hard to preserve their nineteenth century ethos in the modern world.

RAITH ROVERS

v Heart of Midlothian, Scottish Cup Second Round, February 7th 1953
Attendance: 31,306

Raith Rovers: Johnstone, McClure, McNaught, Young, Colville, Leigh, Maule, Kelly, Copland, McIntyre, Penman

In the early 1950s Raith Rovers were developing into a formidable outfit. For several seasons they topped the five-figure mark for average attendances at Stark's Park and there were many fine players for their supporters to enjoy in action. Willie McNaught was an international defender of great versatility who spent over twenty years at Stark's Park. In Ernie Copland Raith possessed one of the most consistent strikers in the game. And Willie Penman was a master craftsman who supplied Copland with ammunition.

Hearts always brought a good travelling support through to Fife and their numbers helped swell the ranks at Stark's Park to 31,306 as the game got under way.

Both sides were hesitant and the only episode of note in the first half-hour came when a Rovers shot hit the woodwork.

After 36 minutes a rare Hearts foray paid off when Willie Bauld put them ahead. Despite much huffing and puffing by both teams no more goals were added and the big crowd departed, lamenting such a poor game.

Writing in the Sunday Mail, the celebrated columnist 'Rex' noted that the crowd figure wouldn't be announced until Monday but he doubted it was a record as there had been no crush and he had noted tickets being handed over to police before the game.

The Stark's Park press box may not be the most lavish such construction but its hidden charms undoubtedly obscured the true extent of the crowd from the reporter's eyes, as the attendance was indeed a new record. It was over a month before Raith played at home again, beating Airdrieonians 3-0 before a (for the times) poor crowd of 8,000.

Stark's Park was given a complete makeover in the 1990s and is now an all-seater with room for 8,473 spectators. Those who can remember the ground before its transition still wonder how on earth over 30,000 supporters ever managed to congregate in such a small space.

RANGERS

v Celtic, Scottish League Division One, January 2nd 1939
Attendance: 118,567

Rangers: Dawson, Gray, Shaw, McKillop, Simpson, Symon, Waddell, Harrison, Thornton, Venters, Kinnear

Glasgow had already witnessed its first big gathering of 1939 before this game took place. Glasgow Cross – the centuries-old traditional venue to see the New Year in – had been discarded in favour of George Square where 50,000 revellers celebrated; unaware it would be the last such peacetime occasion for seven years.

The Glasgow Herald thought that number might be outstripped by the football, saying that 'if the weather conditions are good it is estimated that close on 60,000 spectators will be attracted by this famous "Old Firm" struggle.'

It's often said that newspapers contain half-truths and in this instance the paper got the crowd half-right. The sun shone gloriously and Old Firm fans attended in numbers unprecedented for a League match.

Of course the Old Firm – and the Ne'erday game in particular – have always been associated with big crowds but, by their own high standards, there were times when interest in the fixture flagged. The chief reason for this was Celtic's failure to compete with their rivals for much of the inter-war period.

This resulted in driving attendances down to fewer than 40,000 on occasions. A big crowd by most people's reckoning but not for Scotland's two strongest clubs.

Celtic began to revive in the latter part of the 1930s and had won two of the three previous titles, ensuring an increase in attendances when the old rivals clashed. The last Ne'erday game at Ibrox, in 1937, set a new league record of 94,811. That figure wasn't just beaten this day; it was smashed out of sight.

It wasn't a Scottish record nor was it a record for a club match. But it was a new record for an Old Firm game and for the first time anywhere in the world a six-figure crowd attended a league match. When the counting stopped it had reached the massive total of 118,567.

This figure stayed as an Old Firm record until overtaken by the Scottish Cup Final of May 1963. And in December 1963 it was overtaken as the world record for a league game when over 177,000 saw Fluminense and Flamengo in a Rio State Championship in the Maracana.

Rangers entered the match six points ahead of Celtic who had a game in hand. A Celtic victory would blow the title race wide open. A Rangers triumph would all but confirm the reclamation of the flag.

Rangers were determined not just to retake the title but to avenge a humiliating 6-2 defeat at Parkhead earlier in the season. After all if ever there was a Rangers team that could be described as dyed-in-the-wool bluenoses this was it. Of the starting eleven there were four whose association with the club would go long beyond their playing days. **Davie Kinnear** was on the backroom staff for many years and **Willie Thornton** was assistant manager. But the two who really stood out in the future were **Scot Symon** and **Willie Waddell**, both Rangers

managers in the years ahead and both Ibrox legends to this day.

Rangers' positive attitude, coupled with a catastrophic Celtic selection policy, meant the game was effectively no contest.

Making three changes in personnel and five additional positional alterations too was a risky policy in any circumstances but for an Old Firm game at Ibrox it was plain suicidal. Celtic never got going and Rangers ran the show from start to finish. **Davie Kinnear** and **Alec Venters** scored the goals which gave the home team a 2-1 win which was much more impressive than the deceptively narrow scoreline suggests.

Celtic imploded after this, losing their next two games and fading away from the chase. Rangers' next home game was nine days later when they defeated Arbroath 4-2 to record their sixth successive victory and their twelfth in the last thirteen played.

And how did their supporters demonstrate their loyalty to the team they adored? By staying away in their droves. Only around **5,000** bothered to turn up that afternoon. Even if half the record crowd were Celtic supporters (a doubtful proposition) that still left over 50,000 Rangers fans unaccounted for.

This was one occasion when they chose not to 'follow on.' The title race was virtually over and these supporters had seen many victory processions before. With room for around 120,000 bodies at Ibrox and season tickets the preserve of a small elite, supporters simply picked their games from the fixture menu a la carte. A big variation in crowds could be seen from week to week though the difference was never as wide as it was here.

Amazingly, the aggregate attendance for

Rangers' seven remaining league games after Celtic's visit came to only 107,000 – fewer than had attended just one match!

Rangers strolled on to the inevitable title, finishing eleven points ahead of Celtic – the equivalent of a sixteen-point gap under three points for a win.

Ibrox continued to host huge gates and even burst through the 100,000 barrier three more times but the Ibrox Disaster changed everything. At last spectator safety moved to the head of the agenda as Rangers rebuilt their ground to become the showpiece stadium it is today.

Now capable of seating 50,444 it has fallen behind Celtic Park and remains smaller than Hampden but is still one of the best grounds in Europe.

ROSS COUNTY

v Rangers, Scottish Cup Second Round, February 28th 1966
Attendance: 8,500

Ross County: Sutherland, Borley, Brett, MacNeill, Greig, McMillan, Thomson, McKenzie, Donald, Hosie, Mackay

Highland League Ross County impinged little on the national sporting consciousness prior to the Scottish Cup of 1966. In eight contests with Scottish League clubs they had only a solitary triumph over Dumbarton to their name. Yet by the time they met Rangers they had tripled the number of scalps on their belt.

Their campaign started with their first home win over league opposition when they beat Forfar Athletic 4-3 in a thrilling Victoria Park encounter before 2,945 supporters. That encouraged 800 County fans to make the trek to Alloa by special train in the next round.

They arrived in the Clackmannanshire town only to find the match had been called off. They trudged disappointedly back north but spirits were raised when the draw for the next round gave the winners a home tie with Rangers.

Rejuvenated, the County support set off again, this time in midweek, to see their team knock in the goals once more as they won a terrific tie 5-3 at Recreation Park. In theory they had a game against the mighty Rangers in Dingwall just 48 hours later. In practice they had a bit longer to prepare for the Glaswegians visit as horrendous weather lashed across Scotland. Victoria Park was waterlogged but it wasn't just Dingwall and the Highlands that were affected. Every single Scottish Cup tie scheduled for that day was postponed.

Gradually the weather improved, allowing all the games to be played within the next eleven days bar County's game and the match between Cowdenbeath and St Johnstone. Ironically, the winners of these games were scheduled to meet in the quarter-finals.

The delays did little to diminish anticipation in Dingwall as supporters relished the much-awaited visit from John Greig, Davie Wilson, Willie Johnston and Co. Any trip to the Highlands by one of the Old Firm was a big event and a Scottish Cup tie even more so.

The match was finally re-arranged for the Monday afternoon of February 28th but even that date looked in jeopardy and with the quarter-finals due on the following Saturday, County took drastic action to ensure the game went ahead.

Workmen spent all night removing sodden soil from Victoria Park and laying a covering of peat fibre across the muddy pitch, not finishing till five in the morning. The pitch still took a full forty minutes inspection before being declared playable.

Rangers boss Scot Symon disagreed. He thought it was not only unfit but also downright dangerous and lodged an official objection with match referee JP Barclay. Fortunately, SFA referees supervisor Jack Mowat was taking in the game and he joined Barclay on the pitch for a further nine minutes before finally giving it the go-ahead.

Undeterred by all the fuss and delays the supporters, including a good number of Rangers fans, soon heard that the match was on and turned out in numbers which would have been impressive for many First Division sides on a Monday afternoon in February.

There were around 8,500 present, paying receipts of £2,125 and they saw County get off to a storming start. They won three corners in the first four minutes as Rangers struggled to adjust to the conditions. Crucially, the Ibrox team didn't wilt under this early pressure and gradually began to impose themselves on the game. After 25 minutes Jim Forrest put Rangers ahead. While County were still coming to terms with that loss, George McLean added a second a minute later.

Within the space of those sixty seconds the match altered. From a potential upset it turned into little more than a stroll, as Rangers played out the remaining hour more wary of injury on the dodgy Victoria Park surface than anything County could throw at them. The second half was an anti-climax but the Ross County players and supporters left at the end with heads held high.

Rangers went on to win the Scottish Cup that year. They'd had a scare in the Highlands no doubt but had come through it. Was it ever really feasible that

they, the famous Glasgow Rangers, could seriously have come to grief in the Scottish Cup in a remote footballing backwater at the opposite end of the country? With their reputation?

Next year the draw sent them to Berwick!

As for Ross County they returned to Highland League action, little dreaming that the day would dawn when Scottish League sides made regular visits to Victoria Park.

For the next quarter of a century little was heard of them on a national level. But at the end of the 1980s Ross County re-emerged as a power in the Highlands and victories over League teams in the Scottish Cup, including an astonishing 6-2 win away over Queen of the South, made sure that when the Scottish League expanded its membership in 1994 that County were one of the successful applicants.

Since then they've made a name for themselves in Scottish League football, rising to the First Division and playing in a vastly improved Victoria Park which these days can accommodate 6,900, including 3,000 seated.

ST JOHNSTONE

v Dundee, Scottish Cup Second Round, February 10th 1951
Attendance: 29,972

St Johnstone: Martin, Munro, Blyth, Lindsay, Innes, Pollock, Brydon, McKinlay, Buckley, Malloch, Peat

Demoted by League diktat after the war, St Johnstone had little opportunity to test themselves against the game's leading lights. This was the first occasion a top division side had visited Muirton Park in a cup tie since the outbreak of war.

Still, if the Saints wait had been a long one at least it couldn't have ended with a juicier tie in prospect. Dundee were the undoubted number one team on Tayside. They came into this match lying third in the league while Saints were one place – and one division – lower.

Certainly the tie galvanised the public. Perth had never been noted for football fanaticism. Even in those halcyon post-war days St Johnstone rarely played to more than 6,000. But matches against either of the Dundee teams often reached five figures. This was of a different order entirely as the crowds headed for Muirton swollen by the thousands who had made the journey from Dundee.

The old record of 21,843, set against Aberdeen in 1936, was easily broken as just short of 30,000 entered the ground. Like other grounds of a similar ilk it is difficult for anyone who ever watched a football match at Muirton Park to comprehend that it ever held 29,972 people at a single game.

Yet that was the number in attendance this day and it was the Saints supporters whose roars could be heard the loudest as their heroes took a first minute lead courtesy of **Jackie Malloch**, an ex-Dens Parker.

Dundee were quick to recover though and didn't allow St Johnstone to take a grip on the game. It was, in all respects, an even game from that point until a 28th minute penalty allowed Dundee to draw level.

But just as an early goal had dictated the first half so too did a similar strike determine the second. This time it was Dundee who struck early, within two minutes of the restart to take the lead.

Still, the tie was in the balance and Saints made several attempts to equalise

before Dundee struck again in 66 minutes. At 3-1 they now had some breathing space and saw the game out without further addition to the score. But the match had been a lot closer than the scoreline suggested. Most of the breaks had gone the Dens men's way. As one paper pointed out this had been 'Dundee's day of luck.'

St Johnstone's next game was a 4-2 win over Stirling Albion when the Perth public showed their appreciation of their team's efforts against Dundee by turning up in good numbers. There were 10,500 there that day – a fine crowd for a 'B' Division match.

Muirton Park is gone now and while many St Johnstone fans regard their old ground fondly it certainly didn't bring them any favours when they played Dundee. Not content with ruining St Johnstone's record-breaking day,. Dundee returned there in 1962 to win the Scottish League championship and, in the process, relegate St Johnstone.

Saints waited a long time for revenge but eventually gained it at their new McDiarmid Park home. Built in the late 1980s St Johnstone's ground boasts 10,723 seats and was the first purpose-built all-seater in Scotland.

It saw its biggest crowd on Sunday May 23rd 1999 at the end of the first season of the SPL when Dundee were again the visitors. With a UEFA Cup place at stake, a crowd of 10,545 sat through a nail-biting encounter, There were 72 minutes on the clock before **Paul Kane** scored the only goal of the game to send Saints fans wild. Kane's strike was good enough to secure third place for St Johnstone and bring European football back to Perth after an absence of 28 years.

ST MIRREN

v Celtic, Scottish League Cup Section AA,
August 20th 1949
Attendance: 47,438

St Mirren: Miller, Lapsley, Martin, Crowe,
Telfer, Reid, Burrell, Stewart, Milne,
Deakin, Lesz.

At first glance this is an unlikely
contender for a record crowd. It wasn't a
crucial knockout cup-tie. Neither was it a
vital league game. It had no bearing on
the championship or relegation. There
were no great prizes for the winners and
no disaster lay in store for the losers. It
was, simply, a run-of-the-mill sectional
League Cup game.

It's difficult to understand now just how
fresh and exciting the League Cup
appeared to fans just after the war. But
its sectional format was a novelty in
Scottish football and the competition
was given a further boost this season
with the League itself being delayed until
the League Cup sections had been
completed.

Factor in the inclusion of Rangers in the
section and the fact that Celtic arrived at
Love Street fresh from a thrilling 5-4 win
at Pittodrie and it's easier to understand
why 47,438 spectators jammed into
Love Street this day.

They saw a game in which Celtic
dominated for the opening period
without being able to pierce the Paisley
defence. Yet after twenty minutes they
fell behind. **Johnny Deakin** outsmarted
the Celtic defence at a free kick when he
ghosted past them to put St Mirren
ahead.

Deakin had an unusual claim to fame in
that, while guesting for Glentoran, he'd
played for the Irish League against the
Scottish League. Less than three weeks
after this game he did precisely the

reverse, scoring a hat-trick for the
Scottish League against the Irish League!

There was no hat-trick for Deakin against
Celtic but his one goal was enough to
give the Buddies the points in front of
their record-breaking crowd and deflate
the Celtic support which trudged wearily
home, realising that their promising start
to the season had been yet another false
dawn.

Rangers were the next visitors to Love
Street, ten days later. That game finished
1-1 and, amazingly, at 45,000 the crowd
was almost as big as the Celtic match.

Love Street has seen 40,000-plus gates
on several occasions but to draw as large
a gate twice within ten days
demonstrated clearly the extent of
football's popularity in the late 1940s.
The previous best was just TEN short of
the new record. In March 1925 47,428
had watched St Mirren and Celtic play
out a scoreless Scottish Cup tie IN A
BLIZZARD!

In fact outside of Glasgow and
Edinburgh, no place in Scotland has
attracted as many supporters to a
football match as Paisley. Nor were such
large crowds restricted to just a few years
either side of the Second World War.
Love Street first smashed through the
40,000 barrier in 1924 and 42,653
attended a League match as late as
1968-69. The ground even held 40,000
for a Morton home game when the
Greenock team temporarily shared the
premises in 1949.

Today, St Mirren's home has been
reconstructed into an all-seater capable
of holding 10,752 though the long-term
future of this historic venue is uncertain
as the Buddies consider selling up and
moving to a new stadium.

STENHOUSEMUIR

v East Fife, Scottish Cup Quarter-Final,
March 11th 1950
Attendance: 12,500

Stenhousemuir: W Allan, Jack, Smith, Rice, Paton, Millar, Thomson, Bow, Bannon, McQueen, J Allan.

Stenhousemuir are not a team and Ochilview is not a ground readily associated with large attendances. Even in the post-war boom era they drew the smallest crowds of any league club. Comparatively speaking they were big in relation to attendances in the 21st century with 2,000 and upwards not being an unusual turnout.

At the time the Warriors had a reputation as a handy side in the knockout tournaments and in 1950 they reached a second successive Scottish Cup quarter-final.

With thirteen goals scored in four cup ties Stenhousemuir were an exciting team to watch so when a home tie with East Fife offered the prospect of a semi-final place in the Scottish Cup for the first time since 1903 it was no surprise that their little ground was bursting at the seams come kick-off.

Their visitors were one of the top teams in Scotland at the time and brought a good contingent through from Fife with them, helping the crowd reach a record level of 12,500, producing takings of £937. They saw the home team make most of the early running.

Stenhousemuir were desperately unlucky in the first half. They hit the bar and the post and by some observers reckoning could have gone in at the interval four ahead without being flattered by the scoreline.

Others present were harder to please. The Sunday Mail's 'Rex' was one of them. It was, he opined, 'a game of high wind, light ball and low football.'

By the interval and despite the Warriors best efforts the game remained goalless.

That changed in the second half but not to the liking of the home support as East Fife took the lead. Stenhousemuir weren't out of it yet and when they were awarded a penalty a hush fell over the ground. The mass silence turned into a collective groan as **Peter Smith** directed the spot-kick straight at the delighted keeper.

'Muir's best chance of getting back into the game had gone. This prolific side hadn't run out of ideas – but they had run out of luck. East Fife seized the initiative, scoring two more goals to complete a 3-0 victory which looks a lot easier in print than it was in reality.

Stenhousemuir went back to the everyday world of life in the 'B' Division where they were struggling near the bottom. Two weeks later their magnificent run was paid scant tribute by a sparse crowd of 400 for their next match. And the hangover from their defeat was apparent in a 5-1 beating by Dundee United.

Stenhousemuir have enjoyed better days since then with victories to their credit against Rangers, Dundee, St Johnstone and Aberdeen as well as the memorable day in 1995-96 when they won the Challenge Cup by beating Dundee United.

But they've never played to a crowd of that magnitude again and with Ochilview's current capacity restricted to just 3,776 they never will.

STIRLING ALBION

v Celtic, Scottish Cup Quarter-Final,
March 14th 1959
Attendance: 28,600

Stirling Albion: Stewart, Hailstones,
Pettigrew, McKechnie, Sinclair, Pearson,
Benvie, Kilgannon, Gilmour, Spence,
McPhee

Albion had reached the last eight of the
Scottish Cup for only the second time by
virtue of a hard-fought 4-3 win away to
Fraserburgh and a 3-1 triumph at their
Annfield home over Morton. Their
opponents Celtic weren't exactly an
unknown quantity as they'd played them
three times previously in the Scottish
Cup in the 1950s, losing each time,
including a 7-2 thrashing at Celtic Park
the year before.

These matches had brought out big
crowds at Annfield. There had been
24,763 for a 1-1 draw in 1953 and
25,750 had seen Celtic edge a
magnificent match 4-3 a year later. And
it was their home record against Celts
which gave Albion cause for hope. In
total the teams had met seven times in
competitive matches at Annfield with
honours even at three wins each and a
draw.

The chance for Albion to make history
by reaching the semi-finals helped
bolster the crowd to a new record of
28,600. Some reference books cite the
attendance as lower than this at 26,400
but Stirling Albion's official history is
clear on the subject, saying that over
28,000 tickets were sold and, as is usual
in these circumstances, 'more people are
reckoned to have gained admission
illegally.'

What the exact figure was is unclear but
that there were too many people inside
Annfield that day is beyond doubt. Part
of the retaining wall between the

terracing and the west stand gave way
shortly after kick-off forcing fans to seek
safety by leaping onto the pitch.

There were no serious injuries but that
was more through luck than design as
fifty loose bricks were found afterwards.
Hundreds of supporters watched from
inside the playing area, against the rail
separating the running track from the
terracing slopes.

Whether the events on the terracing
influenced play on the park is debatable
but Celtic were far more experienced in
playing before big audiences than Albion
and although the home team played
reasonably well, it was no great surprise
when Celtic went ahead after seventeen
minutes. With 35 minutes gone Celts
went two ahead and any hope the locals
had of seeing their team pull off an upset
ended in injury time in the first half
when Celtic scored a third.

The second half was a listless affair as,
with the tie won, Celtic eased up. **Jimmy
Kilgannon** scored a consolation for
Albion with nine minutes left to make it
3-1 and give the home fans something
to cheer.

Celtic failed to capitalise on their victory,
losing to St Mirren in the semis and it
was the Buddies who were the next
visitors to Annfield. Two weeks after
losing to Celtic, Albion pulled off a fine
3-0 win in front of a decent-sized crowd
of 8,000. They had one home game left
after this and their final visitors of 1958-
59 were Celtic who won 1-0 but this
time in front of only 7,500.

Albion departed Annfield in the 1990s
for their new Forthbank stadium and its
3,808 capacity including 2,508 seats.
The new ground's record was set on
February 15th 1996 when a full house
saw Albion lose 2-0 to Aberdeen in a
fourth round Scottish Cup tie.

STRANRAER

v Rangers, Scottish Cup First Round,
January 24th 1948
Attendance: 6,500

Stranraer: Park, Kirkland, Dyer, Cox, Milliken, Haxton, Cormack, Jeffrey, Logan, Jones, McGuffie

Even though they were one of the oldest clubs in Scotland, Stranraer were still non-league at the time of this tie. They played in the South of Scotland League and at the time of this match they were the reigning champions.

The Scottish Cup was quite a step up in status for the Blues and in thirteen previous ties with Scottish League clubs in the competition proper Stranraer had lost the lot. Their best performance was in forcing Partick Thistle to a replay in 1938 but the 8-0 beating they received at Firhill was all too typical of the results endured when they faced league opposition.

This tie against the reigning Scottish champions was without doubt the biggest footballing occasion Wigtownshire had ever seen and Stranraer and the surrounding district buzzed with excitement at the impending visit of the mighty Gers. A few even joked that with both clubs holders of their respective league titles this game would determine who Scotland's 'true' champions really were!

No one could accuse Rangers of treating their opponents lightly. They resisted the temptation to field fringe players and sent their full first eleven to do battle at Stair Park.

This was a rare treat for fans in the Stranraer area. The opportunity to see in the flesh defensive giants of the game like George Young and Willie Woodburn, the wing wizard Willie Waddell, noted forwards Torry Gillick and Willie

Thornton and the rest of the Rangers side – all household names – was a once in a lifetime chance. And they took it with gusto.

By the time the game got under way there were a record 6,500 supporters crammed together into the spruce surroundings of Stair Park, easily beating the previous best of 4,200 set when Cowdenbeath visited in the national tournament a year beforehand.

It soon became apparent that Rangers' decision to treat the Blues with respect was the right one. Stranraer set their stall out to take on the Glasgow giants man for man. They harried their opponents all over the park, defended with resolution and in depth and broke forward whenever they had the opportunity. At the end of the first 45 minutes with the game goalless Rangers knew they were in a cup tie all right.

It was much the same after the break and the prospect of a money-spinning replay at Ibrox drew ever closer. But with just twenty minutes remaining Willie Waddell for once eluded his markers and sent over a cross which was firmly planted into the back of the net by Willie Thornton, the finest header of a ball of his era.

Even then Stranraer weren't finished. The Blues rallied and in an attacking flourish claimed an equaliser only for the referee to insist the ball hadn't crossed over the line.

Rangers clung on to their narrow advantage but defeat was no disgrace for battling Stranraer.

Although they lost out in the league to Hibs, Rangers went on to win the Scottish Cup that year – the first of three such victories in succession. Stranraer failed to retain their South of Scotland title, finishing third, but their efforts against the Ibrox team had not gone unnoticed. When the Scottish League split its 'C' Division into two regional sections in 1949, Stranraer (who had regained their southern title) joined the South West section, moving to the B Division in 1955.

Stair Park's capacity today is 5,600 and while the Blues have entertained big crowds against the likes of Ayr United, Kilmarnock and Motherwell their most recent 'full house' signs were posted for the visit of Celtic in the Scottish Cup in the third round in 2001 when the Parkhead team won 4-1 before a crowd of 5,660.

Record Crowds – The Ex-Files

Hundreds of clubs, most long-since gone, have played at various levels of Scottish football for more than 130 years. It would be impossible in a book like this to do justice to them all by attempting to include, for instance, every team that ever played a Scottish Cup tie.

Most of the significant defunct clubs were at one time members of the Scottish Football League (only two teams – Clydesdale and Thornliebank – that ever reached the Scottish Cup Final did not at one time or another join the league). In an attempt to keep this book to manageable proportions the author has decided to include a description of the record attendances of former Scottish League clubs, even if, as many were, these were actually Scottish Cup ties.

Of course not all ex-league teams have similar histories. Some are long-gone but with significant achievements in the game, like Vale of Leven. Others are of more recent vintage and if without great success, still fondly remembered by supporters. The second incarnation of Clydebank falls into this category.

And there are those with both a great a history and a fond memory. The most obvious example here is Third Lanark.

The clubs mentioned above and others like them have their great days retold here in a similar vein to those still playing.

Others, whose existence was much shorter and whose impact was negligible outwith their own localities, like say, Northern or Dumbarton Harp may not have a great tale to tell but they were once part of the fabric of our great national game and as such deserve to have some recollection of their big moments recorded here.

Finally, when is a club not a club? Some teams have changed names over the years. Others have merged. Which should be regarded as extensions of previous names and which should be thought of as separate institutions?

There are no hard and fast answers here. It is all a matter of opinion and, in the full knowledge that others will disagree; here is this author's brief guide to areas of contention.

AIRDRIEONIANS/ AIRDRIE UNITED

Airdrieonians disappeared from the scene in 2002. A few months later a club called Airdrie United started up. They had many of the same players, played at the same ground and are supported by the same fans. Even though they joined the Scottish League by taking over Clydebank it is glaringly obvious that they are a continuation of the previous club. Therefore Airdrieonians do not appear in this section.

AYR UNITED/AYR FC/ AYR PARKHOUSE

This club was formed as a result of a merger between **Ayr FC** and **Ayr Parkhouse** in 1910. Until the League admitted a side from Inverness in 1994 it was the only amalgamation in Scottish football and it remains the only amalgamation between existing League clubs. However, as Ayr were clearly the stronger of the two and brought the bulk of the fans, players and officials into the merged club, not to mention their ground, Ayr United have been regarded as a continuation of Ayr FC. Therefore while Ayr Parkhouse appear in this section, Ayr FC do not.

CLYDEBANK

There was a club with this name in membership of the Scottish League 1914-15 and 1917-31 and another, entirely separate club of the same name in membership 1966-2002. Other than the name, there is no connection between the clubs. They have been treated here as two separate entities with two separate entries in this section.

DUNDEE HIBERNIAN

This is simply an earlier name for **Dundee United** and there is no entry for a club of this name in this section.

ES CLYDEBANK

The one season a club of this name competed in the Scottish League is regarded as part of East Stirlingshire's history and an explanation is given in that club's section.

FERRANTI THISTLE/ MEADOWBANK THISTLE

This club is simply Livingston under an earlier name and no reference appears to them in this section.

In the cases of long-dead clubs it has not always been possible to track down their definitive record attendance and often two or more matches will purport to have attracted a similar number of spectators. The author has done his best to indicate where this is the case and has relied on his researches to provide what is, in his opinion, the record for the club involved.

Finally, some of the names of both teams and grounds in this section will be familiar to followers of junior football. In almost every case there is a direct link between the extinct senior team and the current junior side bearing the same, or similar, name though, for reasons of space, it is not possible to document the exact lineage here.

ABERCORN

v Cambuslang, Scottish Cup Semi-Final, January 14th 1888
Attendance: 8,000

Abercorn: Clark, McIntyre, Brodie, Johnstone, Martin, Gorman, McCormick, Buchanan, Allison, McLardie, Munro

It was in the period leading up to the formation of the Scottish League that Abercorn were at their strongest. They had taken part in the Scottish Cup since 1880 and this was their best season to date.

The early rounds of the competition were regionalised and Abercorn progressed by eliminating Johnstone Harp, Neilston and Kilbirnie. In the 'national' stages they received a fourth round bye before recording an impressive 9-0 win at their Blackstoun Park home over Edinburgh team St Bernard's and followed that up by knocking out Arbroath 3-1 in the quarter-finals.

Up to and including 1911 semi-finals were treated no differently from earlier rounds and the first team drawn received home advantage. There were around 8,000 watching on as Abercorn looked to be in a strong position when a goal from inside-left **Robert Buchanan** gave them the half-time lead.

Buchanan later became the sixth – and last – Abercorn player to be capped by Scotland.

Cambuslang equalised in the second half and won the replay by the embarrassingly large margin of 10-1. Considering that Cambuslang went on to a record 6-1 defeat in the Final against Renton, maybe it was no bad thing that Abercorn lost.

They reached the semi-finals again in 1890 and 1891 but lost, away from home, on both occasions. Abercorn later moved to Underwood Park and that ground was used by Scotland for a 5-0 win over Wales in March 1890 but the attendance that day was estimated at 7,000-7,500, slightly lower than the Blackstoun Park gate.

ARMADALE

v Albion Rovers, Scottish Cup Third Round, February 19th 1921
Attendance: 12,000

Armadale: Short, Harris, Dunsmore, Stubbs, Kirkbride, Gibson, Speirs, Milligan, Wardrope, Sneddon, Williamson

Armadale's best gate at their Volunteer Park home came several months before they joined the Scottish League. This match was a meeting of the then most celebrated 'giant-killers' in the Scottish game.

In the same season as Albion Rovers reached the final, Armadale made a name for themselves with their Scottish Cup exploits, beating no fewer than THREE Scottish League teams – Clyde, Hibernian and Ayr United – to reach the last eight before losing narrowly to eventual winners Kilmarnock.

Their exploits continued this season with a splendid 3-2 win over St Mirren at Love Street then a hard-fought replay triumph over local rivals Bo'ness. So when the draw brought the previous Finalists to West Lothian, local interest was huge.

A crowd of 12,000 saw the two teams embark on a goal spree in the opening 45 minutes which left the sides level at 2-2. No one could have imagined it would be a further five hours before another goal was scored.

But that's exactly what happened. There

were no more goals at Volunteer Park and the replay at Cliftonhill ended goalless before a crowd of 22,000. The two teams trooped off to Hampden for the second replay where they also drew a blank in front of 12,000 fans.

With the next round due just three days later the two teams returned to Hampden the next day and, after another goalless first half, Rovers broke the deadlock by scoring twice after the break to finally clinch the marathon tie to the satisfaction of their fans among the 7,000 present.

Even though subsequent Scottish Cup visitors included Aberdeen and Rangers, Armadale never again drew anything like the crowd in 1921.

ARTHURLIE

v East Fife, Scottish Cup Quarter-Final, March 5th 1927
Attendance: 8,000

Arthurlie: Stevenson, McGowan, McMeekin, Semple Fyfe, Moore, Clark, Armstrong, French, Malloy, GTR Jessiman

Barrhead-based Arthurlie enjoyed something of a renaissance in the 1920s. They had been Scottish Cup entrants for many years and were responsible for the shock of the 19th century when they knocked out Celtic in 1897.

But at times it must have appeared that historic triumph was a curse, as Arthurlie didn't win another Scottish Cup tie until 1925. This season, for a welcome change, the draw benefited them as they reached the last eight without having to play First Division opposition.

Impressively, they alone of the eight surviving teams could claim to have arrived in the quarter-finals without conceding a goal. Considering this was

only the second season since the change in the offside law from three defenders to two and goals were flying in at record levels, this was a notable achievement.

The prospect of a semi-final place and a potential crack at the Scottish Cup Final ensured a record gate at Arthurlie's Dunterlie Park with 8,000 supporters, paying £297 in receipts.

Arthurlie took the opportunity to field **John Moore**, a loan signing from Crystal Palace but also took a big risk by gambling on inside-left **Willie Malloy** who had been carrying an injury. It didn't pay off.

Although the home team had the better of the first half the game was goalless at half-time. With the unfit Malloy taking less and less of a role in the game, East Fife virtually enjoyed a one-man advantage in personnel.

The Fife team dominated the second half but at 0-0 it remained anybody's game. Home hopes were renewed when East Fife missed a penalty but eventually the away team's pressure told and with 69 minutes gone they took the lead. It was the first goal Arthurlie had conceded in over seven hours play in the competition

Arthurlie had no response and in the end were well beaten as their hitherto rock-solid defence caved in, allowing East Fife to add two more goals before the final whistle.

Arthurlie were quickly back in league action, losing 4-1 at home to Albion Rovers three days later when only around 500 bothered to turn up.

Two seasons later financial pressure forced Arthurlie to resign from the Scottish League. Perhaps victory over East Fife would have brought in enough cash to maintain their position and Barrhead may be enjoying Scottish League football to this day.

AYR PARKHOUSE

v Kilmarnock, Scottish Cup Quarter-Final, February 5th 1898
Attendance: 6,000

Ayr Parkhouse: Cochrane, Dick, Orr, Mellon, Paton, Munachen, Fyfe, Long, Crerar, Kay, Muir

Ayrshire football was a thriving scene in the 1890s. There were highly competitive local leagues and knockout cup competitions but the Scottish Cup was still the most highly valued prize of all.

Ayr Parkhouse were the shock troops of the Scottish Cup in 1898 when they reached the last eight of the national tournament. Apart from the celebrated Queen's Park they were the only non-league outfit left.

Five of the eight survivors were First Division teams but the luck of the draw sent the sole Second Division representatives to Beresford Park. They also happened to be Ayrshire's leading side.

Supporters keen to see the first all-Ayrshire quarter-final clash besieged the little ground. Around 6,000 were present as they saw Parkhouse confound expectations by dashing to a two-goal lead.

It was a different game over 100 years ago. Whereas today a team would sit tight on such an advantage and try to hold on to what they had, back then Parkhouse took it as a sign to go foraging up the park in search of more goals.

This backfired badly. Kilmarnock, shocked by the setback, soon regained their composure and rattled in five goals before the break, Killie added two more after the interval to run out easy 7-2 winners in the end.

Parkhouse continued to play at county level before joining the Scottish League in 1903. After just one season they were voted out, replaced by a team the top clubs preferred on account of their potential – Aberdeen.

Parkhouse battled on and were re-admitted to membership in 1906. But life was a continuous struggle. After it was intimated that the authorities would look kindly on an application for First Division membership from a single Ayr side they merged with Ayr to form Ayr United in 1910. Three years later the new team were granted membership of the top flight.

BATHGATE

v Falkirk, Scottish Cup Second Round, February 11th 1922
Attendance: 8,000

Bathgate: Wilkinson, Fergus, Gilmour, Harley, Cameron, Drinnan, Watson, Robertson, J Black, M Connell, R Black

Bathgate were among the clutch of new members of the Scottish League in 1921 and in those optimistic days were hopeful of attracting a decent level of support, Initially at least they did so with league gates averaging over 2,000.

The Scottish Cup was a welcome bonus and Falkirk were a great attraction. Not only were the Bairns a well-established First Division side and former Scottish Cup winners, they also brought a large travelling support with them to Millwall Park. And in their ranks was a player whose presence boosted attendances everywhere.

Syd Puddefoot was one of the top stars of his day and Falkirk smashed the transfer record by paying £5,000 to acquire his signature from West Ham. Supporters all over Scotland were keen to see the English star in action and

Bathgate's were no different.

The tough-tackling Bathgate full-backs were no respecters of reputations and while Puddefoot's Limehouse upbringing ensured he was no stranger to the more 'robust' aspects of the game he struggled to make an impact on the match. 'Puddefoot's cleverness to no avail,' said one match report.

Bathgate were hindered by an injury to inside-right Robertson who was effectively a 'passenger' for all but the opening five minutes yet they matched Falkirk throughout. Thoughts were beginning to turn to a Brockville replay with just ten minutes left when the 'passenger' Robertson scored what proved to be the only goal of the game.

The crowd 'went frantic with delight' according to the same report which appeared the next day under the headline 'Bathgate Bowl Over Bairns,' an apt description considering star man Puddefoot also played cricket at County Championship level for Essex.

Bathgate's reward was a trip to Firhill in the next round two weeks later where they were beaten 3-0 by Partick Thistle in front of a crowd of 16,000. Their next home game was in the following midweek when around 1,500 saw them beat King's Park 3-1. That helped them to an excellent fifth place finish in their first league season.

Four years later another Scottish Cup tie attracted an attendance also reckoned to be around the 8,000 mark when Airdrieonians were the visitors. Again the visit from a nearby First Division side of proven pedigree pulled in the fans.

Airdrie were in the process of finishing runners-up in the Scottish League for the fourth successive season and had won the Scottish Cup in 1924. The legendary Hughie Gallacher had left Broomfield a

couple of months previously but Bob McPhail, later to star for Rangers, was the big attraction in the third round tie on February 20th 1926.

Bathgate were a completely different team. There were no survivors from the 1922 side as this eleven took the field:

Gilchrist, Knox, Gay, Barrie, Davidson, Pearson, Weir, McKinlay, Scouller, Lindsay, Wales

They had also slumped in the league. After finishing comfortably in the top half in their first few seasons, 1925-26 saw them near the bottom. Yet the early pressure was all Bathgate's and they took the lead after fifteen minutes. Airdrie's Somerville struck twice inside a minute to give his side an undeserved half-time lead. The same player scored twice more in the second half as Airdrie ran out 5-2 winners. It wasn't as easy as the score suggests as the next day's headline 'Airdrie survive Bathgate's hurricane start' made clear.

Four days later Bathgate were back on league duty losing 4-0 to bitter local rivals Bo'ness before a crowd of 1,500.

But Bathgate were living on borrowed time. The depression of the 1920s and mass unemployment in West Lothian led to a drastic drop in support and Bathgate resigned from the Scottish League during 1928-29.

Bathgate had one last claim to fame to make. In December 1930 they defeated Dalbeattie Star in front of a crowd of 3,229 at Somerset Park to claim a record-equalling third Qualifying Cup triumph. Just two seasons later they scratched from the same competition and departed the senior ranks for good.

BEITH

v Kilmarnock, Scottish Cup First Round
Replay, February 4th 1905
Attendance: 4,000

Beith: H Higgins, Stevenson, G Higgins, J
McPherson, Chalmers, D McPherson,
Harper, Malcolm, Cameron, Anderson,
Walker

Long before their brief membership of
the Scottish League, North Ayrshire club
Beith enjoyed a sensational Scottish Cup
run when they took on – and defeated –
all three Ayrshire sides in the Scottish
League.

In the Qualifying Cup they travelled to
the county town twice, beating Ayr and
Ayr Parkhouse. Their reward was a trip
to Kilmarnock where they led for long
periods of the match and were unlucky
to only draw 2-2.

The general consensus was that Killie
couldn't play as badly again nor Beith as
well. But that didn't stop an impressive
4,000 or so from attending the replay.
The general consensus turned out to be
right – but only in that Beith played a lot
better and Kilmarnock much worse.

At half-time the teams were level at 1-1
with **John Harper** scoring for Beith. But
the second half belonged to the home
team who scored twice through **Edward
Anderson** and **John Walker**. It was a
sensational 'treble' for Beith and utter
humiliation for Killie.

A 4-0 trouncing of Cowdenbeath
followed and that took them to Ibrox in
the last eight where a 5-1 defeat by
Rangers ended their run.

Their only further achievement of note in
the Scottish Cup was a draw with
Dundee at Dens Park though Beith were
a team to be feared in the Qualifying
Cup. They won the national competition
in 1927 and the Southern version three

times in the 1930s. But neither in the
Scottish Cup nor in the Third Division
did crowds approach anything like the
number that saw them defeat Killie.

BO'NESS

v Falkirk, Scottish League Division One,
August 13th 1927
Attendance: 9,000

Bo'ness: Dempster, Creighton, Ramsay,
Duff, A Walker, Thomson, Lynas,
Cottingham, Martin, Hart, Clark

Like nearby clubs Bathgate and Broxburn
United, Bo'ness' record gate was against
Falkirk. Unlike their neighbours Bo'ness
took on the Bairns, not with the prospect
of a giant-killing in mind, but on equal
terms as proud members of the Scottish
League's top division.

Another of the 1921 intake, Bo'ness had
prospered in the Second Division,
winning the title in 1926-27 by a
comfortable seven point margin and
securing promotion eleven points clear
of third place.

Their Newtown Park home was used to
only modest crowds with 4,000 for the
visits of other West Lothian clubs usually
the best of the season though they had
pulled in a couple of big gates in the
Scottish Cup.

But this opening game of 1927-28
topped the lot. There were around 9,000
inside Newtown Park as the game kicked
off and they saw Bo'ness make a
determined start in their bid to prove
they could live with the elite.

Bo'ness were so much in top that fifteen
minutes had passed before Falkirk had
an attempt on goal. But despite the
home side's dominance they failed to
make it count, even missing a penalty, as
the teams left the field level at 0-0 after
45 minutes.

In the second half the home support's vocal encouragement was finally rewarded when **John Lynas** put them ahead. But with twenty minutes to go Falkirk equalised and suddenly the big day was at risk of being spoiled.

There weren't many goalscorers of international quality to be found in the Scottish Second Division. But Bo'ness had produced one in **Chris Martin**. The centre-forward had scored a club record 31 league goals in 1924-25 and done almost as well with 29 in the promotion campaign but the highlight of his season (promotion aside) was when he turned out in Dublin for the then Irish Free State against the mighty Italy.

If Martin could go up against the best the Italians had to offer, surely he could find a way past Falkirk's defence? And he did, with a glorious header which sent the supporters home ecstatic as Bo'ness claimed victory in their opening game.

Two weeks later the crowd was down to 5,000 when Hamilton visited and left with a point from a 2-2 draw. Despite a formidable home record the step-up in class was just too much for Bo'ness and they narrowly failed to retain their top-flight staus at the end of the season. Crowds slumped as unemployment hit hard and Bo'ness struggled to keep going.

By November 1932 it came to an end as Bo'ness were expelled from the Scottish League and their record expunged for failure to meet financial guarantees to away teams.

They tried to continue as best they could and as late as 1939 a decent gate of 3,451 saw them lose to Hamilton in the Scottish Cup. In 1946-47 their senior days came to an end when, having merged with another local side to form junior team Bo'ness United, they scratched from the Qualifiying Cup.

In their new guise they found almost instant success, winning the Junior Cup in 1948 after losing the 1947 Final.

Those who remembered the League days and the struggle to persuade as many as 1,000 to spend an afternoon at Newtown Park must have scratched their heads in wonder as they watched the junior team perform before gates in excess of 50,000 at Hampden Park three times inside a year. All told Bo'ness United played five Junior Cup games at Hampden Park in 1947 and 1948 before a total attendance of 218,741 – the equivalent of nearly twenty full seasons worth of the kind of support they received in their last days in the Scottish League.

BROXBURN UNITED

v Falkirk, Scottish Cup Third Round, February 21st 1925
Attendance: 9,500

Broxburn United: McKinlay, Reid, Fordyce, Coyle, McBeth, McIlvenny, Hair, Davis, Graham, Wardrop, Walker

Another of the Scottish League intake of 1921, Broxburn United enjoyed fleeting success with average gates of around 2,000 before falling away as recession and unemployment began to bite.

The Scottish Cup provided welcome and much-needed revenue and a club didn't even need to win games to make a profit. In 1922 Broxburn had shared the proceeds from an aggregate attendance of 60,000 in three matches with Hearts which ended in victory for the Edinburgh team.

This year there was no money to be made in a competition which paired them with two Third Division sides – Nithsdale Wanderers and Royal Albert. But it did allow them an easy passage to the last sixteen where Falkirk lay in wait.

The 9,500 in attendance and the £425 taken in receipts were easily both records for their Sports Park home. And those present saw a keenly contested tie in which the home team made most of the early running but which Falkirk dominated after the break.

Most present thought a draw would have been a fair result but just as they had done in Bathgate, Falkirk slipped up once more against West Lothian opposition when Broxburn centre-forward **David Graham** headed the only goal of the game seven minutes form time.

Broxburn played out time without too much difficulty and left the field to a great reception from their supporters Their club treasurer was a happy man too. The takings at this game were greater than those from ties at both Celtic and Kilmarnock the same day.

Before their quarter-final, Broxburn entertained Clyde in a league game the following Saturday which ended 0-0 before a disappointing crowd of 1,000. Seven days later they travelled to Dens Park where their run ended with a narrow 1-0 defeat at the hands of Dundee, watched by a crowd of 15,441.

Inspired by their cup heroics Broxburn climbed the table to finish seventh in the league but the next season they slumped calamitously to the bottom and failed to gain re-election.

CAMBUSLANG

v Abercorn, Scottish Cup Semi-Final Replay, January 21st 1888
Attendance: 5,000

Cambuslang: Dunn, Smith, Semple, McKay, R Gourlay, Jackson, John Buchanan, James Buchanan, Plenderleith, H Gourlay, J Gourlay

Cambuslang had rattled in the goals in the Scottish Cup even before this match. They'd beaten Ayr 10-0 and Our Boys from Dundee 6-0 en route to this, their second appearance in the last four of the Scottish Cup. After drawing away to Abercorn, there was nothing to suggest a similar goal-feast in the replay, as the sides had appeared evenly matched.

That still held true at half-time when the home team led 2-1 but Cambuslang ran riot in the second half, running up eight goals to win by 10-1. Around 5,000 watched the game.

It was their turn to suffer a similar fate in the Final. Two goals down against Renton they scored a minute before half-time to give themselves a fighting chance. But it was to no avail as Renton turned up the heat in the second half to win by 6-1.

Three years earlier Cambuslang had reached thief first semi-final, beating Airdrieonians 10-2 along the way. On that occasion their opponents for a place in the Final were the celebrated Vale of Leven and when they drew 0-0 with Vale away their chances of success looked good.

On February 7th 1885 they met in the replay with an estimated 5,000 looking on. With the scores level at 1-1 at the interval, a place in the Final was still a distinct possibility but the experienced Vale team had much the better of the second half winning 3-1. Vale went on to lose in a replayed Final to Renton.

The Cambuslang eleven for the 1885 contained a few who also appeared in 1888:

Dunn, Semple, Smith, Black, Jackson, Hamilton, Gourlay, Plenderleith, Low, Dalrymple, Buchanan

Cambuslang were founder members of the Scottish League in 1890 and finished fourth in their first season. The second season wasn't as successful and they ended up second bottom. Despite being able to apply for re-election they apparently opted not to and left the league, folding a few years later.

CLACKMANNAN

v Alloa Athletic, August 27th 1921
Attendance: 4,000

Clackmannan: J Muir, Bennett, H Muir, Lamont, Lawrie, Hutchison, Cowan, Balloch, Ferguson, Gettins, McNeill

Here was a clear indication of the Scottish League's level of ambition after the First World War – and the most obvious sign of its total lack of reality.

The newly restarted Division Two contained two clubs from Scotland's smallest county and they met at Chapelhill Park for what was the shortest series of derby matches in league history – this and the return at Recreation Park later in the season.

A good attendance of 4,000 was rewarded with an entertaining 2-2 draw. But there was only really room for one league team in the county and as Alloa ran away with the Second Division title while Clackmannan finished rock bottom there were no prizes for guessing the identity of the winner of this particular contest.

Nor were their attendances much closer than their league placings. Only Cowdenbeath drew more supporters than Alloa in the division and Clackmannan finished bottom of that table as well.

They dropped out of the league but made a game bid to come back when the Third Division was created in 1923, dropping out again when that division folded. Clackmannan soldiered on for a few more years but when they met league teams in the Scottish Cup the scorelines were embarrassing. There was a 10-0 defeat at Third Lanark in 1928, an 8-1 reverse away to Albion Rovers the next year and an 11-2 mauling by Ayr United at Somerset Park in 1931.

After that Clackmannan gave up the ghost, leaving the 'wee county' with just Alloa Athletic as a senior club.

CLYDEBANK (1914-31)

v Celtic, Scottish League Division One, August 22nd 1925
Attendance: 23,193

Clydebank: Gallacher, Murphy, McKendrick, Hogg, Scraggs, Fleming, Evans, Houston, Mackay, Chalmers, McEachran

Attempts to establish Scottish League football in Clydebank have a long and mainly unhappy history, stretching right back to this club's initiation. They had the misfortune to be accepted into membership in 1914 just before the outbreak of war. When the Second Division folded they returned to regional football.

The one real stroke of luck the town ever had in its long on-off association with league football came in 1917 when three clubs withdrew from the single division Scottish League. Clydebank were admitted simply to make up the numbers to an even eighteen.

They grasped the opportunity, doing well at first and finished as high as fifth in 1919-20. Attendances were good too and 18,021 turned out at their Clydeholm ground to see a 0-0 draw with Rangers that season.

But in 1921-22, the first season of automatic promotion and relegation they finished bottom and went down. Clydebank became Scotland's first 'yo-yo' side, winning promotion immediately before being relegated again just as quickly. Twelve months later another promotion brought them another crack at the big time and this, their opening home game with Celtic.

Clydeholm had seen a few big crowds in its time but the feeling of optimism that, this time, Clydebank may be back up for good, allied with a big away support, brought the total to a record 23,193. They saw the home team's defence perform first half heroics, particularly keeper **James Gallacher** who was injured three times in the first 45 minutes yet stayed on the park to make save after save and keep his team in the game.

At half-time it was still 0-0. Two minutes into the second half and the home fans celebrated wildly on the terraces as **Norman Mackay's** fine shot gave Clydebank the lead. They held the advantage for just ten minutes before Celtic equalised.

Then the came the stake through the Clydebank heart when a header from a young Celtic forward found the back of the net. The scorer was **Jimmy McGrory** and two seasons previously, in Clydebank's last top flight campaign, McGrory had been the darling of their supporters. He spent the season on loan from Celtic in order to gain first-team experience.

The man who went on to become British football's all-time top goalscorer defeated his old club in front of their record gate.

Clydebank's next home game was watched by a more modest attendance of 5,000 as St Mirren beat them 2-1.

Clydebank were relegated again at the end of this season but this time there was no way back. Appalling economic conditions took their toll and gates had fallen to below the 800 mark by the time the Bankies faced up to the inevitable and resigned from the League at the end of the 1930-31 season. They weren't to know that an upturn in commercial shipbuilding and a naval build-up as war approached lay just around the corner. If only they could have hung on for a couple of more seasons Clydebank may have survived for good.

CLYDEBANK (1966-2002)

v Celtic, Scottish League Premier Division, November 26th 1977
Attendance: 10,605

Clydebank: Gallacher, Hall, McLaughlin, Cormack, Fallon, Hay, Lumsden, McColl, O'Brien, Larnach, McCallan

Karl Marx was wrong. When history repeated itself in Clydebank the second time wasn't farce but just as tragic as before. As noted elsewhere in this book, East Stirlingshire moved to Clydebank for a season in 1964-65 and took the name ES Clydebank. After 'Shire returned to Falkirk, Clydebank spent a year in the limbo of the Combined Reserve League before being elected to the League in 1966.

By the mid-1970s they had developed into a formidable outfit and after the 1975 reconstruction became the first Scottish side ever to win promotion two years in succession.

That brought them into the Premier Division and a rude introduction to the harsher realities of the game. Bankies struggled throughout the season. Celtic – in Jock Stein's final year in charge – were a pitiful imitation of the great sides of the sixties but their name still carried enough charisma to tempt a record-breaking 10,605 to New Kilbowie on a bitterly cold November day.

And it was the home fans present who had most to cheer about. After thirteen minutes **Mike Larnach** set off on a chase for a ball the Celtic defence assumed was going out of play. Larnach caught the ball at the bye-line and sent over a cross for **Joe McCallan** to side-foot into the net.

Bankies remained on top but six minutes before the interval, a rare Celtic foray forward ended with a powerful header from **Roddy McDonald** which keeper **Jim Gallacher** did well to block. But the loose ball landed at the feet of **Tom McAdam** who fired a volley into the roof of the net to send the teams to the dressing rooms level.

They never re-emerged.

With conditions worsening and even the sanded areas of the pitch beginning to ice up, referee Douglas Browne abandoned the game. The supporters went crazy. This was an all-ticket match with no concessions for seniors or juveniles. Fans set off angrily for the club offices, demanding their money back. To no avail. Because the match had started the club was within its rights to refuse a refund and they did. When the teams met to replay the game near the end of the season, Clydebank charged full admission prices.

The supporters of both teams showed how they felt about this by staying away in their thousands with just under 4,000 actually paying to get in to see the teams share the points.

The largest number to witness a full 90 minutes at Clydebank was also for a Premier Division visit from Celtic – in 1986. Whether the 10,286 present on that occasion received any better value for money than the crowd sent home at half-time is debatable. Celtic struggled to a 1-0 win with a late goal from Mo Johnston as the Sunday Mail commented that 'goals at Kilbowie are as rare as rocking horse droppings'.

Clydebank spent the last few years of their existence as footballing nomads, having lost the use of their ground. In 2002 they were taken over and in theory moved to Airdrie. In practice they were killed off as a senior club and a new Clydebank team emerged back in the junior ranks but aiming at a return to the seniors and a third attempt to bring league football to Clydebank.

COWLAIRS

v Queen's Park, Scottish Cup First Round, January 21st 1893
Attendance: 4,000

Cowlairs: Burnside, Rooney, Maxwell, McFarlane, Shanks, McPherson, Aitken, Edgar, Brown, Lynch, Adams

This team from the Springburn area in the north of Glasgow were one of the more unlikely founder members of the Scottish League and finished bottom in the first season,

By the time of this match they were in the Scottish Alliance League which they won this season. The strength of that body can be gauged by some of the familiar names in it like Airdrieonians, Partick Thistle and Kilmarnock. In fact every club in the Alliance played in the Scottish League at some point in their history.

So it was a strong combination which met with Queen's Park, still regarded by many as the leading club in Scotland despite not being in the Scottish League.

The teams actually first met on November 26th 1891 with Queen's winning easily, 5-2, having been 5-1 up at half-time. But the official referee hadn't turned up and so a replay was ordered.

By the time this took place the competition had moved on. Three of the four quarter-finals were played the same day as this outstanding first round game while for the past two months Kilmarnock cooled their heels, not knowing who their second round opponents would be until this tie was settled.

There had been 3,000 present at the first game and a bigger crowd – some 4,000 strong – assembled for this one. But the wait had done little to alter the two teams strengths and weaknesses. While it wasn't quite as easy as before, Queen's Park triumphed 4-1 and went on to record their tenth (and to date, last) Scottish Cup success.

Buoyed by their success in the Alliance, Cowlairs rejoined the Scottish League as part of its new Second Division in 1893 and finished second in its first season. But plagued by financial problems and poor support they finished bottom in 1894-95, departed the league a second time and disbanded a year later.

DUMBARTON HARP

v Arthurlie, Scottish League Division Three, March 15th 1924
Attendance: 2,000*

Dumbarton Harp: Goodwin, Reid, Hendry, McBride, McInney, Innes, Brooks, Wilson, Brown, Smith, Miller

The decision to admit Dumbarton Harp as a founder member of the Third Division must rank as one of the more obvious acts of folly in the history of the Scottish League. The town of Dumbarton found it hard enough to support one league club and with their long pedigree, Dumbarton FC were always going to be the winners in any battle for survival.

Harp were poorly supported, even by Third Division standards, and the reason for the comparatively large attendance this day was purely down to their visitors. Arthurlie had made a successful return to league football and they were followed to Dumbarton by a special train bearing 800 of their supporters.

It was the Renfrewshire fans who celebrated too, as their team beat the local side 2-0 to clinch the inaugural Third Division championship.

Although Dumbarton Harp had a decent enough playing record theirs was always an unequal struggle to survive and in January 1925, after playing seventeen games, they resigned from the league.

They were the first Third Division club to give up and their withdrawal merely the first in a string of such events which hit both the Third and Second Divisions over the next few seasons.

* There are several matches featuring Dumbarton Harp where an attendance of around this level is claimed. As this was the only match in which the author has been able to trace evidence of a large travelling support to augment the poor home numbers he has assumed this fixture to be the one which produced the record gate.

DUNDEE WANDERERS

v Queen of the South Wanderers, Scottish Cup Fourth Round, November 5th 1887
Attendance: 6,500

Dundee Wanderers: Whitton, Ramsay, Tosh, McMahon, Langlands, Petrie, Hendry, Milne, Paddock, Mudie, Duncan

There seems to be no apparent reason why this game should have attracted such a large attendance as with over 20 clubs still in the Scottish Cup it was hardly anywhere near the final stages and there wouldn't be many travelling fans to account for either. The battle of the Wanderers was won 4-3 by the home team which went on to the last eight where they were beaten by Renton.

Dundee Wanderers spent just one season in the Scottish League, in 1894-95. But this all-amateur combination of several Dundee clubs failed to make a good impression, winning only three times, losing every away game and finishing second bottom.

Seven teams contested the three places up for election and with just three votes, Wanderers finished joint last with Northern. Their brief League career was over with the only attendance noted down the 3,000 who saw one of their rare successes when they beat Partick Thistle 6-5.

Latterly, their Clepington Park ground was taken over by Dundee Hibernian and given a name by which most people today are still familiar with – Tannadice.

DYKEHEAD

v Albion Rovers, Scottish Cup First Round Replay, January 31st 1920.
Attendance: 4,000

Dykenead: Eadon, W Geddes, Watson, Tate, J Geddes, Buttery, Gibson, King, Rennox, Murray, Bennett

Albion Rovers famously reached he Scottish Cup Final in 1920 but they almost came unstuck at the first fence. Drawn at home to Dykehead they were held to a 0-0 draw Cliftonhill and were forced to make the short journey to Shotts for the replay a week later.

The post-war boom, the appearance of a Scottish League side and the possibility of an upset enticed 4,000 supporters along to the game. Rovers calmed their nerves with a first half goal and added another for comfort after the break. But Dykehead pulled one back to keep the spectators interest going right to the end.

Another of the short-lived Third Division sides, Dykehead did little of note in the league though they continued to put in some noted Scottish Cup performances reaching the Qualifying Cup Final in 1923-24 and the Third Round proper the next season.

But times were so hard and support so thin that not even the prospect of a money-spinning tie at Easter Road against Hibs in January 1928 could galvanise them into getting a team together and they scratched from competition.

The 1928-29 Qualifying Cup sums up quite aptly the state of Scottish football as far as teams like Dykehead were concerned. They received a walkover in the first round when Vale of Leven scratched. Dykehead then scratched in turn when drawn against Galston in the second round. The Ayrshire team received another walkover in the third round when Nithsdale Wanderers pulled out and then received a bye in the fourth round. They had reached the quarter-finals, having played one tie (in the first round) of the scheduled four!

EDINBURGH CITY

v St Bernard's, Scottish Cup Second Round, January 30th 1932
Attendance: 6,000

Edinburgh City: R Wann, W Hamilton, D Bannatyne, T Robertson, J MacDonald, R Forrest, R Parry, H Strachan, RR Robson, AB Allan, JM Cumming

In 1931 the Scottish League took the quite bizarre decision to admit Edinburgh City into the Second Division as replacements for Clydebank. It was an unfathomable choice for several reasons. Many of the existing clubs were struggling to survive and the cull that begun in the Third Division in the mid-1920s had not yet run its course. Adding any new club was a risk.

Then there was location. Edinburgh already had four league clubs. This new addition meant the capital now had just one league team fewer than Glasgow – a city twice the size.

Next there was the question of potential for growth, closely related to location. A Highland team or one from the South West or the Borders would have had great swathes of the country to draw on. Edinburgh City had to compete in an already over-subscribed market.

Following on from potential was the question of a club's existing playing record. Put bluntly, were they good enough? The answer as far as Edinburgh City were concerned was a resounding 'NO.'

Formed as recently as 1928 with the avowed all-amateur aim of being the 'Queen's Park of the East' City had little of note to their name, save two appearances in the Scottish Cup proper.

Their greatest attendance was probably a Scottish Cup tie in their first season in the league against local opposition.

St Bernard's were expected to win easily but the novelty of the clash drew an estimated 6,000 to the Powderhall stadium to see the match. At first it followed its predicted course with St Bernard's two goals up inside the opening twenty minutes. But City showed they had some fight in them when **Robert Parry** reduced the leeway on the half-hour mark.

Five minutes into the second half the same player sent over a cross which was glanced home by **Hugh Strachan** for the equaliser. City's hopes of holding out for a draw were crushed by a winner for St Bernard's five minutes from the end.

Two weeks later they were back in action, against King's Park and lost out narrowly 4-3. But the true extent of City's place in the affections of Edinburgh's footballing public can be gauged from the attendance of around just one hundred fans.

They finished the season rock bottom, conceding 146 goals – a tally unmatched either before or since in the annals of Scottish football.

It can certainly be said that Edinburgh City were no quitters and they persevered season after season with little to show for their efforts. In 1935-36 they were having their best ever season in the league and once more a big Scottish Cup game brought a good-sized crowd.

By now they were playing at East Pilton (now the City Park home of Spartans and used for a fourth round Scottish Cup tie as recently as 2004) and the visit of Cowdenbeath for a first round tie on

January 25th 1936 drew a total of 5,740 fans.

Given that the crowd for the St Bernard's game was an estimated figure it is impossible to say with absolute certainty which of the two matches drew the bigger crowd.

The City line-up against the Fife team was:

J Crichton, J McKell, W Hamilton, J Hamilton, R Waterston, JJ McShane, P Carruthers, L Craythorne, R Hope, G Fawcett, HA Gallagher

This time it was City who got off to a flyer. **Peter Carruthers** scored after eight minutes and a penalty converted by right-back **Willie Hamilton** after sixteen minutes gave their supporters that rare feeling –something to cheer about.

But Cowdenbeath hit back – quickly and lethally. In 24 minutes they pulled a goal back then struck twice in succession around the half-hour mark to take the lead. The remainder of the game was played out in sodden conditions with no further addition to the scoring to send the big Cowden contingent back across the Forth Bridge happy.

Seven days later Leith Athletic visited City and won the derby game 3-2 watched by around 800 spectators.

By 1938-39 they had finished bottom six times in eight seasons but they pulled off one momentous victory when they travelled the short distance to Easter Road in 1938 and knocked Hibernian out of the Scottish Cup, winning 3-2.

Perhaps predictably they were then turned over to the tune of 9-2 by Raith Rovers in the next round.

Unsurprisingly, Edinburgh City were one the clubs placed in 'C' Division in 1946. By 1949 they had even ceased to compete at that level and turned junior

before folding in 1955.

In 1986 East of Scotland League side Postal United revived the Edinburgh City name and the 'new' City have done well since, particularly in the Scottish Cup where they have qualified regularly for the competition proper and even reached the last 32 in 1998 after beating East Stirlingshire on penalties. Unfortunately they were then beaten 7-2 by Dunfermline – a result very much in keeping with the Edinburgh City of old.

GALSTON

v Kilmarnock, Scottish Cup First Round, January 26th 1935
Attendance: 4,211

Galston: W Bell, Russell, Strain, Leckie, Falconer, Johnstone, Connell, Reid, A Bell, McGhie, Mair

Like many other Third Division clubs, Galston's biggest gate was recorded in the Scottish Cup rather than the Scottish League. Unlike most in that benighted set-up the Irvine Valley team's big day came some years after their league days were over.

Galston played in the Scottish Alliance and they were familiar with their opponents this day as Kilmarnock's reserve side played in the same league. The familiarity was greater than that however, as a number of the Galston team had been on Killie's books at one time, including some with a fine Scottish Cup pedigree.

Winger **Willie Connell** had the kind of Scottish Cup record few outside the Old Firm could boast. Part of Kilmarnock's winning team of 1929 he had also played for Killie on the losing side in the 1932 Final. Alongside him both that day and this was keeper **Willie Bell**.

This reunion of 'weel-kent' faces

ensured a keen contest lay in store. Galston made that even more certain by refusing to switch the match to Rugby Park. It was fairly common procedure at this time for the 'minnows' to do so for a financial consideration and perfectly above board legally, if ethically dubious.

In any case it's doubtful if many more would have watched this game in Kilmarnock than at Galston's Portland Park where a record 4,211 were in attendance.

Killie prepared for the tie as if they were at home even to the point of the players assembling at Rugby Park and changing into their strips before throwing on overcoats and clambering into the team bus to make the short ride to Galston.

The home team gave a good account of themselves and although on the defensive for most of the match never looked out of their depth against the First Division team. Galston even had opportunities of their own with Connell in particular a thorn in the side of his old team-mates.

It wasn't until the 71st minute that Killie finally made the breakthrough, scoring the goal which took them into the second round.

For Galston it proved there was life outside the Scottish League. They had a long pedigree in knockout football having won the national Qualifying Cup in 1899-1900 – a feat they matched in the Southern Qualifying Cup in 1935-36.

Galston's senior days came to an end when they (and local rivals Beith) were thrown out of the Scottish Alliance thanks to First Division clubs upset at reserve fixtures against the Ayrshire pair being constantly postponed as cup games took precedence. Unlike many, Galston made no attempt to go junior. They played their last Scottish Cup

game, poignantly, at Hampden Park in 1938 when they put up a spirited fight, going down 4-2 to Queen's Park in front of 4,189 supporters.

HELENSBURGH

v Bo'ness, Scottish Cup First Round Replay, January 28th 1925
Attendance: 1,500

Helensburgh: McCallum, Thompson, McLellan, Wilson, McSkimming, Fraser, McKechnie, Kessan, Shaw, Smillie, Miller

Third Division Helensburgh almost pulled off a shock victory over Bo'ness, having led at half-time away from home before being pegged back to 1-1. The prospect of a second round tie away to First Division Raith Rovers was on offer to the winners guaranteeing a bigger than usual gate for the replay at Helensburgh's Ardencaple Park in midweek.

But the 1,500 or so in attendance saw a match in which two evenly-matched sides cancelled each other out. **Harry Smillie** and **William Kessan** had the best chances for Helensburgh but not even the addition of thirty minutes extra time could coax a goal out of either side.

The supporters had to wait six more days for a second replay before Bo'ness finally prevailed 2-0 at Firhill.

Helensburgh's next home game was a 2-1 win over Lochgelly United in the Third Division on February 21st, watched by the usual few hundred enthusiasts.

In the Third Division's final season, Helensburgh were the only team to complete all their fixtures and sat at the top of the table when the division was disbanded.

Although either or both of Forfar or Leith

could have overtaken them had they been able to play their games in hand, it must have been galling for Helensburgh to sit and watch as both these clubs were admitted into the Second Division over the course of the next year while they were stuck out in the cold and forced to revert to amateur football.

Helensburgh played a Scottish Cup tie at Pittodrie after losing their league place, putting up a great fight before going down to Aberdeen 4-2 in front of 14,000 but that was the extent of their life after the league.

In the following season's Qualifying Cup they scratched from their home game against Beith and vanished from the annals of Scottish senior football.

JOHNSTONE

v Queen's Park, Scottish League, Division Two, September 9th 1922
Attendance: 7,000

Johnstone: Carson, Ferrier, McLellan, Stewart, Neave, Craig, Sibbald. McDonald, Murray, Kirk, McGrain

The First World War had punctuated Johnstone's Scottish League membership. They returned to the fray in 1921 as part of a reduced Renfrewshire contingent down from six to three.

They hoped to pick up disaffected fans of the missing teams but the reason for the big turnout this day was less to do with Arthurlie and Abercorn fans hungry for league football than the name and the quality of the opposition.

Although it had been many years since they ruled the roost, Queen's Park were still a team of great standing in Scottish football and their relegation in 1922 had come as a shock to all. Almost until they kicked off the season in Division Two

there were those who thought the authorities would never let Queen's go down and even respected newspaper columnists pontificated on the chicanery at work which would allow the Hampden side to stay in the top league.

It didn't happen and Queen's Park started 1922-23 below stairs. As well as their great name and tradition they were still a well supported side too. There were TWO special trains this day bringing their support through from Glasgow and that helped boost the Newfield Park attendance to an unprecedented 7,000.

They saw the Spiders take control early on and take the lead after twenty minutes. But for the next hour Johnstone hung on grimly, knowing that one goal would change the face of the game. And it did. Unfortunately for Johnstone it was at the other end as Queen's Park cemented their victory with a second goal ten minutes from time. They went on to win the title and regain their top division place at the first time of asking.

The Renfrewshire side rallied in their next game and produced a splendid 4-1 victory against fancied Cowdenbeath in front of 2,000 supporters.

On January 27th 1923 another big crowd, again around the 7,000 mark, gathered at Newfield Park, as Johnstone took on Falkirk in the second round of the Scottish Cup. This was the home eleven:

Carson, Ferrier, McLelland, Allan, Miller, Neave, McDonald, Irvine, Dewtart, Rutherford, Campbell

Their usual line-up was augmented by loan players from their neighbours. Right-half Allan was from Morton and left-winger Campbell from St Mirren and this pair helped Johnstone to make a real game of it. Falkirk scored after fifteen minutes but Johnstone kept taking the game to their opponents without quite being able to make the breakthrough. At the other end keeper Carson was the undoubted star. His heroics made sure Falkirk didn't add to their lead. Even though they lost 1-0 Johnstone emerged from the tie with great credit. 'All Honour to Johnstone' ran a newspaper headline.

It was Johnstone's misfortune to suffer relegation in 1925, thus placing them in the Third Division during that league's last, shambolic season and despite having joined the league as far back as 1912 they went under with the rest.

Johnstone attempted to struggle on but a humiliating 12-0 Scottish Cup defeat in front of a meagre 700 supporters at Cowdenbeath proved to be their sad epitaph.

KING'S PARK

v Airdrieonians, Scottish Cup First Round, January 24th 1925
Attendance: 8,911

King's Park: Arnott, Livingstone, Hay, Brown, Lawson, Waugh, Martin, Abrines, Dodds, Webster, Lamond

This tie brought a rare touch of excitement into the usually mundane world of King's Park. For amid Scottish football's never-ending cycle of teams going bust, new clubs admitted and the annual process of promotion and relegation which defined the inter-war period, the Stirling-based club were a rare constant.

They were one of only three clubs (St Bernard's and Stenhousemuir were the others) to play continuously in the Second Division from its re-launch in 1921 to its wartime closure in 1939.

That stability may have been the envy of those struggling to survive but when a

club seldom threatens promotion, fears relegation or worries about its very survival then an adrenalin injection is needed from somewhere.

Usually, the source of the boost was the Scottish Cup and so it proved this day when Stirling was abuzz with energy and excitement.

Those are not words normally associated with a visit from Airdrieonians but this was no ordinary Airdrie side. This was a team which finished second in the league for four consecutive seasons. This was a team which arrived in Stirling with talents like Hughie Gallacher and Bob McPhail in their ranks. This was a team which descended on King's Park's Forthbank ground bearing the proud title of holders of the Scottish Cup.

A grand total of 8,911 spectators paid £235 in receipts to see the game and for the first quarter of an hour King's Park gave as good as they got. But Airdrie made the breakthrough on sixteen minutes and within another two minutes added a second goal.

Local fans feared the worst – that their team might be the victims of a real 'doing.' But King's Park stuck to their task and for almost an hour repelled the Airdrie offensive even if they seldom looked liked reducing the leeway.

But a forward line like Airdrie's couldn't be held at bay forever and with fifteen minutes remaining, that relentless predator Bob McPhail made it 3-0. With just sixty seconds left on the clock the great Hughie Gallacher burst through the King's Park defence to add a fourth and complete the scoring.

King's Park ended the day well beaten though spared the humiliation that at one stage threatened and their supporters could take some comfort in the knowledge that they left Forthbank having seen in the flesh some of the greatest players of the times. King's Park too could console themselves with the counting of their record receipts.

Seven days later King's Park entertained Dunfermline in the league and won 2-1 before their more usual crowd of 3,000. They finished the season in a position which neatly summed them up. Tenth of twenty with 38 points from 38 matches. The 'Mr Average's' of Scottish football.

And so they stayed until the night a Luftwaffe bomber accidentally destroyed their ground in 1941, bringing about the demise of King's Park and their subsequent replacement by Stirling Albion.

LEITH ATHLETIC

v East Fife, Scottish League Division Two, March 29th 1930
Attendance: 18,079*

Leith Athletic: Steele, Jamieson, Mitchell, McNeill, Reid, Robinson, Carruthers, Marshall, Nicol, Young Johnston

Leith Athletic could moan that they never got a fair shake from the Scottish League. Members since its second season in 1891-92, they'd lost their place in the first division after four seasons when the top clubs clearly decided they preferred the greater pulling power of Hibernian who replaced them.

Two subsequent Second Division titles and four runners-up finishes hadn't been enough to persuade the others to re-elect them to the top and just when it looked like they'd win promotion from the Third Division, that set-up collapsed!

So when Leith made a big promotion push in 1929-30 it was seen as a chance to avenge decades of wrong – 35 years of hurt in fact.

This match against East Fife represented a golden opportunity to reclaim the First Division place lost in 1895. Victory and it was as good as in the bag. Defeat and failure might stamp its imprint on Leith once again.

They went into the match level with East Fife on 52 points but with a superior goal average and a game in hand. Lurking close behind were Albion Rovers, four points adrift but with a game in hand over Leith and two on East Fife.

Leith, who'd played at a number of venues over the years were occupying the Marine Gardens ground at the time and it was to that venue that 18,079 spectators made their way in anticipation of a mighty contest.

Instead, the big crowd was forced to endure a damp squib of a game. East Fife had scored over 100 goals in the league but they arrived this day determined to protect the point they had at kick-off and woeful Leith finishing, particularly from centre-forward Nicol helped them to do so.

It was, said one scribe, 'typical second division stuff.' It's safe to assume that by that he didn't mean free-flowing, attractive, attacking football.

The only consolation the press could find as the teams trudged off after the dullest of 0-0 draws lay in the size of the crowd which was described as 'probably a record for a Second League game'

Albion Rovers failed to capitalise on the stalemate and Leith clung on to their narrow advantage for the remainder of the campaign, edging out East Fife for the title on goal average.

Leith survived for just two seasons in the top flight. Most of their post-war days were in the 'C' Division. Fed up with a diet of games against reserve sides and poor crowds they withdrew from the set-up in 1953 and were expelled from the league as a consequence.

It was a hasty action. As late as January 1953 Leith drew a crowd of 7,377 for a Scottish Cup tie with Airdrie – proof that there was a public out there for them if the opposition was attractive enough.

The next season they played and lost to Fraserburgh in the Scottish Cup and although they entered the competition in 1954-55 they scratched from a tournament they'd played in since 1887.

Ironically, at the end of that season those 'C' Division clubs whose first elevens played in that set-up were all admitted to the 'B' Division.

* The author has seen an estimated figure of 21,000 cited for Leith Athletic's home league game v Celtic on August 8th 1931 but in the absence of evidence of the precise figure has opted to select this match as the record.

LINTHOUSE

v Partick Thistle, Scottish League Division Two, February 27th 1897
Attendance: 3,000

Linthouse: Todd, McNaughton, Mathieson,Boyd, McIntosh, McLaine, Pearson, Brogan, McDonald, Niblo, Barker

Linthouse were a surprise choice for election to the Scottish League in 1895. Of seven clubs contesting three places they came joint top of the poll with Kilmarnock. They finished bottom in their first season and the reason they drew such a comparatively large attendance for this match was that Partick Thistle were in the running for the Second Division title.

Thistle duly won the encounter before a crowd of around 3,000 by 5-3 and went on to secure the title and election to the First Division.

Linthouse had just one more home game left – a 1-1 draw with Kilmarnock a full two months later on April 27th which was watched by a crowd of 1,000.

Linthouse lasted three more years in Division Two, achieving little of consequence and crowds at their Govandale home were usually sparse. They finished bottom in 1899-1900 and resigned from the league.

They entered the Qualifying Cup in 1900-01 and received a walkover into the second round before they themselves scratched from the competition and vanished from Scottish football for good.

A third round Scottish Cup tie against Abercorn which Linthouse lost 4-3 on October 18th 1890 is also reputed to have drawn a crowd of around 3,000.

It is difficult to see why Linthouse were ever considered suitable Scottish League material. They played in Govan, an area of Glasgow which already possessed (and still does) a much more successful, better known and more widely supported club which goes by the name of Rangers!

LOCHGELLY UNITED

v Third Lanark, Scottish Cup Third Round, February 21st 1920
Attendance: 10,000

Lochgelly United: Simpson, Paterson, Archibald, Nicol, Herd, Cannon, McNeill, Russell, Young, Uren, Penman

Lochgelly United joined the Scottish League in 1914 and were left in wartime limbo a year later so by the time the 1920 Scottish Cup rolled round they were again a non-league club.

This first Scottish Cup for six years whetted the appetite of the fans and the game was booming everywhere. Fife was no exception and even though Raith Rovers had a home tie against Morton the same day a huge crowd assembled at Lochgelly's Recreation Park ground.

The Fife team were determined to give a good account of themselves against top class opposition but faded after a bright start, allowing Thirds to take the lead after twenty minutes. The Glasgow side added a second before the break to take charge of the tie and rounded off the day with a third goal midway through the second half for a well-merited 3-0 victory in front of 10,000 fans.

Although they had been well beaten the experience served to renew Lochgelly's thirst for league football and they rejoined the Second Division in 1921. They suffered the double misfortune of relegation to the Third Division in 1924 at the same time as rivals Cowdenbeath won promotion to the First.

This undoubtedly had an effect on Lochgelly's gates which declined sharply from around 3,000 in 1923 to just a few hundred in the lowest league. The loss of derby fixtures against Dunfermline and East Fife as well as Cowdenbeath hurt them even more financially.

There was the odd big crowd such as when Celtic visited in the Scottish Cup and 9,000 saw them win 3-0 but even this competition didn't bring in any great amount of cash for Lochgelly. They were drawn away to Rangers twice but gates didn't exceed 6,000 on either occasion.

Lochgelly United expired soon after the lowest league was disbanded. Attempts were made to resuscitate them as an amateur outfit but despite a brief flurry of activity in the early 1930s this too was unsuccessful.

Today the town has been reduced to a simple mention in a ditty sung to the

'Addams Family' theme by East Fife supporters towards their Cowdenbeath rivals.

'They come fae near Lochgelly
They're dirty and they're smelly
They huvnae got a telly
The Cowden family'

MID-ANNANDALE

v Queen of the South, Scottish League Division Three, November 3rd 1923
Attendance: 2,100

Mid-Annandale: Smith, Fleming, Alexander, Noble, Henderson, McSorland, Tennant, Robb, McLaine, Groves, Simpson

Lockerbie-based Mid-Annandale entered the Third Division in 1923 on a high. They won the Southern Counties League in 1922-23 and reached the Qualifying Cup Final where they lost to Royal Albert before a crowd of 6,700 at Fir Park. Attendances at their Kintail Park ground were never high but Queen of the South were well supported and their appearance in this league match encouraged a crowd of around 2,100 to turn up.

It was the away fans who had most to cheer as their team controlled the game, winning without too much difficulty 3-1.

Appropriately enough the Mids finished mid-table. The nearest they got to repeating the crowd against Queens was in January 1924 when Forres Mechanics made the long trip south for a Scottish Cup game. After a goalless first half Mid-Annandale improved in the second period to win 3-1 before a crowd of around 2,000.

After the collapse of the Third Division the Scottish Cup offered the best opportunities for big crowds. In the 1926-27 Qualifying Cup Mid-Annandale brought the trophy back to Lockerbie by beating Brechin City 4-1 in the Final in front of 4,500 at Tynecastle.

It was proving difficult to survive outside the Scottish League but the final nail in Mid-Annandale's coffin was hammered in by Queen of the South. Their promotion to the First Division in 1933 saw the biggest names in Scottish football visit Dumfriesshire on a regular basis. Mid-Annandale just couldn't compete and folded completely in 1936.

NITHSDALE WANDERERS

v Queen of the South, Scottish League Division Two, September 19th 1925
Attendance: 5,000*

Nithsdale Wanderers: Armour, Vance, Gourlay, McManus, McLaren, Cree, Allan, Ballantyne, McConnel, Wilson, Houston

These two teams both joined the Third Division in 1923 and both won promotion in 1925 with Nithsdale taking the title. And it was the Sanquhar club which had adapted better to life at a higher level when the teams clashed this day.

Nithsdale had enjoyed some decent crowds at their Crawick Holm ground but none quite as high as the 5,000 who gathered for this game. And they saw plenty of action in the opening quarter of an hour as four goals were scored.

Queens took the lead before **Tom Wilson** equalised and **Jimmy McConnel** put the home team ahead before the Dumfries side levelled. The game settled down after this opening burst and one critical reporter even complained about the standard of play on offer even though he admitted there was great excitement both in the crowd and on the field!

The second half was twenty minutes old before another goal was scored when **Tom Allan** gave Nithsdale the lead once more. After that the home team had to hang on as they were reduced to ten men when right-half **Jack McManus** was sent off.

But at the final whistle they had beaten their great rivals 3-2 and with this, their fifth win in succession, gone to the top of the table. For a few giddy weeks Nithsdale Wanderers and their fans allowed themselves to dream of Division One.

Their next home game two weeks later brought a 2-0 win over Albion Rovers before a crowd of 2,000.

But the prospect of First Division football in Sanquhar proved to be a mirage. Nithsdale fell away badly as the season progressed, finishing in twelfth place. Their poor form continued into the next season when they finished last and failed to gain re-election.

Efforts to return to the League were constantly rebuffed with the worst insult coming in 1931 when they were beaten 25-7 by Edinburgh City as the replacements for Clydebank. A humiliating 14-0 Scottish Cup defeat by Dundee United the same year served only to show how far Nithsdale had fallen since the days when they had been knocking at the First Division's door.

They soldiered on into the post-war era and there was the briefest hint of a revival when they pulled in 3,700 for a Scottish Cup tie with holders Aberdeen in 1948 when they lost 5-0. But it was a false dawn. They went down to heavy defeats in the next two qualifying competitions and scratched from the 1950-51 event.

They turned junior in 1951 but this was to be no salvation either and Nithsdale

Wanderers finally departed the game in 1964 though their name has recently been revived in minor football.

*Some reports give the attendance as only 4,000.

NORTHERN

v Partick Thistle, Scottish League Division Two, December 23rd 1893
Attendance: 1,000

Northern: Burnside, Buist, Sinclair, Lamont, Fraser, Mathieson, Neaves, Kyle, Proudfoot, Fyfe, McBride

Northern were from the far north – the far north of Glasgow that is. From Springburn to be precise where they had eked out an existence for almost two decades prior to joining the Second Division in its inaugural season.

Their record wasn't particularly distinguished and Northern's admission to the league was probably more due to geography than playing ability.

This game against their fellow Glaswegians produced a 2-1 victory in front of around 1,000 spectators at their Hyde Park ground.

It was Northern's first league win in nine attempts and hoisted them off the foot of the table. Their next home game wasn't until February 3rd when a 3-3 draw with fellow strugglers Thistle (the OTHER Thistle, not the 'Harry Wraggs') helped them temporarily reach the giddy heights of third from last. But with only three home wins and every away game ending in defeat, Northern ended the season second bottom.

Unsurprisingly, Northern failed to gain re-election and disappeared from sight soon afterwards. They entered the Qualifying Cup in 1896-97 but scratched before the first round.

PEEBLES ROVERS

V Gala Fairydean, Scottish Cup First Round, January 28th 1961
Attendance: 1,750

Peebles Rovers: Lucas, Mair, Robertson, Miller, Moles, Roy, Arnott, Walsh, Sanderson, McWilliam, Reid

That Peebles Rovers biggest crowd came more than thirty years after they departed the Scottish League and that it was fewer than 2,000 speaks volumes about the attendance levels in the Third Division in the 1920s.

Peebles Rovers were founded back in 1893 and have played at Whitestone Park since 1906. Their three league seasons were fairly undistinguished but they put in some sterling performances in the Scottish Cup, including holding Hibernian to a draw in 1923 – the only team to take Hibs to a replay on the Edinburgh club's route to the Final.

Unlike most former Third Division clubs, Rovers actually prospered outside the league, winning the East of Scotland League in 1928-29 then for four consecutive seasons from 1932-36 and adding in a 1945-46 triumph to bring their title tally to six.

They did well in the Qualifying Cup (South) in the post-war period, winning it in 1953-54 and reaching the Final the next time it was played for in 1957-58. They were also losing Finalists in 1959-60 and 60-61.

These achievements gave them regular access to the Scottish Cup proper but here they had fared less well, losing 10-0 away to St Mirren in 1959 and 6-1 at home to Ayr United a year later. At least when the draw paired them with fellow East of Scotland League side Gala Fairydean there was little fear of that kind of result. But the 1,750 supporters who paid £160 in receipts to attend

Whitestone Park were served up a feast of goals.

It was Gala who opened the scoring in ten minutes with a goal engineered by the main reason so many turned up for this borders clash. **Alfie Conn** had enjoyed a magnificent career with Hearts but was now in his footballing twilight days and playing for Gala. The great man still possessed the vision to set up his team-mate Young to put the visitors ahead.

Peebles striker **Renwick Sanderson** equalised to send the sides to the dressing rooms level at 1-1. In the second half Peebles dominated. Sanderson scored twice more to notch up his hat-trick and **William Walsh** added another. But a legend departed the stage with a final flourish. Alfie Conn scored for Gala as the game ended 4-2 in Rovers favour.

Their reward was one Conn would have envied – a trip to Easter Road to face Hibernian in the second round. The Hibees won an embarrassingly one-sided match by an amazing 15-1. Joe Baker helped himself to nine of the goals. As his brother Gerry had scored four for St Mirren against Rovers two years previously Peebles were heartily sick of the sight of the 'fabulous Baker boys.' Consolation came in the form of a handsome cheque as Rovers share of the gate money from the crowd of 10,453.

Rovers Scottish Cup days ended in 1965-66 when they held Dumbarton to a draw before losing the replay in extra time. They turned junior the following year and although they returned to the senior ranks and have been back in the East of Scotland League for over twenty years Whitestone Park no longer meets SFA requirements for Qualifying Cup eligibility.

PORT GLASGOW ATHLETIC

v Rangers, Scottish Cup Quarter-Final, March 10th 1906
Attendance: 11,000

Port Glasgow Athletic: Ward, Robertson, Ritchie, Mainds, G Ross, Allan, Hamilton, McNicoll, Gray, Cunningham, R Ross, O'Brien

Port Glasgow Athletic were founder members of the Second Division in 1893 and enjoyed success at that level, culminating in winning the title in 1902 and subsequently being elected to the First Division.

Port adhered to amateurism though their reasons for doing so were somewhat less lofty than the Corinthian ethos of Queen's Park. Port Glasgow were simply hard up. They were the by far the worst supported side in the top division though this was not something their rivals regretted as the fans they did have weren't exactly noted for the gentility of their behaviour. Police involvement in matches at their Clune Park home was a frequent occurrence, especially in games against other Renfrewshire clubs.

The Scottish Cup of 1906 turned into something of a marathon session for Port. After disposing of Dunblane easily enough it took four matches for them to eliminate Kilmarnock and progress to the last eight. Indeed, they met the Ayrshire team on no less than seven occasions this season – something to ponder for those who think teams meet too often nowadays.

Port were in their usual position near the foot of the table and Rangers were expected to be too powerful for them. Earlier in the season Rangers had won effortlessly at Clune Park 4-1.

That game had been watched by around 3,500. More than three times that number turned up for the cup tie and most were in position well before kick-off. Eventually there were 11,000 spectators present as the teams took the field.

Realists in the home support were hoping simply for a good performance from their favourites. Few expected to win. But Port upset the odds when centre-forward **Albert Cunningham** gave them the lead in the first half, an advantage they maintained at the break.

Rangers shook of their lethargy in the second period and came out all guns blazing. Fortunately for Port, keeper **Robert Ward** was inspired in goal and time and again he saved them when Rangers broke though and all looked lost.

Amazingly, Port hung on to their lead and pulled off what was undoubtedly one of the biggest giant-killings of the early 20th century. Although both clubs were in the same division, it was giant-killing all the same, for Port had never before beaten Rangers.

Victory sparked new life into Port's league efforts and they went on to beat Aberdeen 3-1 in their next home game a week later. Though this was watched by a distinctly smaller and more usual turnout of 2,000.

Port went on to face Hearts for a place in the Final with Clune Park the venue. Another good attendance, of 8,500, watched as the Edinburgh team did what the Glaswegians failed to do and take a grip of the game. Hearts scored once in each half to end Port Glasgow's Scottish Cup dreams.

It was back to league struggle for Port after this and each year saw a constant fight just to maintain their place in the top division. In eight seasons they finished last three times and out of the

bottom four just once.

Eventually their peers tired of re-electing them and in 1910 cast them out into the Second Division. Port survived for just one more year in the League before dropping out altogether and had vanished for good before the outbreak of the First World War.

RENTON

v Queen's Park, Scottish Cup Semi-Final, January 14th 1888
Attendance: 8,000*

Renton: Lindsay, Hannah, A McCall, Kelso, Kelly, McKechnie, McCallum H Campbell, J Campbell, McNee, J McCall

This tie was a meeting of two of the titans of the pre-professional era. In three previous Scottish Cup meetings Renton had never beaten Queen's Park. They'd lost out in the semi-finals in the very first competition back in 1874 and also in the Finals of 1875 and 1886.

Renton had tasted Scottish Cup success themselves with a victory in 1885 and the Dunbartonshire team were hungry for more. This greatly-anticipated game drew a crowd of 8,000 to their Tontine Park home.

Queen's Park were still the lodestar for Scottish football but Renton were a fine team in their own right – seven of this side played for Scotland – and they led 2-0 come half-time.

Queen's were more in the game in the second half but the damage had been done. Renton won by 3-1 to record their first Scottish Cup victory over Queen's Park.

The Final was a one-sided affair as Renton beat Cambuslang 6-1, a record victory that remained unchallenged until Celtic beat Hibs by the same score in

1972. The 'Chicken Bree' (so called because their trainer claimed the secret of their success was chicken broth) had won the Scottish Cup for the second time.

Having demonstrated they were the best in Scotland Renton then responded to a challenge from FA Cup winners West Bromwich Albion to play for the 'Championship of the World' and beat the English team 4-1 at the second Hampden Park (the future Cathkin).

Medals were struck for their players and a plaque proclaiming Renton to be 'Champions of the World' was put up for all to see at Tontine Park. The trophy they won – the 'first World Cup' – is still in existence and now on show at the Scottish Football Museum at Hampden Park.

Renton were at their zenith and two years later one of their heroes of 1888- **Harry Campbell** – made history by becoming the first player to earn Cup winners medals in both Scotland and England when he played in the Blackburn Rovers team that lifted the 1890 FA Cup.

Within a few short years Renton's proud claim rang as hollow as the words of Ozymandias. They joined the Scottish League as founder members in 1890 but were suspended by the SFA for playing a game against a team (St Bernard's operating under a nom de plume) already banned for professionalism. They lost their League place as a consequence but returned in 1891-92.

But the day of the small club was passing. The future belonged to the cities and the larger towns and Renton lost their top division place in 1894.

They rallied one more time to reach the Scottish Cup Final in 1895 where they lost to St Bernard's but by the beginning of 1897-98 they couldn't continue financially. They resigned from the Second Division after just four games and Hamilton Accies took their place.

The two faces of football – the old and the new – were exemplified in the 1904-05 Qualifying Cup Final when Renton were beaten by Aberdeen at Dens Park.

Unlike some early league clubs Renton didn't disappear quickly. They lingered on for some years, still playing occasional Scottish Cup ties and in 1907 girded themselves for one last hurrah, beating St Bernard's and Dundee to reach the last eight of the Scottish Cup where they lost to their old rivals Queen's Park, who themselves were in inevitable decline.

The end for Renton came shortly after the First World War. They made one final appearance in the Scottish Cup in 1921, losing to Motherwell. For the next two seasons their name appeared in the Qualifying Cup draw but they played no games and in 1923-24 even their name was missing from the list of entrants – fifty years after Renton had played and won the very first Scottish Cup tie when they beat Kilmarnock 2-0 back in October 1873.

A sad end for a once-great club.

* Some sources suggest Renton's Scottish Cup Quarter-Final replay against Third Lanark on February 15th 1896 may have attracted a similar crowd.

ROYAL ALBERT

v Dundee, Scottish Cup Second Round, February 11th 1922
Attendance: 7,000

Royal Albert: McKissock, McGowan, McFarlane, Black, Forrest, Falconer, Crosbie, Muir, Dick, Henderson, Bunton

Larkhall team Royal Albert had been in

existence for over forty years achieving little of note by the time of this match yet following on from this tie they embarked on what was, in their own terms, something of a golden age.

Dundee were welcome visitors to their Raploch Park ground as they were a leading First Division team and sure to bring a sizeable contingent of supporters with them as well as entice a few locals along. Royal Albert could certainly do with the cash, having had to undertake a lengthy trip to Buckie in the previous round.

In the event a record 7,000 turned up, paying £238 in receipts and the Royalists gave the home support plenty to cheer. They had the better of the first half and were the more aggrieved of the teams to have left the field with the game goalless.

The second half saw more of the same. It was a 'strenuous struggle' according to the press. Twenty minutes into the second half Dundee managed to sneak a goal and despite intense Royalist pressure held out for a 1-0 win. They had been, it was noted, 'a trifle lucky', as most observers agreed Albert deserved a replay.

The Royalists retired to prepare for the next year's competition. They breezed through the Qualifying Cup and won the trophy by beating Mid-Annandale 4-1 at Fir Park before a crowd of 6,700, most of whom backed the Royalists.

That earned them a tie with Clydebank in the 1922-23 tournament proper and they drew twice before eventually losing in front of a crowd of 15,000 at neutral Firhill.

Games like these cup ties helped Royal Albert gain a place in the Third Division later that year and while they were modestly successful at that level they continued to shine in knockout competitions.

The Qualifying Cup was won again in 1924-25 when they beat Clachnacuddin 2-1 at Pittodrie watched by a 10,000-strong crowd.

But the collapse of the Third Division also saw the end of Albert's success. They spent the next couple of seasons scrabbling around in minor leagues trying to find a suitable home before turning junior in 1928.

That can't have been a unanimous decision by the club as the Royalists (or at least a team bearing their name) continued to enter the Qualifying Cup and last appeared in the Scottish Cup in 1931 when they were on the receiving end of a humiliating 16-0 defeat away to Partick Thistle.

SOLWAY STAR

v Stenhousemuir, Scottish Cup First Round, January 24th 1925
Attendance: 2,000*

Solway Star: Muir, Robinson, Harkins, S Alexander, Duncan, Hardie, W Alexander, Knox, Edgar, Higgins, Smith

v Vale of Leven, Scottish Cup Second Round Replay, February 12th 1925
Attendance: 2,000*

Solway Star: Muir, Robinson, Harkins, S Alexander, Duncan, Hardie, W Alexander, Higgins, Edgar, Black, Smith

Some teams take a long time to achieve anything of note. Others burst brightly onto the scene and pass just as quickly. The aptly named Solway Star belong to the latter category, flaming briefly like a comet across Scottish football's skies before plunging to earth as a pile of scorched cinders, barely a trace of which has been left behind.

Formed in 1912 the team from Annan were quietly plying their trade in the Western League when they were scooped up into the Third Division along with several others from their league. After a moderate first season Star embarked on a memorable campaign in 1924-25.

In the league they were unbeaten in their first ten games and crowds at Kimmeter Green Park regularly topped 1,000. They remained the in the hunt for promotion but turned their attention to the Scottish Cup in the New Year.

Stenhousemuir were the first league team to visit Kimmeter Green Park on Scottish Cup duty and their presence ensured a good turnout. By kick-off there were 2,000 inside the ground and £80 was taken at the gate. Star fell a goal behind in ten minutes and didn't get back on level terms until **Alex Hardie** converted a penalty after half an hour. But just sixty seconds later they conceded again and retired to the dressing room 2-1 down at half-time.

The second half saw an explosive start as goals from **George Higgins** and **Tom Edgar** in the first five minutes gave Star a 3-2 lead. Near the end **Higgins** scored his second goal to give Star a 4-2 triumph. According to the Sunday Mail, 'a thrilling game ended in a well-merited win for Star'.

A thrilling 2-2 draw in Alexandria in the second round brought Vale of Leven south for a replay.

By now the sides knew that the prize on offer for the winners was Celtic away in the next round. Another gate of around 2,000 was present – a fantastic crowd for a place the size of Annan on a midweek afternoon – and they saw Vale, with the wind behind them go in front in the first half. Star couldn't capitalise on the wind advantage after the break and

were staring defeat in the face until **Alex Smith** equalised with just eight minutes remaining.

In extra time Vale seized the initiative again, scoring twice and looked set to book their place at Parkhead. Star fought back into it and were awarded a penalty. To their supporters horror 'Hardie missed. Then, to their delight, the referee ordered the kick re-taken and this time Hardie made no mistake. With five minutes left **Duncan** completed the comeback with an equaliser which sent the crowd wild with delight. In the final furious minutes Vale had a man sent off but the score remained 3-3 after 120 minutes and the teams were sent to Cathkin to do battle again.

The following Monday two goals from **Higgins** were enough to give Star a 2-1 half-time lead which they clung on to and settled the marathon tie in their favour.

So it was that Solway Star arrived at Celtic Park to do battle for a place in the last eight of the Scottish Cup – an unbelievable prospect just a few months previously. Unfortunately the Parkhead punters weren't that enamoured by the romance of Star's progress and only around 7,000 were there to see Celtic take a 2-0 interval lead.

To Star's credit that was how the tie finished and a mightily-relieved Celtic went on to win the Scottish Cup.

Star returned to the promotion battle and a three-way southern dogfight was eventually resolved in Nithsdale's favour as champions while Queen of the South edged out Star on goal average for the second promotion spot.

Solway Star would never see another season like 1924-25. They did their best to live up to that wonderful campaign by reaching the Qualifying Cup Final in

1925-26, losing 3-1 to Leith Athletic at Love Street, watched by around 5,000.

But when the Third Division folded later that season, Star's fortunes faded. Queen of the South's continuing success ate away at their support and Star closed down in 1939. A post-war attempt to revive ended in failure as a new club, Annan Athletic, had been formed during the war and captured what was left of Star's once rock-solid support.

* The same crowd figure was given for both matches and in view of the close relationship between them both are included.

ST BERNARD'S

v Heart of Midlothian, Scottish Cup Semi-Final, March 16th 1895
Attendance: 15,000

St Bernard's: Sneddon, Foyers, Baird, McManus, Robertson, Murdoch, Laing, Paton, Hall Crossan, Clelland

v Hibernian, Scottish League Division Two, November 19th 1932
Attendance: 15,000

St Bernard's: Keenan, Fitzsimmons, Brown, King, Marley, Weir, Davidson, A Robertson, Murray, T Robertson, Eadie

Edinburgh club St Bernard's biggest crowd has been the most elusive of any to track down and ultimately, like Solway Star, it has been impossible to choose between two contenders. Before looking at these matches though, it's necessary to explain why other possible record-breakers have been ruled out.

Two other games, in addition to the two selected here have been mentioned as possible records for St Bernard's. On February 21st 1920 they met Albion Rovers in a Scottish Cup tie. The attendance was reported as close to 20,000 with takings of £770.

These figures are not in dispute but this match was played at Powderhall as St Bernard's usual ground at this time – Old Logie Green – wasn't big enough to accommodate the tie. However, if this is accepted as their record home gate then applying the same principle would mean Celtic's biggest 'home' crowd would be at Hampden Park, Morton's at Love Street and Inverness Caledonian Thistle's at Tannadice to name but three clubs that have played before bigger crowds at temporary 'home' venues than in their recognised home stadium.

Another game cited is St Bernard's home league game against Hibs on New Year's Day 1932 at the Royal Gymnasium ground which they won 1-0. One publication claims the attendance to have been 27,000 which, if true, would easily be the St Bernard's record.

But match reports in the Daily Record and The Scotsman estimate an attendance of 10,000 and 8,000 respectively and while estimates can be off the mark it's difficult to believe that both reports are mistaken by so many. Additionally, The Scotsman describes the attendance at the NOVEMBER 1932 match as a record for the ground.

On the same day Hearts beat Leith Athletic 4-2 at Tynecastle in front of a crowd of 14,258 in a First Division game. To believe that almost twice as many turned up for a Second Division match in the same city is fanciful in the extreme so the 1932 Ne'erday match has also been ruled out.

Which takes us back to 1895. . .

At this time the battle for supremacy in Edinburgh football still hung in the balance though Hearts were generally acknowledged to be the best-supported club in the capital.

Which is why, even though they were

playing at their Logie Green home, St Bernard's were considered outsiders. But they played well and had much the better of the game. The only goal came in the second half when a **George Murdoch** free kick from thirty yards out was glanced in by **Combe Hall**. The press hailed this St Bernard's triumph as 'the greatest victory in its annals.'

If it was then it remained so for just one month as St Bernard's won the Scottish Cup by beating Renton 2-1 in the Final.

These were St Bernard's best days. They joined the league, straight into the First Division in 1893 and remained at that level until 1900 when they failed to gain re-election. Thereafter, no amount of success in Division Two could persuade the top clubs to re-admit them.

By the early 1930s St Bernard's glory days were a dim memory from another era. The same could be said of Hibernian who were relegated in 1931 and had finished BELOW St Bernard's in 1932. The Hi-bees were doing much better in 1932 -33 and this helped encourage a crowd of 15,000 – a record for the 40,000 capacity Royal Gymnasium ground – along for the clubs' meeting in November 1932.

Hibs were the better team but St Bernard's stuffy defence held them at bay for the opening half. Two minutes after the break Hibs finally broke through to score what proved to be the game's only goal.

Hibs regained their First Division place at the end of the season but over the next few years St Bernard's stock in the game rose. They challenged for promotion on several occasions and in 1938 narrowly missed out on the Scottish Cup Final, losing to East Fife in a second replay in the semi-finals.

Those three games – all at Tynecastle –

attracted an aggregate of close to 100,000 but St Bernard's, even when doing well, never played to big crowds as an attendance of 3,600 for their quarter-final win over Motherwell demonstrates.

That lack of support proved to be their wartime death warrant when, along with Leith Athletic, they were axed from the regional set-up in 1942. There was a failed attempt to merge with Leith in 1945 but the sad truth was that in Edinburgh Hearts and Hibs ruled over the city to an even greater extent than the Old Firm in Glasgow.

That still holds true today. In Glasgow Partick Thistle and Queen's Park still survive as they have done for over a century. In Edinburgh each and every attempt to establish a league presence alongside the clubs from Tynecastle and Easter Road has ended in absolute failure.

THIRD LANARK

v Rangers, Scottish Cup Third Round, February 27th 1954
Attendance: 45,591

Third Lanark: Robertson, Balunas, Harrower, Kennedy, Forsyth, Muir, Barclay, Docherty, Kerr, Dick, McLeod

Third Lanark had known great days and big crowds. League champions and twice Scottish Cup winners before the First World War the Hi-Hi had known leaner times in the 1920s and early 30s but had returned to the top flight and entertained large audiences either side of World War Two.

But relegation in 1953 had cast gloom over the Cathkin club and the 1954 Scottish Cup campaign offered a welcome relief from the weekly grind of the 'B' Division.

Interest in this all-Glasgow pairing was immense and Thirds previous best of 45,335, set against Celtic in 1938, was narrowly beaten as 45,591, paying £3,280 16s, somehow managed to find a spot at a crammed Cathkin to watch the game.

They saw a game in which the best chances fell to Thirds, particularly late on. After 72 goalless minutes **Willie Barclay's** shot looked goal-bound till it was palmed away by grounded keeper George Niven and cleared by the defence. Then with a minute to go **Ally McLeod**, five yards from goal, lunged at the ball and missed it totally, watching in agony as it hit off the post and rebounded to a defender.

It was a doubly painful miss for McLeod. Not only had he failed to take a golden opportunity to knock out Rangers, the replay meant he had to turn down the chance to play for Scotland in their 'B' international against England the same day.

Of course it wasn't the end of Ally McLeod's involvement with Scotland but for now his thoughts had to turn to Ibrox. His consolation was to play his part in a classic cup tie.

Two down after seven minutes Thirds fought their way back into the game, eventually scoring with a penalty, after George Young has missed one for Rangers, in the dying minutes to make it 4-4. Thirty minutes of extra time failed to produce any more goals and it was back to Ibrox the following Monday for a second replay.

This time it was Thirds who took a shock lead only for Rangers to equalise with a penalty – Eric Caldow replacing the luckless Young for the spot-kick. Rangers powered to a 3-1 lead but Thirds stormed back in the last few minutes to make it 3-2 and almost forced extra time

again before bowing out with heads held high.

The two replays were certainly better than the first match, after which journalist Willie Allison moaned, 'I cannot recall a match this season when the ball was so often out of play.'

Allison was later to become PRO for Rangers and the laureate of spin (even though the term was not yet in use) for the Ibrox club so his comments may have been designed to mask Rangers struggle against a 'B' Division side.

After Third Lanark regained a place in the top division in 1957 their future seemed bright. The reached the last four of the Scottish Cup in 1959 and later that year were narrowly beaten by Hearts in the League Cup Final. In 1960-61 they were third in the league and scored 100 goals in the process.

Six years later they were dead. The story of Third Lanark's sad demise is material for a book in its own right. Suffice to say that callous mismanagement led them to their doom. They went into liquidation in 1967 for the sake of debts of less than £40,000. Even allowing for inflation since then it wasn't a particularly high figure. To put it into perspective '£40,000 was the transfer fee for a half-decent player in 1967.

In recent years supporters of Airdrieonians and Clydebank have shown that it's possible to fight back from a supposed death sentence and those of Hibs that a cure can be found even when the patient is in intensive care.

But the concept of 'fan power' didn't exist in the 1960s and Thirds supporters were powerless to do anything about the situation.

Their last match was against one of their oldest rivals – Dumbarton at Boghead –

on April 28th 1967. Thirds lost 5-1 in front of a miserable crowd of just 581. **Drew Busby** scored the goal which rang down the curtain on 95 years of history. Thirds had been one of the founding members of the SFA and also the Scottish League (only Vale of Leven could make the same claim).

Their passing was mourned by many both then and still now.

THISTLE

v Queen's Park, Scottish Cup First Round, September 6th 1890
Attendance: 3,000

Thistle: Buchanan, Baker, A McFarlane, McCracken, W McFarlane, S Jackson, Craig, Gillespie, Robb, J Mathieson, W Mathieson

This Glaswegian team had only a fair-to-middling record in the Scottish Cup and the sole reason for a large attendance at their Beechwood Park ground on Dalmarnock Road this day was the presence of their opponents.

Queen's Park were Scottish Cup holders and around 3,000 assembled to see this game. Thistle gave their illustrious opponents a tough game and the teams went in level 1-1 at half-time. But the superior talent and firepower of Queen's brought them through in the end though the final score of 5-3 was no disgrace for Thistle.

Thistle joined the Second Division on its foundation in 1893. Their position as a Glasgow club was very much in their favour in terms of travel but a hindrance in obtaining support as there were many other and better-established teams all playing within a short distance of them.

They had a poor season, winning just two games and they finished bottom of the table. One remarkable result came in

the battle of the Jags when they travelled to face their better-known counterparts from Partick and were demolished 13-1.

They didn't bother to apply for re-election and disbanded soon after.

VALE OF LEVEN

v Dumbarton, Scottish Cup Semi-Final, February 5th 1881
Attendance: 8,000

Vale of Leven: Parlane, McLintock, Strathearn, J McIntyre, McPherson, A McIntyre, Paton, McFarlane, James Baird, JC Baird, Logan.

Vale of Leven had broken Queen's Park's stranglehold on Scottish football and won three successive Scottish Cup tournaments in the late 1870s. They in turn had been challenged by Dumbarton and the rivalry between the two clubs was intense.

In this season's Scottish Cup there were only three teams left and Queen's Park received a bye into the Final where they awaited the winners of this game.

Vale's great team had broken up as age took its toll and they had been playing a younger line-up for most of the season but this game was so important and its consequences so massive that they brought back their tried and tested old guard for the occasion.

It was a profound mistake. For no matter how talented their players were, they were out of condition whereas the Dumbarton team were at their physical peak. It proved to be a disappointing game for the big crowd of 8,000, particularly for the large contingent of press despatched from Glasgow to Alexandria to size up Queen's Park's Final opponents.

Dumbarton won easily, 2-0, and could

have scored more, had they been bothered. It was enough to take them into the Final which, despite it being played twice on account of a successful Sons protest, they lost.

Even at this early stage in the game's history Vale of Leven's best days were behind them. They did manage to reach three more Scottish Cup Finals, losing two and not even turning up for the other!

Just after their last losing Final in 1890 they became founder members of the Scottish League but after failing to win a game in its second season dropped out and declined so rapidly that by 1895 to all extents and purposes they had ceased to exist.

Vale were re-formed a year later and rejoined the league as a Second Division club in 1905. They performed only modestly at this level and were bottom of the table when the division was closed down in 1915.

Rejoining in 1921, Vale were relegated in 1924. They failed to gain promotion the next season and so were sucked into the Third Division maelstrom in 1926.

It was a real struggle to carry on and a home Scottish Cup defeat by lowly Leith Amateurs in front of just 230 spectators at their Millburn Park ground proved to be the last straw.

They were drawn to play Dykehead in the 1928-29 Qualifying Cup but scratched from the competition.

It was a fairly ignominious end for a club that had been one of the greats of the Scottish game.

v England, Home International
Championship, April 17th 1937
Attendance: 149,547

Scotland: Dawson (Rangers), Anderson
(Hearts), Beattie (Preston), Massie
(Aston Villa), Simpson (Rangers) capt,
Brown (Rangers), Delaney (Celtic),
Walker (Hearts), O'Donnell (Preston),
McPhail (Rangers), Duncan (Derby
County)

What better occasion to mark the end of
this book than the game which attracted
more spectators to a football match than
any other – Scotland v England at
Hampden Park on April 17th 1937.

149,547 spectators were in attendance
that day – a new world record. And it
stood for over 13 years until the 1950
World Cup in Brazil when the hosts
match against Spain attracted 152,260 to
the Maracana only to be eclipsed in turn
by the final game when 199,854 saw
Uruguay upset Brazil 2-1.

That Hampden crowd remains the
largest number of people to watch a
football match in Europe though – a
record unlikely ever to be broken.

Yet the match they turned up to see was
not of any particular significance. For
Scotland had seen an impressive two-
year unbeaten run spanning seven
games come to an end at Dens Park the
previous December when they lost 2-1
to Wales.

The Welsh had already beaten England
in Cardiff and followed up with a victory
against Northern Ireland in Wrexham in
March to clinch the International
Championship with maximum points.

All Scotland and England had to fight for
was second place. And, of course, pride.
It had been ten long years since the
English had last won at Hampden but
they fancied their chances this time.
With star names like Cliff Britton and
George Male in defence and the sublime
skills of Raich Carter and the
incomparable Stanley Matthews in
attack, they had every reason to feel
confident.

But Scotland were no mugs. **Jimmy
Delaney, Tommy Walker** and **Dally
Duncan** were all in tremendous form
and **Bob McPhail**, nearing the end of his
career, retained his capacity to terrorise
defences.

Yet for the first 45 minutes, the massive
crowd found little to cheer as England
controlled proceedings. But for all their
territorial advantage, it took until five
minutes from the interval before **Freddie
Steele** put the English ahead.

The second half though was to provide
the stuff of legend. An imperious English

eleven strode out early for the restart but were made to wait by their opponents. When the Scots finally re-emerged, it was to a wall of deafening noise as their 'twelfth man' – the Hampden Roar – came into play.

The players took their lead from the crowd and **Frank O'Donnell** equalised just two minutes after the restart. From then on it was one-way traffic towards Vic Woodley in the English goal.

But the England defence was resilient. Their forwards may have been terrified by the noise but if their defenders were, then they hid it well. Until ten minutes from the end.

Enter **Bob McPhail**. At 31 the Rangers player was considered a veteran. In four previous appearances against England he had failed to score. Indeed, it had been four years since he had last found the net for his country. But, as the Bard said in another context: 'Now's the day and now's the hour.'

McPhail found space just inside the area and unleashed a fifteen-yarder past Woodley to give Scotland the lead. With two minutes remaining, he more than made up for all those non-scoring outings by lashing a header past the keeper to wrap up a 3-1 victory.

Afterwards Matthews paid tribute to the crowd declaring that they had been the real inspiration behind the Scottish triumph.

McPhail couldn't resist a dig at the 'auld enemy.' When one of the crowd complained to him that there had been no room to move on the terracing, Bob replied: 'You should have been where I was. I had plenty of room.'

That remarkable crowd figure has appeared as both 149,547 and 149,415 in record books over the years. Why the discrepancy of 132? The answer, it appears, is that the Press Box at Hampden Park contained room for 132 journalists.

Should reporters be counted as part of the crowd? It's a moot point but on this occasion the answer is clear. For decades Scotland's hacks were derided by their southern counterparts as simply 'fans with typewriters'.

If that's the case and considering this was Scotland v England then let us concede the point to the gentlemen of the English sporting press.

149,547 it is then.